enVision® Mathematics

Volume 1 Topics 1–4

Authors

Robert Q. Berry, III
Professor of Mathematics
Education, Department of
Curriculum, Instruction and
Special Education, University
of Virginia, Charlottesville,
Virginia

Zachary Champagne
Assistant in Research
Florida Center for Research
in Science, Technology,
Engineering, and
Mathematics (FCR-STEM)
Jacksonville, Florida

Eric Milou
Professor of Mathematics
Rowan University,
Glassboro, New Jersey

Jane F. Schielack
Professor Emerita
Department of Mathematics
Texas A&M University,
College Station, Texas

Jonathan A. Wray
Mathematics Supervisor,
Howard County Public
Schools, Ellicott City,
Maryland

Randall I. Charles
Professor Emeritus
Department of Mathematics
San Jose State University
San Jose, California

Francis (Skip) Fennell
Professor Emeritus of
Education and Graduate
and Professional Studies,
McDaniel College
Westminster, Maryland

D1538243

Pearson

Boston, Massachusetts   Chandler, Ariz
Glenview, Illinois   New York, New

CONTENTS

TOPICS

DIGITAL RESOURCES

Go Online

INTERACTIVE STUDENT EDITION
Access online or offline

VISUAL LEARNING
Interact with visual learning animations

ACTIVITY
Use with *Solve & Discuss It, Explore It,* and *Explain It* activities and Examples

VIDEOS
Watch clips to support *3-Act Mathematical Modeling* Lessons and *enVision® STEM Projects*

PRACTICE
Practice what you've learned and get immediate feedback

TUTORIALS
Get help from *Virtual Nerd* any time you need it

MATH TOOLS
Explore math with digital tools

GAMES
Play math games to help you learn

KEY CONCEPT
Review important lesson content

GLOSSARY
Read and listen to English and Spanish definitions

ASSESSMENT
Show what you've learned

realize™
Everything you need for math anytime, anywhere

TOPIC 2

Analyze and Solve Linear Equations

TOPIC 3
Use Functions to Model Relationships

TOPIC 4

Investigate Bivariate Data

TOPIC 5

Analyze and Solve Systems of Linear Equations

Understand and Apply the Pythagorean Theorem

Solve Problems Involving Surface Area and Volume

Math Practices and Problem Solving Handbook

The **Math Practices and Problem Solving Handbook** is available online.

1 Make sense of problems and persevere in solving them.

2 Reason abstractly and quantitatively.

3 Construct viable arguments and critique the reasoning of others.

4 Model with mathematics.

5 Use appropriate tools strategically.

6 Attend to precision.

7 Look for and make use of structure.

8 Look for and express regularity in repeated reasoning.

Stuart is studying cell division. The table below shows the number of cells after a certain number of divisions. He wants to make a chart that shows drawings of the cell divisions through 10 divisions. Is it reasonable to draw this?

Cell Division

Division	Initial Cell	2	3	4	5	6	7
Number of Cells	1	2	4	8	16	32	64

Cell Division

Can I see a pattern or structure in the problem or solution strategy? I see that 1 cell becomes 2 cells and 2 cells become 4 cells, and so on.

How can I use the pattern or structure I see to help me solve the problem? I can write an expression that will show the number of cells after each division.

Do I notice any repeated calculations or steps? Yes; the number of cells after each cell division is the previous number of cells multiplied by 2.

Are there general methods that I can use to solve the problem? I want to show 10 divisions, so I would have to draw 2^{10}, or 1,024 cells. If I try to draw this number of cells on my chart, I could have a really hard time making them fit.

Other questions to consider:
- Are there attributes in common that help me?
- What patterns in numbers can I see and describe?
- How can I see expressions or equations in different ways?

Other questions to consider:
- What can I generalize from one problem to another?
- Can I derive an expression or equation from generalized examples or repeated observations?
- How reasonable are the results that I am getting?

Math Practices and Problem Solving Handbook

Math Practices

1 ▶ **Make sense of problems and persevere in solving them.**

Mathematically proficient students:
- can explain the meaning of a problem
- look for entry points to begin solving a problem
- analyze givens, constraints, relationships, and goals
- make conjectures about the solution
- plan a solution pathway
- think of similar problems, and try simpler forms of the problem
- evaluate their progress toward a solution and change pathways if necessary
- can explain similarities and differences between different representations
- check their solutions to problems.

2 ▶ **Reason abstractly and quantitatively.**

Mathematically proficient students:
- make sense of quantities and their relationships in problem situations:
  - They *decontextualize*—create a coherent representation of a problem situation using numbers, variables, and symbols; and
  - They *contextualize* – attend to the meaning of numbers, variables, and symbols in the problem situation
- know and use different properties of operations to solve problems.

3 ▶ **Construct viable arguments and critique the reasoning of others.**

Mathematically proficient students:
- use definitions and problem solutions when constructing arguments
- make conjectures about the solutions to problems
- build a logical progression of statements to support their conjectures and justify their conclusions
- analyze situations and recognize and use counterexamples
- reason inductively about data, making plausible arguments that take into account the context from which the data arose
- listen or read the arguments of others, and decide whether they make sense
- respond to the arguments of others
- compare the effectiveness of two plausible arguments
- distinguish correct logic or reasoning from flawed, and—if there is a flaw in an argument—explain what it is
- ask useful questions to clarify or improve arguments of others.

4 ▷ Model with mathematics.

Mathematically proficient students:

- can develop a representation—drawing, diagram, table, graph, expression, equation–to model a problem situation
- make assumptions and approximations to simplify a complicated situation
- identify important quantities in a practical situation and map their relationships using a range of tools
- analyze relationships mathematically to draw conclusions
- interpret mathematical results in the context of the situation and propose improvements to the model as needed.

5 ▷ Use appropriate tools strategically.

Mathematically proficient students:

- consider appropriate tools when solving a mathematical problem
- make sound decisions about when each of these tools might be helpful
- identify relevant mathematical resources, and use them to pose or solve problems
- use tools and technology to explore and deepen their understanding of concepts.

6 ▷ Attend to precision.

Mathematically proficient students:

- communicate precisely to others
- use clear definitions in discussions with others and in their own reasoning
- state the meaning of the symbols they use
- specify units of measure, and label axes to clarify their correspondence with quantities in a problem
- calculate accurately and efficiently
- express numerical answers with a degree of precision appropriate for the problem context.

7 ▷ Look for and make use of structure.

Mathematically proficient students:

- look closely at a problem situation to identify a pattern or structure
- can step back from a solution pathway and shift perspective
- can see complex representations, such as some algebraic expressions, as single objects or as being composed of several objects.

8 ▷ Look for and express regularity in repeated reasoning.

Mathematically proficient students:

- notice if calculations are repeated, and look both for general methods and for shortcuts
- maintain oversight of the process as they work to solve a problem, while also attending to the details
- continually evaluate the reasonableness of their intermediate results.

TOPIC 1

REAL NUMBERS

? Topic Essential Question

What are real numbers? How are real numbers used to solve problems?

Topic Overview

1-1 Rational Numbers as Decimals

1-2 Understand Irrational Numbers

1-3 Compare and Order Real Numbers

1-4 Evaluate Square Roots and Cube Roots

1-5 Solve Equations Using Square Roots and Cube Roots

1-6 Use Properties of Integer Exponents

1-7 More Properties of Integer Exponents

1-8 Use Powers of 10 to Estimate Quantities

1-9 Understand Scientific Notation

3-Act Mathematical Modeling: Hard-Working Organs

1-10 Operations with Numbers in Scientific Notation

Topic Vocabulary

- cube root
- irrational number
- Negative Exponent Property
- perfect cube
- perfect square
- Power of Powers Property
- Power of Products Property
- Product of Powers Property
- Quotient of Powers Property
- scientific notation
- square root
- Zero Exponent Property

Lesson Digital Resources

INTERACTIVE STUDENT EDITION
Access online or offline.

INTERACTIVE ANIMATION
Interact with visual learning animations.

ACTIVITY Use with *Solve & Discuss It, Explore It*, and *Explain It* activities, and to explore Examples.

VIDEOS Watch clips to support *3-Act Mathematical Modeling Lessons* and *STEM Projects*.

Go online

Hard-Working Organs

▶ **Hard-Working Organs**

Did you know you have seven pulse points on your body? If you took your pulse recently, you probably used the one in your neck or the one in your wrist. Try to take your resting pulse right now.

Monitoring your pulse while you exercise helps you make sure you are getting the most out of your workout. Your heart rate varies greatly between resting, sleeping, and working out. Think about this during the 3-Act Mathematical Modeling lesson.

PRACTICE Practice what you've learned.

TUTORIALS Get help from *Virtual Nerd*, right when you need it.

MATH TOOLS Explore math with digital tools.

GAMES Play Math Games to help you learn.

KEY CONCEPT Review important lesson content.

GLOSSARY Read and listen to English/Spanish definitions.

ASSESSMENT Show what you've learned.

enVision® STEM Project

Did You Know?

Natural resources are materials that occur in nature, such as water, fossil fuels, wood, and minerals. Natural resources not only meet basic human needs, but also support industry and economy.

Minerals are used in the manufacturing of all types of common objects, including cell phones, computers, light bulbs, and medicines.

Water, oil, and forests are some of the natural resources that are **in danger of someday being depleted.**

Each person in the United States needs **over 48,000 pounds of minerals each year.**

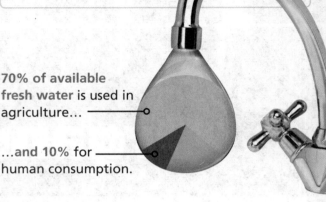

70% of available fresh water is used in agriculture…

…and 10% for human consumption.

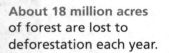

About 18 million acres of forest are lost to deforestation each year.

Solar power, wind power and other renewable energy sources are **helping to lessen the dependency on oil and fossil fuels.**

Fossil fuels are expected to **supply almost 80% of world** energy use through 2040.

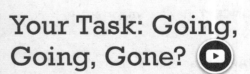

Your Task: Going, Going, Gone? ▶

Natural resource depletion is an important issue facing the world. Suppose a natural resource is being depleted at the rate of 1.333% per year. If there were 300 million tons of this resource in 2005, and there are no new discoveries, how much will be left in the year 2045? You and your classmates will explore the depletion of this resource over time.

Review What You Know!

Vocabulary

Choose the best term from the box. Write it on the blank.

fraction
integer
repeating decimal
terminating decimal

1. A(n) _____ is a decimal that ends in repeating zeros.

2. A(n) _____ is a decimal in which a digit or digits repeat endlessly.

3. A(n) _____ is either a counting number, the opposite of a counting number, or zero.

4. A(n) _____ is a number that can be used to describe a part of a whole, a part of a set, a location on a number line, or a division of whole numbers.

Terminating and Repeating Decimals

Determine whether each decimal is terminating or repeating.

5. 5.692

6. −0.222222…

7. 7.0001

8. $7.2\overline{8}$

9. $1.\overline{178}$

10. −4.03479

Multiplying Integers

Find each product.

11. $2 \cdot 2$

12. $-5 \cdot (-5)$

13. $7 \cdot 7$

14. $-6 \cdot (-6) \cdot (-6)$

15. $10 \cdot 10 \cdot 10$

16. $-9 \cdot (-9) \cdot (-9)$

Simplifying Expressions

Simplify each expression.

17. $(4 \cdot 10) + (5 \cdot 100)$

18. $(2 \cdot 100) + (7 \cdot 10)$

19. $(6 \cdot 100) - (1 \cdot 10)$

20. $(9 \cdot 1,000) + (4 \cdot 10)$

21. $(3 \cdot 1,000) - (2 \cdot 100)$

22. $(2 \cdot 10) + (7 \cdot 100)$

Language Development

Fill in the word map with new terms, definitions, and supporting examples or illustrations.

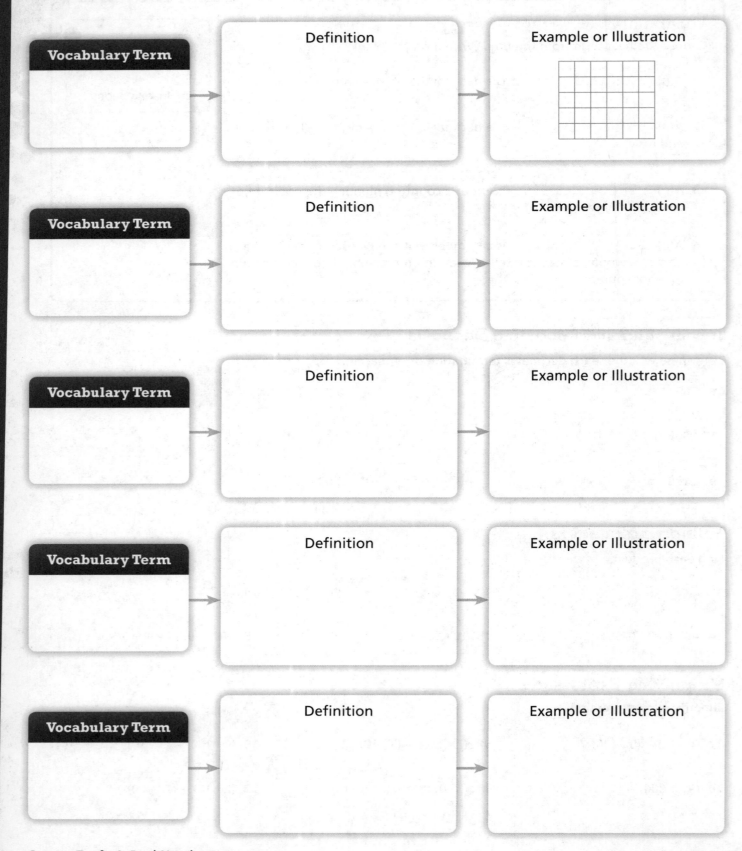

Vocabulary Term	Definition	Example or Illustration

PROJECT 1A

Who is your favorite poet, and why?

PROJECT: WRITE A POEM

PROJECT 1B

If you moved to a tiny house, what would you bring with you?

PROJECT: DESIGN A TINY HOUSE

PROJECT 1C

If you could travel anywhere in space, where would you go?

PROJECT: PLAN A TOUR OF THE MILKY WAY

PROJECT 1D

Why do you think people tell stories around a campfire?

PROJECT: TELL A FOLK STORY

Solve & Discuss It! 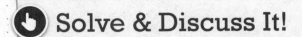 ACTIVITY

Jaylon has a wrench labeled 0.1875 inch and bolts labeled in fractions of an inch. Which size bolt will fit best with the wrench? Explain.

0.1875 in.

$\frac{3}{8}$ in. $\frac{1}{8}$ in. $\frac{3}{16}$ in. $\frac{1}{4}$ in.

I can...
write repeating decimals as fractions.

Reasoning How can you write these numbers in the same form?

Focus on math practices

Reasoning Why is it useful to write a rational number as a fraction or as a decimal?

? Essential Question How can you write repeating decimals as fractions?

VISUAL LEARNING   ASSESS

EXAMPLE 1 **Write Repeating Decimals as Fractions**

Scan for Multimedia

The Sluggers baseball team ended the season with the highest win percentage in their division. What is the Slugger's winning percentage written as a fraction?

Statistics are often rounded. Here, the decimal 0.555... or $0.\overline{5}$ is rounded to the thousandths place.

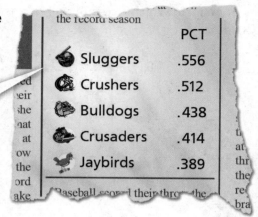

the record season

		PCT
	Sluggers	.556
	Crushers	.512
	Bulldogs	.438
	Crusaders	.414
	Jaybirds	.389

Baseball scored their throw the...

Locate 0.555... on a number line.

The decimal number 0.555... is between 0.5 and 0.6; so it is between $\frac{1}{2}$, or $\frac{5}{10}$, and $\frac{6}{10}$.

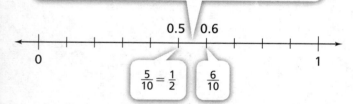

0.5   0.6

0   1

$\frac{5}{10} = \frac{1}{2}$ $\frac{6}{10}$

Reasoning How do you know that the repeating decimal 0.555... can be written as a fraction?

Write the repeating decimal as a fraction.

Assign a variable to represent the repeating decimal.

Let $x = 0.\overline{5}$.

$10 \cdot x = 10 \cdot 0.\overline{5}$

Because $0.\overline{5}$ has 1 repeating digit, multiply each side of the equation by 10^1, or 10.

$10x = 5.\overline{5}$

$10x - x = 5.\overline{5} - 0.\overline{5}$

Subtract $0.\overline{5}$ from each side of the equation, then solve for x. Because $x = 0.\overline{5}$, you can subtract x from one side and $0.\overline{5}$ from the other side.

$9x = 5$

$\frac{9x}{9} = \frac{5}{9}$

$x = \frac{5}{9}$

The Sluggers won $\frac{5}{9}$ of their games.

✓ Try It!

In another baseball division, one team had a winning percentage of 0.444.... What fraction of their games did this team win?

The team won [ ] of their games.

Convince Me! How do you know what power of ten to multiply by in the second step at the right?

Let $x = 0.\overline{4}$.

[ ] $\cdot x =$ [ ] $\cdot 0.\overline{4}$

[ ] $x =$ [ ]

[ ] $- x =$ [ ] $- 0.\overline{4}$

[ ] $x =$ [ ]

$x =$ [ ]

EXAMPLE 2 — Write Repeating Decimals with Nonrepeating Digits as Fractions

Sabine entered a division expression into her calculator. The quotient is shown on the calculator screen. What expression could Sabine have entered?

0.266666666667

Let $x = 0.2\overline{6}$.

$10x = 2.\overline{6}$

> Multiply by 10^1, or 10, because the decimal has 1 repeating digit.

$10x - x = 2.\overline{6} - 0.2\overline{6}$

> Subtract $0.2\overline{6}$ from each side of the equation, and then solve for x. Because $x = 0.2\overline{6}$, you can subtract x from one side and $0.2\overline{6}$ from the other side.

$9x = 2.4$

$\dfrac{9x}{9} = \dfrac{2.4}{9}$

$x = \dfrac{24}{90}$

> Write an equivalent fraction so that the numerator and denominator are integers.

Sabine could have entered $24 \div 90$, or an equivalent expression such as $8 \div 30$.

Try It!

Write the repeating decimal 0.63333… as a fraction.

EXAMPLE 3 — Write Decimals with Multiple Repeating Digits as Fractions

Write $2.\overline{09}$ as a mixed number.

Let $x = 2.\overline{09}$.

$100 \cdot x = 100 \cdot 2.\overline{09}$

> The repeating decimal has 2 repeating digits, so multiply each side of the equation by 10^2, or 100.

$100x - x = 209.\overline{09} - 2.\overline{09}$

$99x = 207$

$x = \dfrac{207}{99}$ or $2\dfrac{1}{11}$

> Subtract x from one side of the equation and its equivalent $2.\overline{09}$ from the other side of the equation.

> **Use Structure** How do you know that subtracting x from one side of the equation and subtracting $2.\overline{09}$ from the other side results in an equivalent equation?

Try It!

Write the repeating decimal 4.1363636… as a fraction.

Because repeating decimals are rational numbers, you can write them in fraction form.

STEP 1 Assign a variable to represent the repeating decimal.

STEP 2 Write an equation: *variable = decimal*.

STEP 3 Multiply each side of the equation by 10^d, where d is the number of repeating digits in the repeating decimal.

STEP 4 Subtract equivalent expressions of the variable and the repeating decimal from each side of the equation.

STEP 5 Solve for the variable. Write an equivalent fraction so that the numerator and denominator are integers, if necessary.

Do You Understand?

1. ❓ **Essential Question** How can you write repeating decimals as fractions?

2. **Use Structure** Why do you multiply by a power of 10 when writing a repeating decimal as a rational number?

3. **Be Precise** How do you decide by which power of 10 to multiply an equation when writing a decimal with repeating digits as a fraction?

Do You Know How?

4. A survey reported that $63.\overline{63}\%$ of moviegoers prefer action films. This percent represents a repeating decimal. Write it as a fraction.

5. A student estimates the weight of astronauts on the Moon by multiplying their weight by the decimal 0.16666.... What fraction can be used for the same estimation?

6. Write 2.3181818... as a mixed number.

Name: _____

Practice & Problem Solving

Leveled Practice In **7** and **8**, write the decimal as a fraction or mixed number.

7. Write the number 0.21212121… as a fraction.

Let $x = $ [　　　　].

$100x = $ [　　　　]

$100x - x = $ [　　　　] − [　　　　]

$99x = $ [　　　　]

$x = $ [　　　　]

So 0.2121… is equal to [　　　　].

8. Write 3.7 as a mixed number.

Let $x = $ [　　　　].

$10x = $ [　　　　]

$9x = $ [　　　　]

$x = $ [　　　　]

So 3.$\overline{7}$ is equal to [　　　　].

9. Write the number shown on the scale as a fraction.

10. Tomas asked 15 students whether summer break should be longer. He used his calculator to divide the number of students who said yes by the total number of students. His calculator showed the result as 0.9333….

a. Write this number as a fraction.

b. How many students said that summer break should be longer?

11. Write 0.$\overline{87}$ as a fraction.

12. Write 0.$\overline{8}$ as a fraction.

13. Write $1.\overline{48}$ as a mixed number.

14. Write $0.\overline{6}$ as a fraction.

15. A manufacturer determines that the cost of making a computer component is $2.161616. Write the cost as a fraction and as a mixed number.

$2.161616

16. Reasoning When writing a repeating decimal as a fraction, does the number of repeating digits you use matter? Explain.

17. Higher Order Thinking When writing a repeating decimal as a fraction, why does the fraction always have only 9s or 9s and 0s as digits in the denominator?

☑ Assessment Practice

18. Which decimal is equivalent to $\frac{188}{11}$?

Ⓐ $17.\overline{09}$

Ⓑ $17.0\overline{09}$

Ⓒ $17.\overline{1709}$

Ⓓ $17.\overline{17090}$

19. Choose the repeating decimal that is equal to the fraction on the left.

	$0.1\overline{7}$	$0.3\overline{51}$	$0.\overline{17}$	$0.\overline{351}$	$0.35\overline{1}$
$\frac{58}{165}$	☐	☐	☐	☐	☐
$\frac{79}{225}$	☐	☐	☐	☐	☐
$\frac{13}{37}$	☐	☐	☐	☐	☐
$\frac{8}{45}$	☐	☐	☐	☐	☐
$\frac{17}{99}$	☐	☐	☐	☐	☐

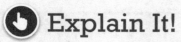 **Explain It!**

 ACTIVITY

Sofia wrote a decimal as a fraction. Her classmate Nora says that her method and answer are not correct. Sofia disagrees and says that this is the method she learned.

$$0.1211211121112.... =$$
$$x = 0.12$$
$$100 \cdot x = 100 \cdot 0.12$$
$$100x = 12.12$$
$$99x = 12$$
$$x = \frac{12}{99}$$

I can...
identify a number that is irrational.

A. Construct Arguments Is Nora or Sofia correct? Explain your reasoning.

B. Use Structure What is another nonterminating decimal number that can not be written as a fraction.

Focus on math practices

Construct Arguments Is 0.12112111211112... a rational number? Explain.

VISUAL LEARNING   ASSESS

Scan for Multimedia

EXAMPLE 1   Identify Irrational Numbers

The Venn diagram shows the relationships among rational numbers.

How would you classify the number 0.24758326... ?

Reasoning How can you use the definition of each number set to classify numbers?

Rational Numbers: $-\frac{4}{5}$, 0.75, 31.8

Integers: -5, $-\frac{16}{4}$, $-1{,}000$

Whole Numbers: 0

Natural Numbers: 19, $\sqrt{4}$

0.24758326...

The decimal expansion does not terminate or repeat, so it cannot be written as a ratio of two integers.

The number 0.24758326... is not a rational number.

Numbers that are not rational are called *irrational*. An **irrational number** is a number that cannot be written in the form $\frac{a}{b}$, where a and b are integers and $b \neq 0$.

Rational Numbers: $-\frac{4}{5}$, 0.75, 31.8

Integers: -5, $-\frac{16}{4}$, $-1{,}000$

Whole Numbers: 0

Natural Numbers: 19, $\sqrt{4}$

Irrational Numbers: $\sqrt{2}$, 1.121121112..., π, $-\sqrt{3}$

The number 0.24758326... is irrational because the decimal expansion is nonrepeating and nonterminating.

☑ Try It!

Classify each number as rational or irrational.

π 3.565565556...

0.04053661... -17

$0.\overline{76}$ 3.275

Rational	Irrational

Convince Me! Construct Arguments Jen classifies the number 4.567 as irrational because it does not repeat. Is Jen correct? Explain.

EXAMPLE **2**

Identify Square Roots as Irrational Numbers

Classify √3.

√3 means "the nonnegative square root of 3."

The **square root** of a number is a number that when multiplied by itself equals the original number. The radical symbol √ is used to denote the nonnegative square root.

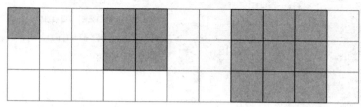

$1 \cdot 1 = 1$ $2 \cdot 2 = 4$ $3 \cdot 3 = 9$

$\sqrt{1} = 1$ $\sqrt{4} = 2$ $\sqrt{9} = 3$

The number 3 is not a perfect square, so √3 cannot be written as an integer. So, √3 is irrational.

> A **perfect square** is a number that is the square of an integer. The first three integer perfect squares are 1, 4, and 9.

> **Generalize** For any whole number b that is not a perfect square, $\sqrt{b}$ is irrational.

EXAMPLE **3**

Classify Numbers as Rational or Irrational

Classify each number as rational or irrational. Explain how you classified each number.

   −81,572   √11   5.636336333...   √16

> −81,572 is an integer and can be written as the fraction $\frac{-81,572}{1}$, so it is rational.

Rational	Irrational
−81,572	√11
√16	5.636336333...

> 11 is not a perfect square, so √11 is irrational.

> The number 16 is a perfect square, so √16 = 4 is rational.

> This decimal expansion does not repeat or terminate, so it is irrational.

 Try It!

Classify each number as rational or irrational and explain.

$\frac{2}{3}$ √25   −0.7$\overline{5}$ √2   7,548,123

Numbers that are not rational are called **irrational numbers**.

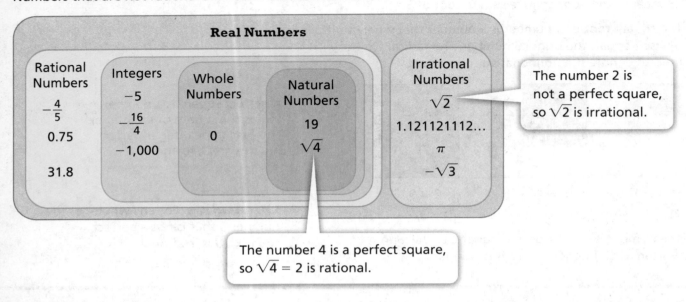

Real Numbers

Rational Numbers
$-\dfrac{4}{5}$
0.75
31.8

Integers
-5
$-\dfrac{16}{4}$
$-1,000$

Whole Numbers
0

Natural Numbers
19
$\sqrt{4}$

Irrational Numbers
$\sqrt{2}$
1.121121112...
π
$-\sqrt{3}$

The number 2 is not a perfect square, so $\sqrt{2}$ is irrational.

The number 4 is a perfect square, so $\sqrt{4} = 2$ is rational.

Do You Understand?

1. **? Essential Question** How is an irrational number different from a rational number?

2. **Reasoning** How can you tell whether a square root of a whole number is rational or irrational?

3. **Construct Arguments** Could a number ever be both rational and irrational? Explain.

Do You Know How?

4. Is the number 65.4349224... rational or irrational? Explain.

5. Is the number $\sqrt{2,500}$ rational or irrational? Explain.

6. Classify each number as rational or irrational.

$4.2\overline{7}$ 0.375   0.232342345... $\sqrt{62}$ $\dfrac{13}{1}$

Rational	Irrational

Practice & Problem Solving

7. Is 5.787787778... a rational or irrational number? Explain.

8. Is $\sqrt{42}$ rational or irrational? Explain.

9. A teacher places seven cards, lettered A–G, on a table. Which cards show irrational numbers?

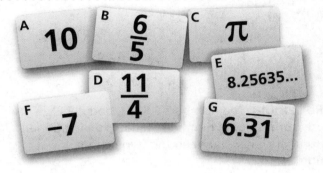

10. Circle the irrational number in the list below.

$7.\overline{27}$ $\dfrac{5}{9}$ $\sqrt{15}$ $\sqrt{196}$

11. Lisa writes the following list of numbers.

$5.737737773..., 26, \sqrt{45}, -\dfrac{3}{2}, 0, 9$

a. Which numbers are rational?

b. Which numbers are irrational?

12. Construct Arguments Deena says that 9.565565556... is a rational number because it has a repeating pattern. Do you agree? Explain.

13. Is $\sqrt{1,815}$ rational? Explain.

14. Is the decimal form of $\frac{13}{3}$ a rational number? Explain.

15. Write the side length of the square rug as a square root. Is the side length a rational or irrational number? Explain.

Area = 100 ft ^{2}

16. Reasoning The numbers 2.888... and 2.999... are both rational numbers. What is an irrational number that is between the two rational numbers?

17. Higher Order Thinking You are given the expressions $\sqrt{76 + n}$ and $\sqrt{2n + 26}$. What is the smallest value of n that will make each number rational?

✓ Assessment Practice

18. Which numbers are rational?

I.   1.1111111...

II. 1.567

III. 1.101101110...

Ⓐ II and III

Ⓑ III only

Ⓒ II only

Ⓓ I and II

Ⓔ I only

Ⓕ None of the above

19. Determine whether the following numbers are rational or irrational.

	Rational	Irrational
$\frac{8}{5}$	☐	☐
π	☐	☐
0	☐	☐
$\sqrt{1}$	☐	☐
4.46466...	☐	☐
−6	☐	☐
$\sqrt{2}$	☐	☐

Solve & Discuss It!  ACTIVITY

Courtney and Malik are buying a rug to fit in a 50-square-foot space. Which rug should they purchase? Explain.

$99 Rug Sale!

7 ft x 7 ft   8 ft diameter   6 ft x $8\frac{1}{2}$ ft

Rug Emporium has your floors covered.

I can...
compare and order rational and irrational numbers.

Focus on math practices

Make Sense and Persevere How did you decide which rug Courtney and Malik should purchase?

? **Essential Question** How can you compare and order rational and irrational numbers?

 VISUAL LEARNING   ✓ ASSESS

EXAMPLE 1 👁 **Approximate an Irrational Number**

Scan for Multimedia

Darcy wants to add the ribbon shown along the diagonal of the rectangular flag she is designing. Does Darcy have enough ribbon? Explain.

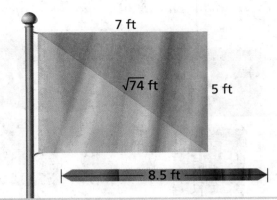

7 ft

√74 ft   5 ft

← 8.5 ft →

Approximate √74 using perfect squares.

Because 74 lies between the two consecutive perfect squares 64 and 81, √74 is located between √64 and √81.

> Because 74 is closer to 81 than 64, √74 is closer to √81, or 9.

√64   √74   √81
├────────────●──────────┤
8   9

Find a better approximation by squaring decimals between 8 and 9. Then compare.

Reasoning Which decimals can you use to find a better approximation?

8.5 × 8.5 = 72.25
This approximation is too low.

8.6 × 8.6 = 73.96
This is a good approximation.

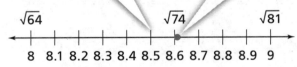

√64   √74   √81
├──┼──┼──┼──┼──┼──●──┼──┼──┼──┤
8 8.1 8.2 8.3 8.4 8.5 8.6 8.7 8.8 8.9 9

The length of the diagonal, √74, is about 8.6 feet. Darcy does not have enough ribbon.

✓ **Try It!**

Between which two whole numbers is √12?

☐ < 12 < ☐

☐ < √12 < ☐

☐ < √12 < ☐

Convince Me! Which of the two numbers is a better estimate for √12? Explain.

EXAMPLE **2** **Compare Irrational Numbers**

  ACTIVITY ASSESS

Compare $\sqrt{32}$ and 5.51326... . Plot each number at its approximate location on a number line.

STEP 1 Approximate $\sqrt{32}$ by using perfect squares.

$$25 < 32 < 36$$
$$\sqrt{25} < \sqrt{32} < \sqrt{36}$$
$$5 < \sqrt{32} < 6$$

> **Look for Relationships**
> To compare irrational numbers and locate them on a number line, you can use their rational approximations.

Then find a better approximation by using decimals.

$$5.5 \times 5.5 = 30.25 \qquad 5.6 \times 5.6 = 31.36 \qquad 5.7 \times 5.7 = 32.49$$
$$5.6 < \sqrt{32} < 5.7$$

STEP 2 Approximate 5.51326... as a rational number by rounding to the nearest tenth.

$$5.51326... \approx 5.5$$

STEP 3 Plot each approximation on a number line to compare.

So, $5.51326... < \sqrt{32}$.

EXAMPLE **3** **Compare and Order Rational and Irrational Numbers**

Compare and order the numbers below.

$$\pi^2, 9\frac{1}{2}, 9.8, 9.\overline{5}, \sqrt{94}$$

STEP 1 Use rational approximation to estimate the values of irrational numbers.

$$\pi^2 \approx 3.14 \times 3.14 \approx 9.8596$$
$$9\frac{1}{2} = 9.5$$
$$9.8$$
$$9.\overline{5} = 9.5555...$$
$$\sqrt{94} \approx 9.7$$

STEP 2 Plot each approximation on a number line.

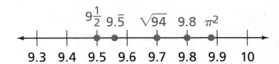

So, $9\frac{1}{2} < 9.\overline{5} < \sqrt{94} < 9.8 < \pi^2$.

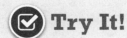 **Try It!**

Compare and order the following numbers:

$$\sqrt{11}, 2\frac{1}{4}, -2.5, 3.\overline{6}, -3.97621 ...$$

To compare rational and irrational numbers, you must first find rational approximations of the irrational numbers. You can approximate irrational numbers using perfect squares or by rounding.

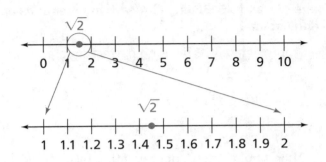

Do You Understand?

1. **? Essential Question** How can you compare and order rational and irrational numbers?

2. **Reasoning** The "leech" is a technical term for the slanted edge of a sail. Is the length of the leech shown closer to 5 meters or 6 meters? Explain.

3. **Construct Arguments** Which is a better approximation of $\sqrt{20}$, 4.5 or 4.47? Explain.

Do You Know How?

4. Approximate $\sqrt{39}$ to the nearest whole number.

5. Approximate $\sqrt{18}$ to the nearest tenth and plot the number on a number line.

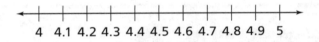

6. Compare 5.7145… and $\sqrt{29}$. Show your work.

7. Compare and order the following numbers:

   5.2, $-5.\overline{6}$, $3\frac{9}{10}$, $\sqrt{21}$

Practice & Problem Solving

8. Leveled Practice Find the rational approximation of $\sqrt{15}$.

a. Approximate using perfect squares.

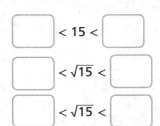

$\boxed{} < 15 < \boxed{}$

$\boxed{} < \sqrt{15} < \boxed{}$

$\boxed{} < \sqrt{15} < \boxed{}$

b. Locate and plot $\sqrt{15}$ on a number line.

Find a better approximation using decimals.

$3.8 \times 3.8 = \boxed{}$

$3.9 \times 3.9 = \boxed{}$

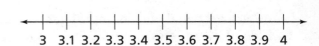

3 3.1 3.2 3.3 3.4 3.5 3.6 3.7 3.8 3.9 4

9. Compare $-1.96312\ldots$ and $-\sqrt{5}$.
Show your work.

10. Does $\frac{1}{6}$, -3, $\sqrt{7}$, $-\frac{6}{5}$, or 4.5 come first when the numbers are listed from least to greatest? Explain.

11. A museum director wants to hang the painting on a wall. To the nearest foot, how tall does the wall need to be?

$\sqrt{90}$ ft

12. Dina has several small clay pots. She wants to display them in order of height, from shortest to tallest. What will be the order of the pots?

$\sqrt{8}$ in. $2\frac{1}{3}$ in. $\sqrt{5}$ in.   2.5 in.

13. Rosie is comparing $\sqrt{7}$ and 3.44444... . She says that $\sqrt{7} > 3.44444...$ because $\sqrt{7} = 3.5$.

a. What is the correct comparison?

b. **Critique Reasoning** What mistake did Rosie likely make?

14. **Model with Math** Approximate $-\sqrt{23}$ to the nearest tenth. Draw the point on the number line.

15. **Higher Order Thinking** The length of a rectangle is twice the width. The area of the rectangle is 90 square units. Note that you can divide the rectangle into two squares.

Area = 90 square units

a. Which irrational number represents the length of each side of the squares?

b. Estimate the length and width of the rectangle.

☑ Assessment Practice

16. Which list shows the numbers in order from least to greatest?

Ⓐ $-4, -\frac{9}{4}, \frac{1}{2}, 3.7, \sqrt{5}$

Ⓑ $-4, -\frac{9}{4}, \frac{1}{2}, \sqrt{5}, 3.7$

Ⓒ $-\frac{9}{4}, \frac{1}{2}, 3.7, \sqrt{5}, -4$

Ⓓ $-\frac{9}{4}, -4, \frac{1}{2}, 3.7, \sqrt{5}$

17. The area of a square poster is 31 square inches. Find the length of one side of the poster. Explain.

PART A

To the nearest whole inch

PART B

To the nearest tenth of an inch

👆 Solve & Discuss It!

 👆 ACTIVITY

Matt and his dad are building a tree house. They buy enough flooring material to cover an area of 36 square feet. What are all possible dimensions of the floor?

I can...
find square roots and cube roots of rational numbers.

Look for Relationships
Can different floor dimensions result in the same area?

Focus on math practices

Reasoning Why is there only one set of dimensions for a square floor when there are more sets for a rectangular floor? Are all the dimensions reasonable? Explain.

VISUAL LEARNING

ASSESS

EXAMPLE 1 **Evaluate Cube Roots to Solve Problems**

Scan for Multimedia

Leah is building a bird house for purple martins, birds that prefer cube-shaped birdhouses. What are the dimensions of each square piece of wood Leah needs to build the 216 cubic-inch birdhouse?

Reasoning What do you know about the length, width, and height of the birdhouse?

Draw and label a cube to represent the birdhouse.

$V = 216$ in.^{3}

s

s

s

$216 = s \cdot s \cdot s$

$216 = s^3$

A number that is a cube of an integer is a **perfect cube**.

The number 216 is also a perfect cube.

To find the value of s, find the cube root of 216. The **cube root** of a number is a number whose cube is equal to that number.

The symbol $\sqrt[3]{\ }$ means the cube root of a number.

$\sqrt[3]{216} = \sqrt[3]{6 \cdot 6 \cdot 6}$

$= \sqrt[3]{6^3}$

$= 6$

Taking the cube root and cubing a number are inverse operations.

The dimensions of each square piece of wood are 6 inches by 6 inches.

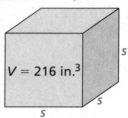 **Try It!**

A cube-shaped art sculpture has a volume of 64 cubic feet. What is the length of each edge of the cube?

The length of each edge is ⬜ feet.

$\sqrt[3]{64} = \sqrt[3]{\boxed{} \cdot \boxed{} \cdot \boxed{}}$

$\sqrt[3]{64} = \sqrt[3]{\boxed{}^{3}}$

$\sqrt[3]{64} = \boxed{}$

Convince Me! How can you find the cube root of 64?

EXAMPLE 2 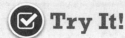 Evaluate Perfect Squares and Perfect Cubes

Evaluate.

A. $\sqrt[3]{64}$

$\sqrt[3]{64} = \sqrt[3]{4 \cdot 4 \cdot 4}$

$= \sqrt[3]{4^3}$

$= 4$

B. $\sqrt{100}$

$\sqrt{100} = \sqrt{10 \cdot 10}$

$= \sqrt{10^2}$

$= 10$

C. $\sqrt{49}$

$\sqrt{49} = \sqrt{27 \cdot 7}$

$= \sqrt{7^2}$

$= 7$

D. $\sqrt[3]{8}$

$\sqrt[3]{8} = \sqrt[3]{2 \cdot 2 \cdot 2}$

$= \sqrt[3]{2^3}$

$= 2$

Try It!

Evaluate.

a. $\sqrt[3]{27}$

b. $\sqrt{25}$

c. $\sqrt{81}$

d. $\sqrt[3]{1}$

EXAMPLE 3 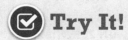 Evaluate Square Roots to Solve Problems

Sean cuts one sheet of colorful poster paper to cover the bulletin board exactly. What are the dimensions of the poster paper?

Find the square root of the area to find the side lengths of the bulletin board.

$\sqrt{144} = \sqrt{12 \cdot 12}$

$= \sqrt{12^2}$

$= 12$

Each side of the bulletin board measures 12 inches. Sean will need to cut a 12-inch by 12-inch sheet of poster paper.

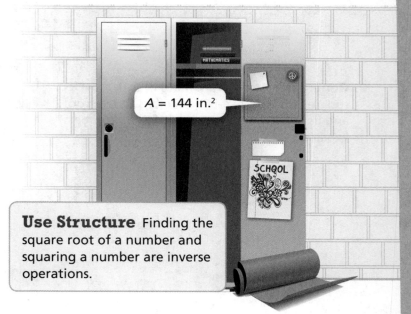

$A = 144$ in.^{2}

Use Structure Finding the square root of a number and squaring a number are inverse operations.

Try It!

Emily wants to buy a tablecloth to cover a square card table. She knows the tabletop has an area of 9 square feet. What are the minimum dimensions of the tablecloth Emily needs?

Emily should buy a tablecloth that measures at least ☐ feet by ☐ feet.

$\sqrt{9} = \sqrt{\boxed{} \cdot \boxed{}}$

$= \sqrt{\boxed{}^2}$

$= \boxed{}$

The cube root of a number is a number whose cube is equal to that number.

$$\sqrt[3]{125} = \sqrt[3]{5 \cdot 5 \cdot 5}$$
$$= \sqrt[3]{5^3}$$
$$= 5$$

> Cubing a number and taking the cube root of the number are inverse operations.

The square root of a number is a number whose square is equal to that number.

$$\sqrt{4} = \sqrt{2 \cdot 2}$$
$$= \sqrt{2^2}$$
$$= 2$$

> Squaring a number and taking the square root of the number are inverse operations.

Do You Understand?

1. **? Essential Question** How do you evaluate cube roots and square roots?

2. **Generalize** A certain number is both a perfect square and a perfect cube. Will its square root and its cube root always be different numbers? Explain.

3. **Critique Reasoning** A cube-shaped box has a volume of 27 cubic inches. Bethany says each side of the cube measures 9 inches because $9 \times 3 = 27$. Is Bethany correct? Explain your reasoning.

Do You Know How?

4. A cube has a volume of 8 cubic inches. What is the length of each edge of the cube?

5. Below is a model of the infield of a baseball stadium. How long is each side of the infield?

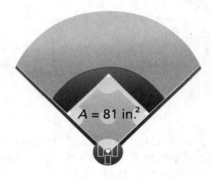

$A = 81 \text{ in.}^2$

6. Julio cubes a number and then takes the cube root of the result. He ends up with 20. What number did Julio start with?

Practice & Problem Solving

Scan for
Multimedia

Leveled Practice In 7 and 8, evaluate the cube root or square root.

7. Relate the volume of the cube to the length of each edge.

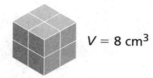

$V = 8 \text{ cm}^3$

Edge length   Edge length   Edge length

☐ cm × ☐ cm × ☐ cm

$\sqrt[3]{8} = $ ☐

8. Relate the area of the square to the length of each side.

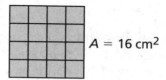

$A = 16 \text{ cm}^2$

Side length   Side length

☐ cm × ☐ cm

$\sqrt{16} = $ ☐

9. Would you classify the number 169 as a perfect square, a perfect cube, both, or neither? Explain.

10. The volume of a cube is 512 cubic inches. What is the length of each side of the cube?

11. A square technology chip has an area of 25 square centimeters. How long is each side of the chip?

12. Would you classify the number 200 as a perfect square, a perfect cube, both, or neither? Explain.

13. A company is making building blocks. What is the length of each side of the block?

$V = 1 \text{ ft}^3$

14. Mrs. Drew wants to build a square sandbox with an area of 121 square feet. What is the total length of wood Mrs. Drew needs to make the sides of the sandbox?

15. Construct Arguments Diego says that if you cube the number 4 and then take the cube root of the result, you end up with 8. Is Diego correct? Explain.

16. Higher Order Thinking Talia is packing a moving box. She has a square-framed poster with an area of 9 square feet. The cube-shaped box has a volume of 30 cubic feet. Will the poster lie flat in the box? Explain.

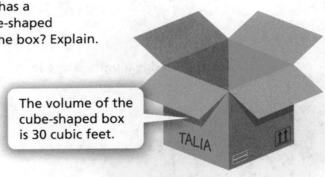

The volume of the cube-shaped box is 30 cubic feet.

TALIA

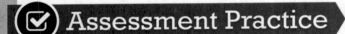
☑ Assessment Practice

17. Which expression has the greatest value?

Ⓐ $\sqrt{49} \cdot 2$

Ⓑ $\sqrt{49} - \sqrt{16}$

Ⓒ $\sqrt{25} + \sqrt{16}$

Ⓓ $\sqrt{25} \cdot 3$

18. A toy has various shaped objects that a child can push through matching holes. The area of the square hole is 8 square centimeters. The volume of a cube-shaped block is 64 cubic centimeters.

PART A

Which edge length can you find? Explain.

PART B

Will the block fit in the square hole? Explain.

Solve & Discuss It! 📶 👆 ACTIVITY

Janine can use up to 150 one-inch blocks to build a solid, cube-shaped model. What are the dimensions of the possible models that she can build? How many blocks would Janine use for each model? Explain.

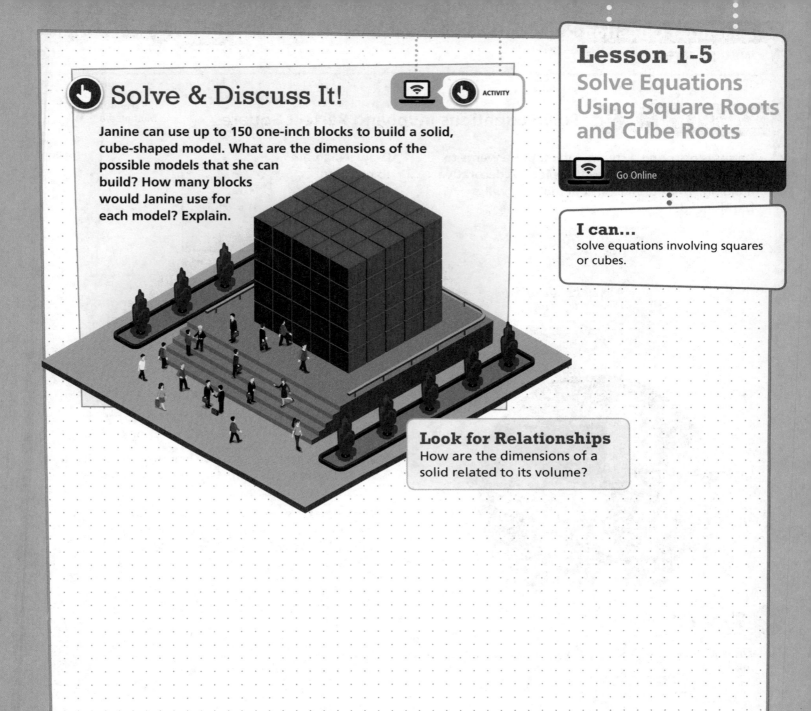

I can...
solve equations involving squares or cubes.

Look for Relationships
How are the dimensions of a solid related to its volume?

Focus on math practices

Reasoning Janine wants to build a model using $\frac{1}{2}$-inch cubes. How many $\frac{1}{2}$-inch cubes would she use to build a solid, cube-shaped model with side lengths of 4 inches? Show your work.

? **Essential Question** How can you solve equations with squares and cubes?

 VISUAL LEARNING   ASSESS

EXAMPLE 1 Solve Equations Involving Perfect Squares

Scan for Multimedia

Darius is restoring a square tabletop. He wants to finish the outside edges with a piece of decorative molding. What total length of molding will Darius need?

A = 25 ft²

Draw a diagram to represent the tabletop.

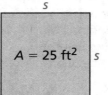

s

$A = 25$ ft² s

Use the formula $A = s^2$ to find each side length. To solve, take the square root of both sides of the equation.

$$A = s^2$$
$$25 = s^2$$
$$\sqrt{25} = \sqrt{s^2}$$
$$\pm 5 = s$$

Because $5^2 = 5 \times 5 = 25$ and $(-5)^2 = -5 \times -5 = 25$, $s = 5$ and $s = -5$, or $s = \pm 5$.

Since length is positive, each side length of the tabletop is 5 feet. Darius needs 20 feet of decorative molding.

Generalize In general, an equation of the form $x^2 = p$, where p is a positive rational number, has two solutions, $x = \pm \sqrt{p}$.

☑ Try It!

What is the side length, s, of the square below?

A = 100 m²

$$A = s^2$$
$$\boxed{} = s^2$$
$$\boxed{} = \sqrt{s^2}$$
$$\pm \boxed{} = s$$

Each side of the square measures $\boxed{}$ meters.

Convince Me! Why are there two possible solutions to the equation $s^2 = 100$? Explain why only one of the solutions is valid in this situation.

EXAMPLE **2** Solve Equations Involving Perfect Cubes   ACTIVITY ASSESS

Kyle has a large, cube-shaped terrarium for his iguana. He wants to cover the opening with a square screen. What are the dimensions, s, for the screen?

$V = s^3$

$343 = s^3$

$\sqrt[3]{343} = \sqrt[3]{s^3}$

$7 = s$

The value of s is not $\pm \sqrt[3]{343}$ because $(-7)^3 = -7 \times -7 \times -7 = -343$.

Each edge of the terrarium is 7 feet, so the dimensions of the screen are 7 feet by 7 feet.

$V = 343 \text{ ft}^3$

 Try It!

Solve $x^3 = 64$.

 EXAMPLE **3** **Solve Equations Involving Imperfect Squares and Cubes**

Solve for x.

A. $x^2 = 50$

$\sqrt{x^2} = \sqrt{50}$

$x = \pm \sqrt{50}$

Because 50 is not a perfect square, write the solution using the square root symbol.

There are two possible solutions, $x = +\sqrt{50}$ and $x = -\sqrt{50}$.

B. $x^3 = 37$

$\sqrt[3]{x^3} = \sqrt[3]{37}$

$x = \sqrt[3]{37}$

$x = \sqrt[3]{37}$ is an exact solution of the equation.

There is one possible solution, $x = \sqrt[3]{37}$.

 Try It!

a. Solve $a^3 = 11$.

b. Solve $c^2 = 27$.

You can use square roots to solve equations involving squares.

$$x^2 = a$$
$$\sqrt{x^2} = \sqrt{a}$$
$$x = +\sqrt{a}, -\sqrt{a}$$

You can use cube roots to solve equations involving cubes.

$$x^3 = b$$
$$\sqrt[3]{x^3} = \sqrt[3]{b}$$
$$x = \sqrt[3]{b}$$

Do You Understand?

1. **? Essential Question** How can you solve equations with squares and cubes?

2. **Be Precise** Suri solved the equation $x^2 = 49$ and found that $x = 7$. What error did Suri make?

3. **Construct Arguments** There is an error in the work shown below. Explain the error and provide a correct solution.

$$x^3 = 125$$
$$\sqrt[3]{x^3} = \sqrt[3]{125}$$
$$x = 5 \text{ and } x = -5$$

4. Why are the solutions to $x^2 = 17$ irrational?

Do You Know How?

5. If a cube has a volume of 27 cubic centimeters, what is the length of each edge? Use the volume formula, $V = s^3$, and show your work.

6. Darius is building a square launch pad for a rocket project. If the area of the launch pad is 121 square centimeters, what is its side length? Use the area formula, $A = s^2$, and show your work.

$A = 121 \text{ cm}^2$

7. Solve the equation $x^3 = -215$.

Practice & Problem Solving

Leveled Practice In **8** and **9**, solve.

8. $z^2 = 1$

$$\sqrt{\boxed{}} = \sqrt{\boxed{}}$$

$$z = \pm\boxed{}$$

The solutions are $\boxed{}$ and $\boxed{}$.

9. $a^3 = 216$

$$\sqrt[3]{\boxed{}} = \sqrt[3]{\boxed{}}$$

$$a = \boxed{}$$

10. Solve $v^2 = 47$.

11. The area of a square photo is 9 square inches. How long is each side of the photo?

12. Solve the equation $y^2 = 81$.

13. Solve the equation $w^3 = 1{,}000$.

14. The area of a square garden is shown. How long is each side of the garden?

$A = 121 \text{ ft}^2$

s

15. Solve $b^2 = 77$.

16. Find the value of c in the equation $c^3 = 1{,}728$.

17. Solve the equation $v^3 = 12$.

18. Higher Order Thinking Explain why $\sqrt[3]{-\frac{8}{27}}$ is $-\frac{2}{3}$

19. Critique Reasoning Manolo says that the solution of the equation $g^2 = 36$ is $g = 6$ because $6 \times 6 = 36$. Is Manolo's reasoning complete? Explain.

20. Evaluate $\sqrt[3]{-512}$.

  a. Write your answer as an integer.

  b. Explain how you can check that your result is correct.

21. Yael has a square-shaped garage with 228 square feet of floor space. She plans to build an addition that will increase the floor space by 50%. What will be the length, to the nearest tenth, of one side of the new garage?

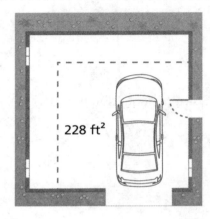

228 ft²

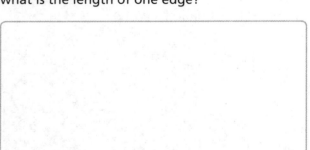

Assessment Practice

22. The Traverses are adding a new room to their house. The room will be a cube with a volume of 6,859 cubic feet. They are going to put in hardwood floors, which costs $10 per square foot. How much will the hardwood floors cost?

23. While packing for their cross-country move, the Chen family uses a crate that has the shape of a cube.

PART A

If the crate has the volume $V = 64$ cubic feet, what is the length of one edge?

PART B

The Chens want to pack a large, framed painting. If the framed painting has the shape of a square with an area of 12 square feet, will the painting fit flat against a side of the crate? Explain.

Name: ______________________

MID-TOPIC CHECKPOINT

TOPIC 1

1. **Vocabulary** How can you show that a number is a rational number? *Lesson 1-2*

2. Which shows $0.2\overline{3}$ as a fraction? *Lesson 1-1*

Ⓐ $\frac{2}{33}$

Ⓑ $\frac{7}{33}$

Ⓒ $\frac{23}{99}$

Ⓓ $\frac{7}{30}$

3. Approximate $\sqrt{8}$ to the nearest hundredth. Show your work. *Lesson 1-3*

4. Solve the equation $m^2 = 14$. *Lesson 1-5*

5. A fish tank is in the shape of a cube. Its volume is 125 ft^3. What is the area of one face of the tank? *Lessons 1-4 and 1-5*

6. Write $1.\overline{12}$ as a mixed number. Show your work. *Lesson 1-1*

How well did you do on the mid-topic checkpoint? Fill in the stars. ☆☆☆

MID-TOPIC
PERFORMANCE TASK

Six members of the math club are forming two teams for a contest. The teams will be determined by having each student draw a number from a box.

Student	Number Drawn
Lydia	$\sqrt{38}$
Marcy	$6.3\overline{4}$
Caleb	$\sqrt{36}$
Ryan	6.343443444...
Anya	$6.\overline{34}$
Chan	$\sqrt{34}$

PART A

The table shows the results of the draw. The students who drew rational numbers will form the team called the Tigers. The students who drew irrational numbers will form the team called the Lions.

List the members of each team.

PART B

The student on each team who drew the greatest number will be the captain of that team. Who will be the captain of the Tigers? Show your work.

PART C

Who will be the captain of the Lions? Show your work.

 Solve & Discuss It!

One band's streaming video concert to benefit a global charity costs $1.00 to view.

The first day, the concert got 2,187 views. The second day, it got about three times as many views. On the third day, it got 3 times as many views as on the second day. If the trend continues, how much money will the band raise on Day 7?

I can...
use the properties of exponents to write equivalent expressions.

Focus on math practices

Use Structure Use prime factorization to write an expression equivalent to the amount of money raised by the band on the last day of the week.

VISUAL LEARNING

ASSESS

EXAMPLE 1 👁 **Multiply Exponential Expressions: Same Base**

Scan for Multimedia

The weight of a juvenile alligator is shown on the right. The adult alligator weighs about 2^6 times more than the juvenile. How can you determine the weight of the adult alligator?

2^3 pounds

Look for Relationships How do the two weights relate?

ONE WAY Write the two expressions in expanded form.

2^3 2^6

$2 \times 2 \times 2 \times$ $2 \times 2 \times 2 \times 2 \times 2 \times 2$

2 is multiplied 3 times   2 is multiplied 6 times

Join the two expressions.

$\underbrace{2 \times 2 \times 2 \times 2 \times 2 \times 2 \times 2 \times 2 \times 2}_{\text{2 is multiplied 9 times}} = 2^9$

ANOTHER WAY Use the Product of Powers Property.

$2^3 \times 2^6 = 2^{3+6} = 2^9$

The **Product of Powers Property** states that when multiplying two powers with the same base, add the exponents.

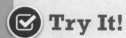 **Try It!**

The local zoo welcomed a newborn African elephant that weighed 3^4 kg. It is expected that at adulthood, the newborn elephant will weigh approximately 3^4 times as much as its birth weight. What expression represents the expected adult weight of the newborn elephant?

Convince Me! Explain why the Product of Powers Property makes mathematical sense.

Find the volume in cubic inches of a cube with edge length of 2 feet.

$V = 2^3$ cubic feet   1 cubic foot = 12^3 cubic inches

$2^3 \times 12^3 = \underbrace{2 \times 2 \times 2 \times 12 \times 12 \times 12}$

$= (2 \times 12) \times (2 \times 12) \times (2 \times 12)$ ◄ Use the Associative and Commutative Properties.

$= (2 \times 12)^3$

$= 24^3$ cubic inches ◄ Use the **Power of Products Property:** when multiplying two exponential expressions with the same exponent and different bases, multiply the bases and keep the exponent the same.

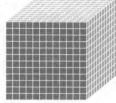

1 cubic foot

12^3 cubic inches

EXAMPLE **3** **Find the Power of a Power**

Write an equivalent expression for $(5^2)^4$.

$(5^2)^4 = \underbrace{(5^2)(5^2)(5^2)(5^2)}_{5^2 \text{ multiplied 4 times}}$

$= 5^{(2+2+2+2)}$ ◄ Use the Product of Powers Property to add the exponents.

$= 5^8$ ◄ The **Power of Powers Property** states that to find the power of a power, multiply the exponents.

EXAMPLE **4** **Divide Exponential Expressions: Same Base**

Write an equivalent expression for $6^5 \div 6^3$.

$6^5 \div 6^3 = \dfrac{6^5}{6^3}$ ◄ Write as a fraction.

$= \dfrac{\overbrace{6 \times 6 \times 6 \times 6 \times 6}^{6 \text{ multiplied 5 times}}}{\underbrace{6 \times 6 \times 6}_{6 \text{ multiplied 3 times}}}$

Remember, $\dfrac{6}{6} = 1$.

$= \dfrac{6 \times \boxed{6 \times 6 \times 6} \times 6}{\boxed{6 \times 6 \times 6}}$ ◄ The **Quotient of Powers Property** states that when dividing two exponential expressions with the same base, subtract the exponents.

$= 6 \times 6$ or 6^2

 Try It!

Write equivalent expressions using the properties of exponents.

a. $(7^3)^2$ **b.** $(4^5)^3$ **c.** $9^4 \times 8^4$ **d.** $8^9 \div 8^3$

Use these properties when simplifying expressions with exponents (when a, m, and $n \neq 0$).

Product of Powers Property

When the bases are the same, $a^m \times a^n = a^{m+n}$ add the exponents.

Power of Products Property

When the bases are different, $a^n \times b^n = (a \times b)^n$ multiply the bases and keep the exponent the same.

Power of a Power Property

To find the power of a power, $(a^m)^n = a^{m \times n}$ multiply the exponents.

Quotient of Powers Property

When the bases are the same, $a^m \div a^n = a^{m-n}$ subtract the exponents.

Do You Understand?

1. **? Essential Question** How do properties of integer exponents help you write equivalent expressions?

2. **Look for Relationships** If you are writing an equivalent expression for $2^3 \cdot 2^4$, how many times would you write 2 as a factor?

3. **Construct Arguments** Kristen wrote 5^8 as an expression equivalent to $(5^2)^4$. Her math partner writes 5^6. Who is correct?

4. **Critique Reasoning** Tyler says that an equivalent expression for $2^3 \times 5^3$ is 10^9. Is he correct? Explain.

Do You Know How?

5. Write an equivalent expression for $7^{12} \cdot 7^4$.

6. Write an equivalent expression for $(8^2)^4$.

7. A billboard has the given dimensions.

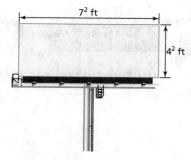

Using exponents, write two equivalent expressions for the area of the rectangle.

8. Write an equivalent expression for $18^9 \div 18^4$.

Name: _____

Practice & Problem Solving

Leveled Practice In **9–12**, use the properties of exponents to write an equivalent expression for each given expression.

9. $2^8 \cdot 2^4$

$$2^8 \cdot 2^4 = 2^{8\,\boxed{}\,4}$$

$$= \boxed{}^{\boxed{}}$$

10. $\dfrac{8^7}{8^3}$

$$\dfrac{8^7}{8^3} = 8^{7\,\boxed{}\,3}$$

$$= \boxed{}^{\boxed{}}$$

11. $(3^4)^5$

$$(3^4)^5 = 3^{4\,\boxed{}\,5}$$

$$= \boxed{}^{\boxed{}}$$

12. $3^9 \cdot 2^9$

$$3^9 \cdot 2^9 = \left(\boxed{} \cdot \boxed{}\right)^{\boxed{}}$$

13. a. How do you multiply powers that have the same base?

b. How do you divide powers that have the same base?

c. How do you find the power of a power?

d. How do you multiply powers with different bases but the same exponent?

14. Which expressions are equivalent to 2^{11}? Select all that apply.

☐ $\dfrac{2^{23}}{2^{12}}$

☐ $2^7 \cdot 2^4$

☐ $\dfrac{2^9}{2^2}$

☐ $2^2 \cdot 2^9$

In **15–18**, use the properties of exponents to write an equivalent expression for each given expression.

15. $(4^4)^3$

16. $\dfrac{3^{12}}{3^3}$

17. $4^5 \cdot 4^2$

18. $6^4 \cdot 2^4$

19. Critique Reasoning Alberto incorrectly stated that $\frac{5^7}{5^4} = 1^3$. What was Alberto's error? Explain your reasoning and find the correct answer.

20. Is the expression 8×8^5 equivalent to $(8 \times 8)^5$? Explain.

21. Is the expression $(3^2)^{-3}$ equivalent to $(3^3)^{-2}$? Explain.

22. Is the expression $3^2 \cdot 3^{-3}$ equivalent to $3^3 \cdot 3^{-2}$? Explain.

23. Model with Math What is the width of the rectangle written as an exponential expression?

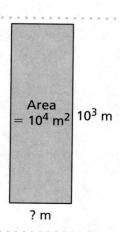

Area = 10^4 m² | 10^3 m

? m

24. Simplify the expression $\left(\left(\frac{1}{2}\right)^3\right)^3$.

25. Higher Order Thinking Use a property of exponents to write $(3b)^5$ as a product of powers.

26. Select all the expressions equivalent to $4^5 \cdot 4^{10}$.

☐ $4^5 + 4^{10}$

☐ $4^3 \cdot 4^5$

☐ $4^3 \cdot 4^{12}$

☐ $4^3 + 4^{12}$

☐ $4^{18} - 4^3$

☐ 4^{15}

27. Your teacher asks the class to evaluate the expression $(2^3)^1$. Your classmate gives an incorrect answer of 16.

PART A Evaluate the expression.

PART B What was the likely error?

Ⓐ Your classmate divided the exponents.

Ⓑ Your classmate multiplied the exponents.

Ⓒ Your classmate added the exponents.

Ⓓ Your classmate subtracted the exponents.

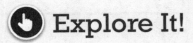 **Explore It!**

Calvin and Mike do sit-ups when they work out. They start with 64 sit-ups for the first set and do half as many each subsequent set.

Look for Relationships Determine whether the relationship shown for Set 1 is also true for Sets 2–5.

Lesson 1-7
More Properties of Integer Exponents

I can...
write a number with a negative or zero exponent a different way.

A. What representation can you use to show the relationship between the set number and the number of sit-ups?

B. What conclusion can you make about the relationship between the number of sit-ups in each set?

Focus on math practices

Use Structure How could you determine the number of sit-up sets Calvin and Mike do?

VISUAL LEARNING   ASSESS

EXAMPLE 1 ◉ **The Zero Exponent Property**

Scan for Multimedia

Marchella is playing a card-matching game with some classmates. Four matches have been made. It is Marchella's turn, and she chooses 3^0. What card would complete her match?

Organize the information in a table and look for a pattern.

Exponent Form	Simplified Form
3^4	81
3^3	27
3^2	9
3^1	3
3^0	?

$÷ 3$
$÷ 3$
$÷ 3$
$÷ 3$

As the exponent decreases by one, the product is divided by 3.

$3 ÷ 3 = 1$, so $3^0 = 1$.

ANOTHER WAY Use the Quotient of Powers Property.

$3^3 ÷ 3^3$

$= 3^{3-3} = 3^0$

When dividing two exponential expressions with the same base, subtract the exponents.

and

$$\frac{3^3}{3^3} = \frac{3 × 3 × 3}{3 × 3 × 3} = 1$$

so $3^0 = 1$

The **Zero Exponent Property** states that $a^0 = 1$ (assuming $a ≠ 0$).

☑ Try It!

Evaluate.

a. $(-7)^0$ b. $(43)^0$ c. 1^0 d. $(0.5)^0$

Convince Me! Why is $2(7^0) = 2$?

EXAMPLE 2   The Negative Exponent Property

Simplify the expression $4^3 \div 4^5$.

$$4^3 \div 4^5 = \frac{4^3}{4^5}$$

> Remember, $\frac{4}{4} = 1$.

$$= \frac{\boxed{4 \times 4 \times 4}}{4 \times \boxed{4 \times 4 \times 4} \times 4} = \frac{1}{16}$$

and

$$4^3 \div 4^5 = 4^{(3-5)} = 4^{-2}$$

> Use the Quotient of Powers Property.

So, $4^{-2} = \frac{1}{16}$.

> The **Negative Exponent Property** states that $a^{-n} = \frac{1}{a^n}$ (assuming $a \neq 0$).

Try It!

Write each expression using positive exponents.

a. 8^{-2} b. 2^{-4} c. 3^{-5}

EXAMPLE 3   Expressions with Negative Exponents

Write the expression $\frac{1}{7^{-3}}$ **with a positive exponent.**

$$\frac{1}{7^{-3}} = \frac{1}{\frac{1}{7^3}}$$

> Use the Negative Exponent Property.

$$= 1 \cdot \frac{7^3}{1}$$

> Multiply by the reciprocal of the denominator.

$$= 7^3$$

Try It!

Write each expression using positive exponents.

a. $\frac{1}{5^{-3}}$ b. $\frac{1}{2^{-6}}$

Use these additional properties when simplifying or generating equivalent expressions with exponents (when $a \neq 0$ and $n \neq 0$).

Zero Exponent Property	Negative Exponent Property
$a^0 = 1$	$a^{-n} = \dfrac{1}{a^n}$

Do You Understand?

1. **? Essential Question** What do the Zero Exponent and Negative Exponent Properties mean?

2. **Reasoning** In the expression 9^{-12}, what does the negative exponent mean?

3. **Reasoning** In the expression $3(2^0)$, what is the order of operations? Explain how you would evaluate the expression.

Do You Know How?

4. Simplify $1,999,999^0$.

5. **a.** Write 7^{-6} using a positive exponent.

   b. Rewrite $\dfrac{1}{10^{-3}}$ using a positive exponent.

6. Evaluate $27x^0y^{-2}$ for $x = 4$ and $y = 3$.

Name: _____

Practice & Problem Solving ✏️ ⏻

Leveled Practice In 7–8, complete each table to find the value of a nonzero number raised to the power of 0.

7.

Exponent	Simplified
4^4	256
4^3	☐
4^2	☐
4^1	☐
4^0	☐

8.

Exponent	Simplified
$(-2)^4$	16
$(-2)^3$	☐
$(-2)^2$	☐
$(-2)^1$	☐
$(-2)^0$	☐

9. Given: $(-3.2)^0$

   a. Simplify the given expression.

   b. Write two expressions equivalent to the given expression. Explain why the three expressions are equivalent.

10. Simplify each expression for $x = 6$.

   a. $12x^0(x^{-4})$

   b. $14(x^{-2})$

In **11** and **12**, compare the values using >,<, or =.

11. 3^{-2} ☐ 1

12. $(\frac{1}{4})^0$ ☐ 1

In **13** and **14**, rewrite each expression using a positive exponent.

13. 9^{-4}

14. $\frac{1}{2^{-6}}$

15. Given: $9y^0$

   a. Simplify the expression for $y = 3$.

   b. **Construct Arguments** Will the value of the given expression vary depending on y? Explain.

16. Simplify each expression for $x = 4$.

a. $-5x^{-4}$

b. $7x^{-3}$

17. Evaluate each pair of expressions.

a. $(-3)^{-8}$ and -3^{-8}

b. $(-3)^{-9}$ and -3^{-9}

18. Be Precise To win a math game, Lamar has to pick a card with an expression that has a value greater than 1. The card Lamar chooses reads $\left(\frac{1}{2}\right)^{-4}$. Does Lamar win the game? Explain.

19. Simplify the expression. Assume that x is nonzero. Your answer should have only positive exponents.

$x^{-10} \cdot x^6$

20. Higher Order Thinking

a. Is the value of the expression $\left(\frac{1}{4^{-3}}\right)^{-2}$ greater than 1, equal to 1, or less than 1?

b. If the value of the expression is greater than 1, show how you can change one sign to make the value less than 1. If the value is less than 1, show how you can change one sign to make the value greater than 1. If the value is equal to 1, show how you can make one change to make the value not equal to 1.

☑ Assessment Practice

21. Which expressions are equal to 5^{-3}? Select all that apply.

- ☐ 125
- ☐ 125^{-1}
- ☐ 5^3
- ☐ $\frac{1}{5^3}$
- ☐ $\frac{1}{125}$

22. Which expressions have a value less than 1 when $x = 4$? Select all that apply.

- ☐ $\left(\frac{3}{x^2}\right)^0$
- ☐ $\frac{x^0}{3^2}$
- ☐ $\frac{1}{6^{-x}}$
- ☐ $\frac{1}{x^{-3}}$
- ☐ $3x^{-4}$

Lesson 1-8
Use Powers of 10 to Estimate Quantities

 Go Online

I can...
estimate large and small quantities using a power of 10.

🔘 **Explain It!**

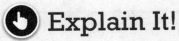 ACTIVITY

Keegan and Jeff did some research and found that there are approximately 7,492,000,000,000,000,000 grains of sand on Earth. Jeff says that it is about 7×10^{15} grains of sand. Keegan says that this is about 7×10^{18} grains of sand.

7,492,000,000,000,000,000

A. How might Jeff have determined his estimate? How might Keegan have determined his estimate?

B. Whose estimate, Jeff's or Keegan's, is more logical? Explain.

Focus on math practices

Be Precise Do you think the two estimates are close in value? Explain your reasoning.

53

VISUAL LEARNING · ASSESS

EXAMPLE 1 Estimate Very Large Quantities

Scan for Multimedia

Janelle is comparing the estimated populations of Japan and China. The estimated population of Japan is 126,818,019. The estimated population of China is shown. How can Janelle compare the two populations more easily?

Use Structure You can estimate large quantities and write them in a format that is easier to compare.

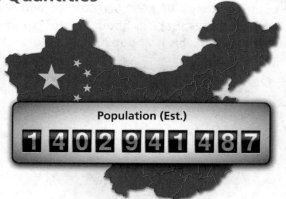

Population (Est.)

1 4 0 2 9 4 1 4 8 7

STEP 1 Estimate each population by rounding to the greatest place value. Then write the number as a single digit times a power of 10.

Population of China

1,402,941,487

rounds to 1,000,000,000

1×10^9

Count the zeros to determine the power of 10.

Population of Japan

126,818,019

rounds to 100,000,000

1×10^8

STEP 2 Compare the estimated values.

$$10^9 > 10^8$$

$$1 \times 10^9 > 1 \times 10^8$$

Janelle can use estimates using powers of 10 to compare the populations more easily.

☑ Try It!

Light travels 299,792,458 meters per second. Sound travels at 332 meters per second. Use a power of 10 to compare the speed of light to the speed of sound.

299,792,458 rounded to the greatest place value is [   ].

322 rounded to the greatest place value is [   ].

There are [ ] zeros in the rounded number.

The estimated speed of light

is [ ] × 10^[ ] meters per second.

There are [ ] zeros in the rounded number.

The estimated speed of sound

is [ ] × 10^[ ] meters per second.

$3 \times 10^{[\ ]} > 3 \times 10^{[\ ]}$, so the speed of light is faster than the speed of sound.

Convince Me! Country A has a population of 1,238,682,005 and Country B has a population of 1,106,487,394. How would you compare these populations?

EXAMPLE **2** **Estimate Very Small Quantities**

  ACTIVITY ASSESS

Matthias used a laser to measure the average thickness of a human hair. A sheet of paper is about 0.0013 meter thick. How do the two thicknesses compare?

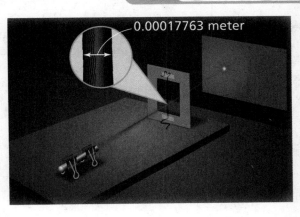

0.00017763 meter

Write the estimated thickness of a human hair using a single digit and a power of 10.

Round 0.00017763 to 0.0002.

Write 0.0002 as 2×10^{-4}.

Compare the estimates.

$2 \times 10^{-4} < 1 \times 10^{-3}$

A human hair is thinner than a sheet of paper.

Write the estimated thickness of a sheet of paper using a single digit and a power of 10.

Round 0.0013 to 0.001.

Write 0.001 as 1×10^{-3}.

EXAMPLE **3** **Find How Many Times as Much**

How does the Gross Domestic Product (GDP) of Canada compare to that of the United States?

Gross Domestic Product	
Canada	$1,785,387,000,000,000
USA	$17,348,075,000,000,000

STEP 1 Write each GDP as a single digit times a power of 10.

Canada: $1,785,387,000,000,000 \approx 2,000,000,000,000,000$
$$= 2 \times 10^{15}$$

> Count the zeros to determine the power of 10.

USA: $17,348,075,000,000,000 \approx 20,000,000,000,000,000$
$$= 2 \times 10^{16}$$

STEP 2 Compare the two estimates.

$$(2 \times 10^{16}) > (2 \times 10^{15})$$

The U.S. GDP is about 10 times greater than that of Canada.

 Try It!

There are approximately 1,020,000,000 cars in the world. The number of cars in the United States is approximately 239,800,000.

Compare the number of cars in the world to that in the United States.

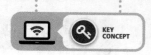

You can estimate a very large or very small number by rounding the number to its greatest place value, and then writing that number as a single digit times a power of 10.

Very Large Numbers

$3{,}564{,}879{,}000 \approx 4{,}000{,}000{,}000$

$\approx 4 \times 10^9$

> Count the number of zeros to determine the power of 10.

> The number is greater than 1, so the exponent is positive.

Very Small Numbers

$0.000000235 \approx 0.0000002$

$\approx 2 - 10^{-7}$

> The number is less than 1, so the exponent is negative.

Do You Understand?

1. **Essential Question** When would you use powers of 10 to estimate a quantity?

2. **Construct Arguments** Kim writes an estimate for the number 0.00436 as 4×10^3. Explain why this cannot be correct.

3. **Be Precise** Raquel estimated 304,900,000,000 as 3×10^8. What error did she make?

Do You Know How?

4. Use a single digit times a power of 10 to estimate the height of Mt. Everest to the nearest ten thousand feet.

Mt. Everest is 29,035 feet tall.

5. A scientist records the mass of a proton as 0.0000000000000000000000016726231 gram. Use a single digit times a power of 10 to estimate the mass.

6. The tanks at the Georgia Aquarium hold approximately 8.4×10^6 gallons of water. The tanks at the Audubon Aquarium of the Americas hold about 400,000 gallons of water. Use a single digit times a power of 10 to estimate how many times greater the amount of water is at the Georgia Aquarium.

Practice & Problem Solving

Leveled Practice In 7–9, use powers of 10 to estimate quantities.

7. A city has a population of 2,549,786 people. Estimate this population to the nearest million. Express your answer as the product of a single digit and a power of 10.

Rounded to the nearest million, the population is about ⬚ .

Written as the product of a single digit and a power of ten, this number is ⬚ × 10^⬚ .

8. Use a single digit times a power of 10 to estimate the number 0.00002468.

Rounded to the nearest hundred thousandth, the number is about ⬚ .

Written as a single digit times a power of ten, the estimate is ⬚ × 10^⬚ .

9. The approximate circumferences of Earth and Saturn are shown. How many times greater is the circumference of Saturn than the circumference of Earth?

The circumference of Saturn is ⬚ × 10^⬚ km.

Saturn's circumference is about ⬚ times greater than the circumference of Earth.

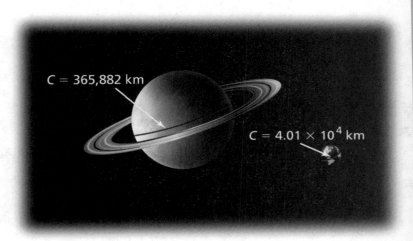

C = 365,882 km

C = 4.01 × 10^4 km

10. Estimate 0.037854921 to the nearest hundredth. Express your answer as a single digit times a power of ten.

11. Compare the numbers 6×10^{-6} and 2×10^{-8}.

a. Which number has the greater value?

b. Which number has the lesser value?

c. How many times greater is the greater number?

12. Taylor made $43,785 last year. Use a single digit times a power of ten to express this value rounded to the nearest ten thousand.

13. The length of plant cell A is 8×10^{-5} meter. The length of plant cell B is 0.000004 meter. How many times greater is plant cell A's length than plant cell B's length?

14. **Critique Reasoning** The diameter of one species of bacteria is shown. Bonnie approximates this measure as 3×10^{-11} meter. Is she correct? Explain.

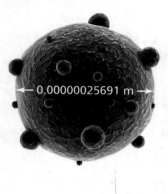

← 0.00000025691 m →

15. The populations of Cities A and B are 2.6×10^5 and 1,560,000, respectively. The population of City C is twice the population of City B.

The population of City C is how many times the population of City A?

Assessment Practice

16. Earth is approximately 5×10^9 years old. For which of these ages could this be an approximation?

Ⓐ 4,762,100,000 years

Ⓑ 48,000,000,000 years

Ⓒ 4.45×10^9 years

Ⓓ 4.249999999×10^9 years

17. **PART A**

Express 0.000000298 as a single digit times a power of ten rounded to the nearest ten millionth.

PART B

Explain how negative powers of 10 can be helpful when writing and comparing small numbers.

Solve & Discuss It!  ACTIVITY

Scientists often write very large or very small numbers using exponents. How might a scientist write the number shown using exponents?

I can...
use scientific notation to write very large or very small quantities.

Use Structure How can you use your knowledge of powers of 10 to rewrite the number?

Focus on math practices

Look for Relationships What does the exponent in 10^{15} tell you about the value of the number?

VISUAL LEARNING   ASSESS

EXAMPLE 1 **Write Large Numbers in Scientific Notation**

Scan for Multimedia

Louisa is researching the approximate distance between Earth and the Sun. Her father told her that the distance is 9.296×10^7 miles. In an astronomy book, she found the following.

Which distance is correct?

92,960,000 miles

Louisa's father used **scientific notation** to express the approximate distance because the distance is so great. Numbers in scientific notation have two factors.

$$9.296 \times 10^7$$

The first factor is always a number greater than or equal to 1 and less than 10.

The second factor is always a power of 10.

Write the number in standard form in scientific notation.

Place the decimal point after the first nonzero digit.

7 digits

9.2,960,000

Count the number of digits after the decimal point to determine the power of 10.

$$9.296 \times 10^7$$

The two numbers represent the same distance.

 Try It!

The height of Angel Falls, the tallest waterfall in the world, is 3,212 feet. How do you write this number in scientific notation?

☐.☐☐☐ × 10^☐

Convince Me! Why do very large numbers have positive exponents when written in scientific notation? Explain.

EXAMPLE 2 — Write Small Numbers in Scientific Notation

What is the width of a red blood cell written in scientific notation?

Write the number as the product of two factors.

Place the decimal after the first nonzero digit.	Count the number of digits before the decimal point to determine the power of 10.

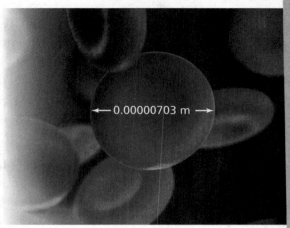
← 0.00000703 m →

0.00000703 → 7.03

6 digits
0.000007.03
$\times$ 10^{-6}

The width of the red blood cell, expressed in scientific notation, is 7.03×10^{-6} meter.

Try It!

A common mechanical pencil lead measures about 0.005 meter in diameter. How can you express this measurement using scientific notation?

EXAMPLE 3 Convert Scientific Notation to Standard Form

A. Kelly used a calculator to multiply large numbers. How can she write the number on her calculator screen in standard form?

$3.5 \times 10^{15} = 3{,}500{,}000{,}000{,}000{,}000$

The exponent is positive so move the decimal point to the right.

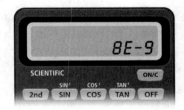
3.5 E15

B. How can Charlie write the number on the calculator screen in standard form?

$8 \times 10^{-9} = 0.000000008$

The exponent is negative so move the decimal point to the left.

8E-9

Use Appropriate Tools Certain calculators may display scientific notation using the symbol EE or E. The number that follows is the power of 10.

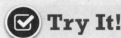 Try It!

Write the numbers in standard form.

a. 9.225×10^{18} b. 6.3×10^{-8}

Scientific notation is a way to write very large numbers or very small numbers. Scientists use scientific notation as a more efficient and convenient way of writing such numbers.

A number in scientific notation is the product of two factors. The first factor must be greater than or equal to 1 and less than 10. The second factor is a power of 10.

> Count the number of digits **after** the decimal point. The exponent is positive.

7 digits

$6.5,000,000 \rightarrow 6.5 \times 10^7$

> Place the decimal point after the first nonzero digit.

> Count the number of digits **before** the decimal point. The exponent is negative.

5 digits

$0.00009.87 \rightarrow 9.87 \times 10^{-5}$

> Place the decimal point after the first nonzero digit.

To write a number in scientific notation in standard form, multiply the decimal number by the power of 10.

Do You Understand?

1. **? Essential Question** What is scientific notation and why is it used?

2. **Critique Reasoning** Taylor states that 2,800,000 in scientific notation is 2.8×10^{-6} because the number has six places to the right of the 2. Is Taylor's reasoning correct?

3. **Construct Arguments** Sam will write 0.000032 in scientific notation. Sam thinks that the exponent of 10 will be positive. Do you agree? Construct an argument to support your response.

Do You Know How?

4. Express 586,400,000 in scientific notation.

5. The genetic information of almost every living thing is stored in a tiny strand called DNA. Human DNA is 3.4×10^{-8} meter long. Write the length in standard form.

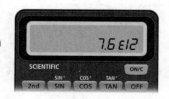

6. The largest virus known to man is the Megavirus, which measures 0.00000044 meter across. Express this number in scientific notation.

7. How would you write the number displayed on the calculator screen in standard form?

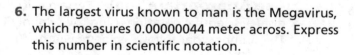

Practice & Problem Solving

Leveled Practice In **8** and **9**, write the numbers in the correct format.

8. The Sun is 1.5×10^8 kilometers from Earth.

1.5×10^8 is written as [   ] in standard form.

9. Brenna wants an easier way to write 0.0000000000000000587.

0.0000000000000000587 is written as [   ] $\times$ 10[   ] in scientific notation.

10. Is 23×10^{-8} written in scientific notation? Justify your response.

11. Is 8.6×10^7 written in scientific notation? Justify your response.

12. Simone evaluates an expression using her calculator. The calculator display is shown at the right. Express the number in standard form.

13. Express the number 0.00001038 in scientific notation.

14. Express the number 80,000 in scientific notation.

15. Peter evaluates an expression using his calculator. The calculator display is shown at the right. Express the number in standard form.

16. a. What should you do first to write 5.871×10^{-7} in standard form?

b. Express the number in standard form.

17. Express 2.58×10^{-2} in standard form.

18. At a certain point, the Grand Canyon is approximately 1,600,000 centimeters across. Express this number in scientific notation.

1,600,000 cm

19. The length of a bacterial cell is 5.2×10^{-6} meter. Express the length of the cell in standard form.

20. Higher Order Thinking Express the distance 4,300,000 meters using scientific notation in meters, and then in millimeters.

☑ Assessment Practice

21. Which of the following numbers are written in scientific notation?

☐ 12×10^6

☐ 12

☐ 6.89×10^6

☐ 6.89

☐ 0.4

☐ 4×10^{-1}

22. Jeana's calculator display shows the number to the right.

PART A

Express this number in scientific notation.

5.49 E-14

PART B

Express this number in standard form.

3-ACT MATH ▶ ▶ ▶

ACT 1

1. After watching the video, what is the first question that comes to mind?

2. Write the Main Question you will answer.

3. Construct Arguments Predict an answer to this Main Question. Explain your prediction.

4. On the number line below, write a number that is too small to be the answer. Write a number that is too large.

Too small   Too large

5. Plot your prediction on the same number line.

6. What information in this situation would be helpful to know? How would you use that information?

7. Use Appropriate Tools What tools can you use to solve the problem? Explain how you would use them strategically.

8. Model with Math Represent the situation using mathematics. Use your representation to answer the Main Question.

9. What is your answer to the Main Question? Is it greater or less than your prediction? Explain why.

10. Write the answer you saw in the video.

11. Reasoning Does your answer match the answer in the video? If not, what are some reasons that would explain the difference?

12. Make Sense and Persevere Would you change your model now that you know the answer? Explain.

Reflect

13. Model with Math Explain how you used a mathematical model to represent the situation. How did the model help you answer the Main Question?

14. Generalize What pattern did you notice in your calculations? How did that pattern help you solve the problem?

15. Use Structure How many times does a heart beat in a lifetime? Use your solution to the Main Question to help you solve.

Solve & Discuss It!

 ACTIVITY

The homecoming committee wants to fly an aerial banner over the football game. The banner is 1,280 inches long and 780 inches tall. How many different ways can the area of the banner be expressed?

I can...
perform operations with numbers in scientific notation.

Focus on math practices

Be Precise Which of the solutions is easiest to manipulate?

? **Essential Question** How does using scientific notation help when computing with very large or very small numbers?

EXAMPLE 1 **Add or Subtract Numbers in Scientific Notation**

Scan for Multimedia

The mass of Earth and the mass of the Moon are shown. How much greater is the mass of Earth than that of the Moon?

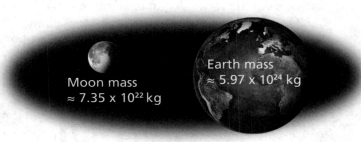

Moon mass ≈ 7.35×10^{22} kg

Earth mass ≈ 5.97×10^{24} kg

Use Structure What does the exponent tell you about the magnitude of the number?

ONE WAY Write the masses in standard form and then subtract.

$5.97 \times 10^{24} = 5{,}970{,}000{,}000{,}000{,}000{,}000{,}000{,}000$

$7.35 \times 10^{22} = 73{,}500{,}000{,}000{,}000{,}000{,}000{,}000$

$$\begin{array}{r} 5{,}970{,}000{,}000{,}000{,}000{,}000{,}000{,}000 \\ -\ 73{,}500{,}000{,}000{,}000{,}000{,}000{,}000 \\ \hline 5{,}896{,}500{,}000{,}000{,}000{,}000{,}000{,}000 \end{array}$$

The difference is about 5.8965×10^{24} kilograms.

ANOTHER WAY Write the masses using the same power of 10. Then subtract.

5.97×10^{24}

$= (5.97 \times 10^{2}) \times 10^{22}$

$= 597 \times 10^{22}$

> Use a property of exponents to write 10^{24} as $10^{2} \times 10^{22}$.

$(597 \times 10^{22}) - (7.35 \times 10^{22})$

$= (597 - 7.35) \times 10^{22}$

$= 589.65 \times 10^{22}$

$= 5.8965 \times 10^{24}$

> Remember, the first factor must be greater than or equal to 1 and less than 10.

The difference is about 5.8965×10^{24} kilograms.

 Try It!

The planet Venus is on average 2.5×10^{7} kilometers from Earth. The planet Mars is on average 2.25×10^{8} kilometers from Earth. When Venus, Earth, and Mars are aligned, what is the average distance from Venus to Mars?

$2.25 \times 108 = (2.25 \times \boxed{} \times \boxed{})$

$\qquad = \boxed{} \times 10^{7}$

$2.5 \times 10^{7} + \boxed{} \times 10^{7} = (2.5 + \boxed{}) \times 10^{7}$

$\qquad\qquad = \boxed{} \times 10^{7}$

$\qquad\qquad = \boxed{} \times \boxed{}$

Convince Me! In Example 1 and the Try It, why did you move the decimal point to get the final answer?

EXAMPLE 2

Multiply Numbers in Scientific Notation

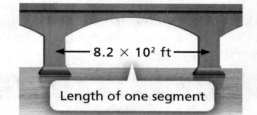

The Confederation Bridge connects New Brunswick to Prince Edward Island. The main part of the bridge rests on piers that form 43 segments. What is the approximate length of the main part of the bridge? Express your answer in scientific notation.

8.2×10^2 ft

Length of one segment

STEP 1 Write an expression to represent the problem situation.

$(8.2 \times 10^2) \times 43$

$= (8.2 \times 10^2) \times (4.3 \times 10^1)$ ← Express both numbers in scientific notation.

STEP 2 Multiply.

$(8.2 \times 10^2) \times (4.3 \times 10^1)$

$= (8.2 \times 4.3) \times (10^2 \times 10^1)$

$= 35.26 \times (10)^{2+1}$

Remember: The Product of Powers Property states that when multiplying powers with the same base, you add the exponents.

$= 35.26 \times 10^3$

$= 3.526 \times 10^4$

The first factor must be less than 10 and greater than or equal to 1.

The length of the main part of the bridge is approximately 3.5×10^4 feet.

EXAMPLE 3 **Divide Numbers in Scientific Notation**

A queen ant lays 1.83×10^6 eggs over a period of 30 days. Assuming she lays the same number of eggs each day, about how many eggs does she lay in one day? Express your answer in scientific notation.

First, write 30 in scientific notation: 3.0×10^1

Then, divide.

$$(1.83 \times 10^6) \div (3.0 \times 10^1)$$

$$\frac{1.83 \times 10^6}{3.0 \times 10^1}$$

$$\frac{1.83}{3.0} \times \frac{10^6}{10^1}$$

$$(1.83 \div 3.0) \times (10^6 \div 10^1)$$

The Quotient of Powers Property states that when dividing powers with the same base, you subtract the exponents.

$$0.61 \times 10^5$$

$$6.1 \times 10^4$$

The queen ant lays about 6.1×10^4 eggs per day.

☑ Try It!

There are 1×10^{14} good bacteria in the human body. There are 2.6×10^{18} good bacteria among the spectators in a soccer stadium. About how many spectators are in the stadium? Express your answer in scientific notation.

Operations with very large or very small numbers can be carried out more efficiently using scientific notation. The properties of exponents apply when carrying out operations.

Addition or Subtraction	Multiplication	Division
$(2.3 \times 10^6) + (1.6 \times 10^9)$	$(2.3 \times 10^6) \times (1.6 \times 10^9)$	$(2.3 \times 10^6) \div (1.6 \times 10^9)$
$(2.3 \times 10^6) + (1.6 \times 10^3) \times 10^6$	$(2.3 \times 1.6) \times (10^6 \times 10^9)$	$(2.3 \div 1.6) \times (10^6 \div 10^9)$
$(2.3 \times 10^6) + (1{,}600 \times 10^6)$	$3.68 \times 10^{6+9}$	$1.4375 \times 10^{6-9}$
$(2.3 + 1{,}600) \times 10^6$	3.68×10^{15}	1.4375×10^{-3}
$1{,}602.3 \times 10^6$		
1.6023×10^9		

Use the Product of Powers Property. (Addition or Subtraction)

Use the Product of Powers Property. (Multiplication)

Use the Quotient of Powers Property. (Division)

Do You Understand?

1. **?** **Essential Question** How does using scientific notation help when computing with very small or very large numbers?

2. **Use Structure** When multiplying and dividing two numbers in scientific notation, why do you sometimes have to rewrite one factor?

3. **Use Structure** For the sum of (5.2×10^4) and (6.95×10^4) in scientific notation, why will the power of 10 be 10^5?

Do You Know How?

4. A bacteriologist estimates that there are 5.2×10^4 bacteria growing in each of 20 petri dishes. About how many bacteria in total are growing in the petri dishes? Express your answer in scientific notation.

5. The distance from Earth to the Moon is approximately 1.2×10^9 feet. The Apollo 11 spacecraft was approximately 360 feet long. About how many spacecraft of that length would fit end to end from Earth to the Moon? Express your answer in scientific notation.

6. The mass of Mars is 6.42×10^{23} kilograms. The mass of Mercury is 3.3×10^{23} kilograms.

   a. What is the combined mass of Mars and Mercury expressed in scientific notation?

   b. What is the difference in the mass of the two planets expressed in scientific notation?

Practice & Problem Solving

Leveled Practice In **7** and **8**, perform the operation and express your answer in scientific notation.

7. $(7 \times 10^{-6})(7 \times 10^{-6})$

$$\left(\boxed{} \cdot \boxed{}\right) \times \left(10^{\boxed{}} \cdot 10^{\boxed{}}\right)$$

$$\boxed{} \times 10^{\boxed{}}$$

$$4.9 \times 10^{\boxed{}}$$

8. $(3.76 \times 10^5) + (7.44 \times 10^5)$

$$\left(\boxed{} + \boxed{}\right) \times \left(10^{\boxed{}}\right)$$

$$\boxed{} \times \boxed{}$$

$$1.12 \times 10^{\boxed{}}$$

9. What is the value of n in the equation $1.9 \times 10^7 = (1 \times 10^5)(1.9 \times 10^n)$?

10. Find $(5.3 \times 10^3) - (8 \times 10^2)$. Express your answer in scientific notation.

11. What is the mass of 30,000 molecules? Express your answer in scientific notation.

Mass of one molecule of oxygen $= 5.3 \times 10^{-23}$ gram

12. Critique Reasoning Your friend says that the product of 4.8×10^8 and 2×10^{-3} is 9.6×10^{-5}. Is this answer correct? Explain.

13. Find $\dfrac{7.2 \times 10^{-8}}{3 \times 10^{-2}}$. Write your answer in scientific notation.

14. A certain star is 4.3×10^2 light years from Earth. One light year is about 5.9×10^{12} miles. How far from Earth (in miles) is the star? Express your answer in scientific notation.

15. The total consumption of fruit juice in a particular country in 2006 was about 2.28×10^9 gallons. The population of that country that year was 3×10^8. What was the average number of gallons consumed per person in the country in 2006?

16. The greatest distance between the Sun and Jupiter is about 8.166×10^8 kilometers. The greatest distance between the Sun and Saturn is about 1.515×10^9 kilometers. What is the difference between these two distances?

17. What was the approximate number of pounds of garbage produced per person in the country in one year? Express your answer in scientific notation.

Garbage generated in country:
6.958×10^{10} pounds
Population of country:
4.57×10^6 people

18. Higher Order Thinking

    a. What is the value of n in the equation $1.5 \times 10^{12} = (5 \times 10^5)(3 \times 10^n)$?

    b. Explain why the exponent on the left side of the equation is not equal to the sum of the exponents on the right side.

☑ Assessment Practice

19. Find $(2.2 \times 10^5) \div (4.4 \times 10^{-3})$. When you regroup the factors, what do you notice about the quotient of the decimal factors? How does this affect the exponent of the quotient?

20. Which expression has the least value?

    Ⓐ $(4.7 \times 10^4) + (8 \times 10^4)$

    Ⓑ $(7.08 \times 10^3) + (2.21 \times 10^3)$

    Ⓒ $(5.43 \times 10^8) - (2.33 \times 10^8)$

    Ⓓ $(9.35 \times 10^6) - (6.7 \times 10^6)$

? Topic Essential Question

What are real numbers? How are real numbers used to solve problems?

Vocabulary Review

Draw lines to connect each vocabulary word with its definition.

Vocabulary Word	Definition
1. cube root	a number that cannot be written in the form $\frac{a}{b}$, where a and b are integers and $b \neq 0$
2. irrational number	a way to express a number as the product of two factors, one greater than or equal to 1 and less than 10, and the other a power of 10
3. Product of Powers Property	a number that when multiplied by itself equals the original number
4. perfect cube	the cube of an integer
5. perfect square	a number whose cube equals the original number
6. Power of Powers Property	To multiply two powers with the same base, keep the common base and add the exponents.
7. Powers of Products Property	To multiply two powers with the same exponent and different bases, multiply the bases and keep the exponent.
8. scientific notation	a number that is the square of an integer
9. square root	When you have an exponent raised to a power, keep the base and multiply the exponents.

Use Vocabulary in Writing

Use vocabulary words to explain how to find the length of each side of a square garden with an area of 196 square inches.

Concepts and Skills Review

Rational Numbers as Decimals

Quick Review

You can write repeating decimals in fraction form by writing two equations. You multiply each side of one equation by a power of 10. Then you subtract the equations to eliminate the repeating decimal.

Example

Write 1.0505… as a mixed number.

$x = 1.\overline{05}$

$100 \cdot x = 100 \cdot 1.\overline{05}$

$100x = 105.\overline{05}$

$100x - x = 105.\overline{05} - 1.\overline{05}$

$99x = 104$

$x = \dfrac{104}{99}$ or $1\dfrac{5}{99}$

Practice

Write each number as a fraction or a mixed number.

1. $0.\overline{7}$

2. $.0.0\overline{4}$

3. $4.\overline{45}$

4. $2.191919…$

Understand Irrational Numbers

Quick Review

An **irrational number** is a number that cannot be written in the form $\dfrac{a}{b}$, where a and b are integers and $b \neq 0$. Rational and irrational numbers together make up the real number system.

Real Numbers

Rational Numbers	Integers	Whole Numbers	Natural Numbers	Irrational Numbers
$-\dfrac{4}{5}$	-5			$\sqrt{2}$
0.75	$-\dfrac{16}{4}$	0	19	$1.121121112…$
31.8	$-1,000$		$\sqrt{4}$	π
				$-\sqrt{3}$

Example

Classify $-\sqrt{50}$ as rational or irrational.

The number $-\sqrt{50}$ is irrational because 50 is not the square of any integer.

Practice

1. Determine which numbers are irrational. Select all that apply.

☐ $\sqrt{36}$

☐ $\sqrt{23}$

☐ $-4.232323…$

☐ $0.151551555…$

☐ $0.3\overline{5}$

☐ π

2. Classify $-0.\overline{25}$ as rational or irrational. Explain.

Quick Review

To compare and order real numbers, it helps to first write each number in decimal form.

Example

Compare and order the following numbers. Locate each number on a number line.

$7.\overline{8}$, $7\frac{4}{5}$, $\sqrt{56}$

Write each number in decimal form.

$7.\overline{8} = 7.8888...$

$7\frac{4}{5} = 7.8$

$\sqrt{56} \approx 7.5$

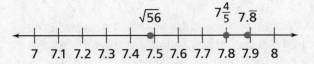

So, $\sqrt{56} < 7\frac{4}{5} < 7.\overline{8}$.

Practice

1. Between which two whole numbers does $\sqrt{89}$ lie?

$\sqrt{89}$ is between ☐ and ☐.

2. Compare and order the following numbers. Locate each number on a number line.

$2.\overline{3}$, $\sqrt{8}$, 2.5, $2\frac{1}{4}$

Quick Review

Remember that a perfect square is the square of an integer. A square root of a number is a number that when multiplied by itself is equal to the original number. Similarly, a perfect cube is the cube of an integer. A cube root of a number is a number that when cubed is equal to the original number.

Example

A monument has a cube shape with a volume of 729 cubic meters. What is the length of each edge of the monument?

$\sqrt[3]{729} = \sqrt[3]{9 \cdot 9 \cdot 9}$

$\qquad = \sqrt[3]{9^3}$

$\qquad = 9$

So, the length of each edge is 9 meters.

Practice

Classify each number as a perfect square, a perfect cube, both, or neither.

1. 27

2. 100

3. 64

4. 24

5. A gift box is a cube with a volume of 512 cubic inches. What is the length of each edge of the box?

LESSON 1-5 ▸ Solve Equations Using Square Roots and Cube Roots

Quick Review

You can use square roots to solve equations involving squares. You can use cube roots to solve equations involving cubes. Equations with square roots often have two solutions. Look at the context to see whether both solutions are valid.

Example

Mattie wants to build a square deck to make a kiddie play area of 144 square feet. What will be the length of each side of the deck?

Use the formula $A = s^2$ to find each side length.

$144 = s2$

$\sqrt{144} = \sqrt{s^2}$

$\pm 12 = s$

Length cannot be negative, so the length of each side of the deck will be 12 feet.

Practice

Solve for x.

1. $x^3 = 64$

2. $x^2 = 49$

3. $x^3 = 25$

4. $x^2 = 125$

5. A container has a cube shape. It has a volume of 216 cubic inches. What are the dimensions of one face of the container?

LESSON 1-6 ▸ Use Properties of Integer Exponents

Quick Review

These properties can help you write equivalent expressions that contain exponents.

Product of Powers Property

$a^m \cdot a^n = a^{m+n}$

Power of Powers Property

$(a^m)^n = a^{mn}$

Power of Products Property

$a^n \cdot b^n = (a \cdot b)^n$

Quotient of Powers Property

$a^m \div a^n = a^{m-n}$, when $a \neq 0$

Example

Write an equivalent expression for $(4^3)^2$.

$(4^3)^2 = (4^3)(4^3)$

$\quad = (4 \cdot 4 \cdot 4)(4 \cdot 4 \cdot 4)$

$\quad = 4^6$

Practice

Use the properties of exponents to write an equivalent expression for each given expression.

1. $6^4 \cdot 6^3$

2. $(3^6)^{-2}$

3. $7^3 \cdot 2^3$

4. $4^{10} \div 4^4$

Quick Review

The **Zero Exponent Property** states that any nonzero number raised to the power of 0 is equal to 1. The **Negative Exponent Property** states that for any nonzero rational number a and integer n, $a^{-n} = \frac{1}{a^n}$.

Example

Evaluate the expression for $x = 2$ and $y = 4$.

$$\frac{2}{y^{-2}} + 5x^0 = \frac{2}{(4)^{-2}} + 5(2)^0$$

$$= \frac{2(4^2)}{1} + 5(1)$$

$$= 2(16) + 5(1)$$

$$= 32 + 5$$

$$= 37$$

Practice

Write each expression using positive exponents.

1. 9^{-4}

2. $\frac{1}{3^{-5}}$

Evaluate each expression for $x = 2$ and $y = 5$

3. $-4x^{-2} + 3y^0$

4. $2x^0y^{-2}$

Quick Review

You can estimate very large and very small quantities by writing the number as a single digit times a power of 10.

Example

Keisha is about 1,823,933 minutes old. Write this age as a single digit times a power of 10.

First round to the greatest place value. 1,823,933 is about 2,000,000.

Write the rounded number as a single digit times a power of 10.

$$2,000,000 = 2 \times 10^6$$

654321

Keisha is about 2×10^6 minutes old.

Practice

1. In the year 2013 the population of California was about 38,332,521 people. Write the estimated population as a single digit times a power of 10.

2. The wavelength of green light is about 0.00000051 meter. What is this estimated wavelength as a single digit times a power of 10?

3. The land area of Connecticut is about 12,549,000,000 square meters. The land area of Rhode Island is about 2,707,000,000 square meters. How many times greater is the land area of Connecticut than the land area of Rhode Island?

Understand Scientific Notation

Quick Review

A number in scientific notation is written as a product of two factors, one greater than or equal to 1 and less than 10, and the other a power of 10.

Example

Write 65,700,000 in scientific notation.

First, place the decimal point to the right of the first nonzero digit.

Then, count the number of digits to the right of the decimal point to determine the power of 10.

65,700,000 in scientific notation is 6.57×10^7.

Practice

1. Write 803,000,000 in scientific notation.

2. Write 0.0000000068 in scientific notation.

3. Write 1.359×10^5 in standard form.

4. The radius of a hydrogen atom is 0.000000000025 meter. How would you express this radius in scientific notation?

Operations with Numbers in Scientific Notation

Quick Review

When multiplying and dividing numbers in scientific notation, multiply or divide the first factors. Then multiply or divide the powers of 10. When adding and subtracting numbers in scientific notation, first write the numbers with the same power of 10. Then add or subtract the first factors, and keep the same power of 10.

If the decimal part of the result is not greater than or equal to 1 and less than 10, move the decimal point and adjust the exponent.

Example

Multiply $(4.2 \times 10^5) \times (2.5 \times 10^3)$.

$(4.2 \times 10^5) \times (2.5 \times 10^3)$

$= (4.2 \times 2.5) \times (10^5 \times 10^3)$

$= 10.5 \times 10^8$

$= 1.05 \times 10^9$

Practice

Perform each operation. Express your answers in scientific notation.

1. $(2.8 \times 10^4) \times (4 \times 10^5)$

2. $(6 \times 10^9) \div (2.4 \times 10^3)$

3. $(4.1 \times 10^4) + (5.6 \times 10^6)$

4. The population of Town A is 1.26×10^5 people. The population of Town B is 2.8×10^4 people. How many times greater is the population of Town A than the population of Town B?

Crisscrossed

Solve each equation. Write your answers in the cross-number puzzle below. Each digit, negative sign, and decimal point of your answer goes in its own box.

I can...
solve one-step equations, including those involving square roots and cube roots.

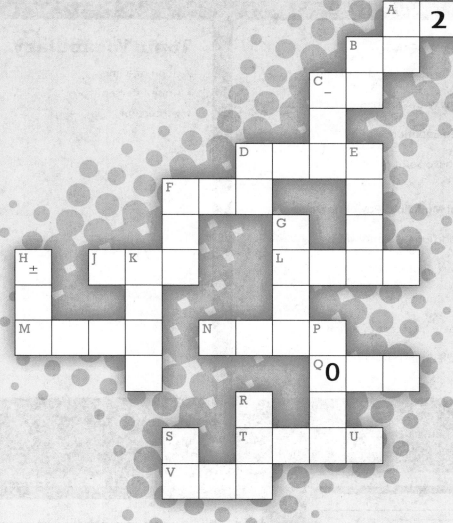

Across

A $-377 = x - 1,000$

B $x^3 = 1,000$

C $x^3 = -8$

D $x + 7 = -209$

F $x + 19 = -9$

J $14 + x = -19$

L $m - 2.02 = -0.58$

M $-3.09 + x = -0.7$

N $-2.49 = -5 + x$

Q $x - 3.5 = -3.1$

T $q - 0.63 = 1.16$

V $8.3 + x = 12.1$

Down

A $y - 11 = 49$

B $x + 8 = 20$

C $z^3 = -1,331$

D $11 + x = 3$

E $x - 14 = -7.96$

F $14 + x = -9$

G $d + 200 = 95$

H $x^2 = 144$

K $-12 = t - 15.95$

P $0.3 + x = 11$

R $x - 3 = -21$

S $-7 = -70 + y$

TOPIC 2

ANALYZE AND SOLVE LINEAR EQUATIONS

? Topic Essential Question

How can we analyze connections between linear equations, and use them to solve problems?

Topic Overview

2-1 Combine Like Terms to Solve Equations

2-2 Solve Equations with Variables on Both Sides

2-3 Solve Multistep Equations

2-4 Equations with No Solutions or Infinitely Many Solutions

3-Act Mathematical Modeling: Powering Down

2-5 Compare Proportional Relationships

2-6 Connect Proportional Relationships and Slope

2-7 Analyze Linear Equations: $y = mx$

2-8 Understand the y-Intercept of a Line

2-9 Analyze Linear Equations: $y = mx + b$

Topic Vocabulary

- slope of a line
- slope-intercept form
- y-intercept

Lesson Digital Resources

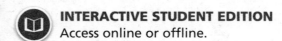

INTERACTIVE STUDENT EDITION
Access online or offline.

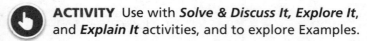

VISUAL LEARNING ANIMATION
Interact with visual learning animations.

ACTIVITY Use with *Solve & Discuss It, Explore It,* and *Explain It* activities, and to explore Examples.

VIDEOS Watch clips to support *3-Act Mathematical Modeling Lessons* and *STEM Projects*.

 Go online

Powering Down

Powering Down

Do you know that feeling when you realize you left your charger at home?
Uh-oh. It's only a matter of time before your device runs out of power.
Your battery percentage is dropping, but you still have so much left to do.
Think about this during the 3-Act Mathematical Modeling lesson.

PRACTICE Practice what you've learned.

TUTORIALS Get help from *Virtual Nerd*, right when you need it.

MATH TOOLS Explore math with digital tools.

GAMES Play Math Games to help you learn.

KEY CONCEPT Review important lesson content.

GLOSSARY Read and listen to English/Spanish definitions.

ASSESSMENT Show what you've learned.

ēnVision STEM Project

Did You Know?

Demography is the study of changes, such as the number of births, deaths, or net migration, occurring in the human population over time.

Births Worldwide in 2015 (estimated)

13,760,000 in more developed countries

132,213,000 in less developed countries

145,973,000

57,052,000

44,769,000 in less developed countries

12,283,000 in more developed countries

Deaths Worldwide in 2015 (estimated)

Emigration is the act of leaving one's country to settle elsewhere. In 2015, 244 million people, or 3.3% of the world's population, lived outside their country of origin.

Emigration

Immigration is the act of entering and settling in a foreign country. The United States has the largest immigrant population in the world.

Immigration

Your Task: Modeling Population Growth

Human population numbers are in constant flux. Suppose a country has a population of 20 million people at the start of one year and during the year there are 600,000 births, 350,000 deaths, 100,000 immigrants, and 5,000 emigrants. You and your classmates will determine the total population at the end of the year and then model expected change over a longer period.

Review What You Know!

Vocabulary

Choose the best term from the box to complete each definition.

inverse operations
like terms
proportion
variables

1. In an algebraic expression, _____ are terms that have the same variables raised to the same exponents.

2. Quantities that represent an unknown value are _____.

3. A _____ is a statement that two ratios are equal.

4. Operations that "undo" each other are _____.

Identify Like Terms

Complete the statements to identify the like terms in each expression.

5. $4x + 7y - 6z + 6y - 9x$

$4x$ and ☐ are like terms.

$7y$ and ☐ are like terms.

6. $\frac{1}{2}s - (6u - 9u) + \frac{1}{10}t + 2s$

$\frac{1}{2}s$ and ☐ are like terms.

$6u$ and ☐ are like terms.

Solve One-Step Equations

Simplify each equation.

7. $2x = 10$

8. $x + 3 = 12$

9. $x - 7 = 1$

Simplify Fractions

10. **Explain how to simplify the fraction $\frac{12}{36}$.**

Language Development

Fill in the Venn diagram to compare and contrast linear equations of the form $y = mx$ and $y = x + b$.

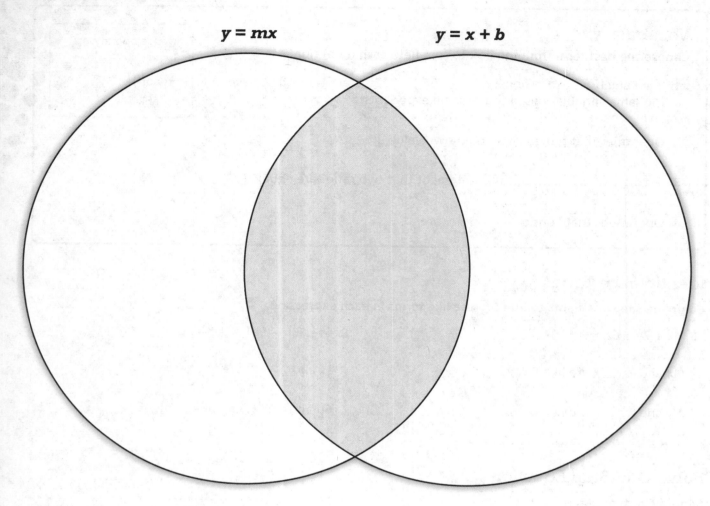

$y = mx$　　　　　$y = x + b$

In the box below, draw graphs to represent each form of the linear equations.

PROJECT 2A

If you had to escape from a locked room, how would you start?

PROJECT: DESIGN AN ESCAPE-ROOM ADVENTURE

PROJECT 2B

What animal would you most like to play with for an hour? Why?

PROJECT: PLAN A PET CAFÉ

PROJECT 2C

If you wrote a play, what would it be about?

PROJECT: WRITE A PLAY

PROJECT 2D

How many tiny steps does it take to cross a slack line?

PROJECT: GRAPH A WALKING PATTERN

Explore It!

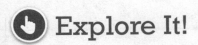 **Explore It!**

ACTIVITY

A superintendent orders the new laptops shown below for two schools in her district. She receives a bill for $7,500.

I can...
solve equations that have like terms on one side.

A. Draw a representation to show the relationship between the number of laptops and the total cost.

B. Use the representation to write an equation that can be used to determine the cost of one laptop.

Focus on math practices

Reasoning Why is it important to know that each laptop costs the same amount?

EXAMPLE 1 Combine Like Terms to Solve Addition Equations   Scan for Multimedia

Gianna has 36 yards of fabric to make sets of matching placemats and napkins. How many matching sets can she make?

> **Look for Relationships** Why can you use the same variable to represent the number of placements and to represent the number of napkins?

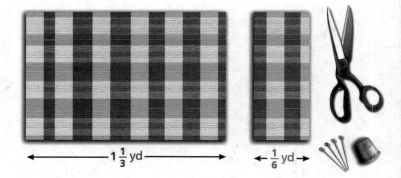

$1\frac{1}{3}$ yd $\frac{1}{6}$ yd

Draw a bar diagram to show how the quantities are related.

36 yd

| $1\frac{1}{3}x$ | $\frac{1}{6}x$ |

Yards of fabric needed to make x placemats

Yards of fabric needed to make x napkins

Use the diagram to write and solve an equation.

$$1\frac{1}{3}x + \frac{1}{6}x = 36$$
$$\frac{8}{6}x + \frac{1}{6}x = 36$$
$$\frac{9}{6}x = 36 \quad \text{Combine like terms.}$$
$$\frac{6}{9} \cdot \left(\frac{9}{6}\right)x = \frac{6}{9} \cdot (36)$$
$$x = 24$$

Gianna has enough fabric to make 24 matching sets of placemats and napkins.

Try It!

Selena spends $53.94 to buy a necklace and bracelet set for each of her friends. Each necklace costs $9.99, and each bracelet costs $7.99. How many necklace and bracelet sets, s, did Selena buy?

Selena buys necklace and bracelet sets for ☐ friends.

Convince Me! Suppose the equation is $9.99s + 7.99s + 4.6 = 53.94$. Can you combine the s terms and 4.6? Explain.

☐ $s +$ ☐ $s = 53.94$

☐ $s = 53.94$

$s =$ ☐

EXAMPLE **2**  **Combine Like Terms to Solve Subtraction Equations**

ACTIVITY   ASSESS

Selene bought a computer screen on sale for 35% off the original price. What was the price of the computer screen before the sale?

Draw a bar diagram to represent the situation.

> Let p be the price of the screen before the sale.

SALE PRICE
$130

SALE
35% OFF

p

$130	0.35p

Use the bar diagram to write an equation. Then solve.

$$p - 0.35p = 130$$
$$0.65p = 130 \quad \longleftarrow \text{Combine like terms.}$$
$$\frac{0.65p}{0.65} = \frac{130}{0.65}$$
$$p = 200$$

> **Look for Relationships** How do the original price and the sale price relate?

The price of the computer screen before the sale was $200.

 **Try It!**

Nat's grocery bill was $150, which included a 5% club discount. What was Nat's bill before the discount? Write and solve an equation.

EXAMPLE **3** **Combine Like Terms with Negative Coefficients to Solve Equations**

Solve the equation $-3.5y - 6.2y = -87.3$.

$$-3.5y - 6.2y = -87.3$$
$$-9.7y = -87.3$$
$$\frac{-9.7y}{-9.7} = \frac{-87.3}{-9.7}$$
$$y = 9$$

> To combine like terms with negative coefficients, use the rules that you learned for adding and subtracting rational numbers.

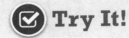 **Try It!**

Solve for d.

a. $-\frac{1}{4}d - \frac{2}{5}d = 39$

b. $-9.76d - (-12.81d) = 8.54$

In an equation with variable terms on one side, you can combine like terms before using inverse operations and properties of equality to solve the equation.

$$0.8n + 0.6n = 42$$

$$1.4n = 42 \quad \text{Combine like terms.}$$

$$\frac{1.4n}{1.4} = \frac{42}{1.4}$$

$$n = 30$$

Do You Understand?

1. **? Essential Question** How do you solve equations that contain like terms?

2. **Look for Relationships** How do you recognize when an equation has like terms?

3. **Make Sense and Persevere** In the equation $0.75s - \frac{5}{8}s = 44$, how do you combine the like terms?

Do You Know How?

4. Henry is following the recipe card to make a cake. He has 95 cups of flour. How many cakes can Henry make?

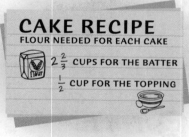

CAKE RECIPE
FLOUR NEEDED FOR EACH CAKE

$2\frac{2}{3}$ CUPS FOR THE BATTER

$\frac{1}{2}$ CUP FOR THE TOPPING

5. A city has a population of 350,000. The population has decreased by 30% in the past ten years. What was the population of the city ten years ago?

6. Solve the equation $-12.2z - 13.4z = -179.2$.

Practice & Problem Solving

Scan for
Multimedia

Leveled Practice In **7** and **8**, complete the steps to solve for *x*.

7. $\frac{4}{5}x - \frac{1}{4}x = 11$

$\dfrac{\boxed{}}{20}x = 11$

$\dfrac{\boxed{}}{\boxed{}}\left(\dfrac{\boxed{}}{20}x\right) = \dfrac{\boxed{}}{\boxed{}}(11)$

$x = \boxed{}$

8. $-0.65x + 0.45x = 5.4$

$\boxed{}x = 5.4$

$x = \dfrac{5.4}{\boxed{}}$

$x = \boxed{}$

In **9–12**, solve for *x*.

9. $\frac{4}{9}x + \frac{1}{5}x = 87$

10. $-3.8x - 5.9x = 223.1$

11. $x + 0.15x = 3.45$

12. $-\frac{3}{5}x - \frac{7}{10}x + \frac{1}{2}x = -56$

---

13. A contractor buys 8.2 square feet of sheet metal. She used 2.1 square feet so far and has $183 worth of sheet metal remaining. Write and solve an equation to find out how much sheet metal costs per square foot.

14. Make Sense and Persevere Clint prepares and sells trail mixes at his store. This week, he uses $\frac{3}{8}$ of his supply of raisins to make regular trail mix and $\frac{1}{4}$ of his supply to make spicy trail mix. If Clint uses 20 pounds of raisins this week, how many pounds of raisins did he have at the beginning of the week?

---

15. Make Sense and Persevere A submarine descends to $\frac{1}{6}$ of its maximum depth. Then it descends another $\frac{2}{3}$ of its maximum depth. If it is now at 650 feet below sea level, what is its maximum depth?

650 ft

16. Model with Math Write an equation that can be represented by the bar diagram, then solve.

$$\overset{-3.78}{\boxed{\begin{array}{|c|c|} \hline -1.2y & -4.2y \\ \hline \end{array}}}$$

17. Higher Order Thinking Solve $\frac{2}{3}h - 156 = 3\frac{13}{24}$.

18. Model with Math Nathan bought one notebook and one binder for each of his college classes. The total cost of the notebooks and binders was $27.08. Draw a bar diagram to represent the situation. How many classes is Nathan taking?

Notebook $0.95
Binder $5.82

---

19. Construct Arguments Your friend incorrectly says the solution to the equation $-\frac{3}{5}y - \frac{1}{7}y = 910$ is $y = 676$. What error did your friend make?

Ⓐ Added $-\frac{1}{7}$ to $-\frac{3}{5}$

Ⓑ Subtracted $\frac{1}{7}$ from $-\frac{3}{5}$

Ⓒ Multiplied 910 by $\frac{26}{35}$

Ⓓ Multiplied 910 by $\frac{35}{26}$

20. A 132-inch board is cut into two pieces. One piece is three times the length of the other. Find the length of the shorter piece.

PART A

Draw a bar diagram to represent the situation.

PART B

Write and solve an equation to find the length of the shorter piece.

Solve & Discuss It!

 ACTIVITY

Jaxson and Bryon collected an equal amount of money during a car wash. They collected cash and checks as shown below. If each check is written for the same amount, x, what is the total amount of money collected by both boys? Explain.

 Go Online

I can...
solve equations with variables on both sides of the equal sign.

Reasoning How can you use an equation to show that expressions are equal?

Focus on math practices

Model with Math What expressions can you write to represent the amount of money collected by each boy? How can you use these expressions to write an equation?

Essential Question How do you use inverse operations to solve equations with variables on both sides?

  VISUAL LEARNING ASSESS

EXAMPLE 1 Solve Equations with Fractional Coefficients

Scan for Multimedia

Jonah and Lizzy are making smoothies that have the same number of fluid ounces. Jonah uses 4 containers of yogurt to make his smoothie. Lizzy uses $2\frac{1}{2}$ containers of yogurt to make her smoothie. How many ounces of yogurt, x, are in each container?

Jonah's Smoothie   Lizzy's Smoothie

6 ounces of juice →   ← 12 ounces of juice

yogurt →   ← yogurt

ONE WAY Draw a bar diagram to represent the situation. Use the diagram to solve for x.

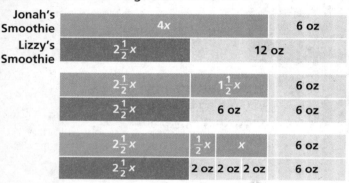

Jonah's Smoothie | $4x$ | 6 oz
Lizzy's Smoothie | $2\frac{1}{2}x$ | 12 oz

| $2\frac{1}{2}x$ | $1\frac{1}{2}x$ | 6 oz |
| $2\frac{1}{2}x$ | 6 oz | 6 oz |

| $2\frac{1}{2}x$ | $\frac{1}{2}x$ | x | 6 oz |
| $2\frac{1}{2}x$ | 2 oz 2 oz 2 oz | 6 oz |

The bar for x is equal to the two bars of 2.

ANOTHER WAY Write an equation and use inverse operations to solve for x.

$$4x + 6 = 2\frac{1}{2}x + 12$$

$$4x - 2\frac{1}{2}x + 6 = 2\frac{1}{2}x - 2\frac{1}{2}x + 12$$

$$1\frac{1}{2}x + 6 = 12$$

$$1\frac{1}{2}x + 6 - 6 = 12 - 6$$

$$1\frac{1}{2}x = 6$$

$$\frac{2}{3} \cdot \frac{3}{2}x = \frac{2}{3} \cdot 6$$

$$x = 4$$

Subtract $2\frac{1}{2}x$ from both sides to get the variable terms on one side of the equation.

Subtract 6 from both sides to get all of the constant terms on one side of the equation.

There are 4 ounces of yogurt in each container.

✓ Try It!

Class A was given a sunflower with a height of 8 centimeters that grows at a rate of $3\frac{1}{2}$ centimeters per week. Class B was given a sunflower with a height of 10 centimeters that grows at a rate of $3\frac{1}{4}$ centimeters per week. After how many weeks are the sunflowers the same height?

Let w = the number of weeks.

☐ $w + 8 = $ ☐ $w + 10$

☐ $w + 8 = 10$

☐ $w = $ ☐

$w = $ ☐

The sunflowers are the same height after ☐ weeks.

Convince Me! How can you check your work to make sure the value of the variable makes the equation true? Explain.

EXAMPLE 2 — Solve Equations with Decimal Coefficients

Teresa earns a weekly salary of $925 and a 5% commission on her total sales. Ramón earns a weekly salary of $1,250 and a 3% commission on sales. What amount of sales, x, will result in them earning the same amount for the week?

$0.05x$	925
$0.03x$	1,250

$$0.05x + 925 = 0.03x + 1,250$$

$$0.05x - 0.03x + 925 = 0.03x - 0.03x + 1,250$$

$$0.02x + 925 = 1,250$$

> Use inverse operations to combine like terms on both sides of the equals sign.

$$0.02x + 925 - 925 = 1,250 - 925$$

$$0.02x = 325$$

$$0.02x \div 0.02 = 325 \div 0.02$$

$$x = 16,250$$

Teresa and Ramón each need $16,250 of sales in order to earn the same amount for the week.

EXAMPLE 3 — Solve Equations with Negative Coefficients

Kelsey withdraws $25 per week from her bank account. Each week, Kris deposits $15 of his allowance and $20 earned from dog walking into his bank account. After how many weeks will they have the same amount of money in the bank?

Bank Statement Saving Account Number: 012 000 054 2036
Name : Kelsey Jones

DATE	DESCRIPTION	WITHDRAWAL	DEPOSIT	BALANCE
	PREVIOUS BALANCE			$550.00
WEEK 1	WITHDRAWAL	–$25.00		$525.00
WEEK 2	WITHDRAWAL	–$25.00		$500.00
WEEK 3	WITHDRAWAL	–$25.00		$475.00

> Kelsey's amount after x weeks

> Kris's amount after x weeks

$$550 - 25x = 10 + 15x + 20x$$

$$550 - 25x = 10 + 35x$$

> Combine like terms.

$$550 - 25x + 25x = 10 + 35x + 25x$$

$$550 = 10 + 60x$$

$$550 - 10 = 10 - 10 + 60x$$

$$540 = 60x$$

$$540 \div 60 = 60x \div 60$$

$$9 = x$$

Bank Statement Saving Account Number: 012 000 054 3169
Name : Kris Jones

DATE	DESCRIPTION	WITHDRAWAL	DEPOSIT	BALANCE
	PREVIOUS BALANCE			$10.00
WEEK 1	DEPOSIT		$35.00	$45.00
WEEK 2	DEPOSIT		$35.00	$80.00
WEEK 3	DEPOSIT		$35.00	$115.00

After 9 weeks, Kelsey and Kris will have the same amount of money in their bank accounts.

☑ Try It!

Solve the equation $96 - 4.5y - 3.2y = 5.6y + 42.80$.

When two expressions represent equal quantities, they can be set equal to each other. Then you can use inverse operations and properties of equality to combine like terms and solve for the unknown.

$$3x + 15 = 4x + 12$$
$$3x - 3x + 15 = 4x - 3x + 12$$
$$15 = x + 12$$
$$15 - 12 = x + 12 - 12$$
$$3 = x$$

Do You Understand?

1. **❓ Essential Question** How do you use inverse operations to solve equations with variables on both sides?

2. **Reasoning** Why are inverse operations and properties of equality important when solving equations? Explain.

3. **Model with Math** Cynthia earns $680 in commissions and is paid $10.25 per hour. Javier earns $410 in commissions and is paid $12.50 per hour. What will you find if you solve for x in the equation $10.25x + 680 = 12.5x + 410$?

Do You Know How?

4. Maria and Liam work in a banquet hall. Maria earns a 20% commission on her food sales. Liam earns a weekly salary of $625 plus a 10% commission on his food sales. What amount of food sales will result in Maria and Liam earning the same amount for the week?

5. Selma's class is making care packages to give to victims of a natural disaster. Selma packs one box in 5 minutes and has already packed 12 boxes. Her friend Trudy packs one box in 7 minutes and has already packed 18 boxes. How many more minutes does each need to work in order to have packed the same number of boxes?

6. Solve the equation $-\frac{2}{5}x + 3 = \frac{2}{3}x + \frac{1}{3}$.

7. Solve the equation $-2.6b + 4 = 0.9b - 17$.

Practice & Problem Solving

Leveled Practice In **8** and **9**, solve each equation.

8. $6 - 4x = 6x - 8x + 2$

$6 - 4x = \boxed{} + 2$

$6 = \boxed{} + 2$

$\boxed{} = \boxed{}$

$\boxed{} = x$

9. $\frac{5}{3}x + \frac{1}{3}x = 13\frac{1}{3} + \frac{8}{3}x$

$\boxed{}x = 13\frac{1}{3} + \frac{8}{3}x$

$\boxed{} = \frac{8}{3}x - \boxed{}x$

$-\frac{40}{3} = \boxed{}x$

$\boxed{} \cdot \left(-\frac{40}{3}\right) = \boxed{} \cdot \frac{2}{3}x$

$\boxed{} = x$

10. Two towns have accumulated different amounts of snow. In Town 1, the snow depth is increasing by $3\frac{1}{2}$ inches every hour. In Town 2, the snow depth is increasing by $2\frac{1}{4}$ inches every hour. In how many hours will the snowfalls of the towns be equal?

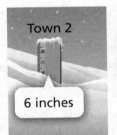

Town 2

Town 1

6 inches

5 inches

11. Solve the equation $5.3g + 9 = 2.3g + 15$.

a. Find the value of g.

b. Explain how you can check that the value you found for g is correct. If your check does not work, does that mean that your result is incorrect? Explain.

12. Solve the equation $6 - 6x = 5x - 9x - 2$.

13. Model with Math The population of one town in Florida is 43,425. About 125 people move out of the town each month. Each month, 200 people on average move into town. A nearby town has a population of 45,000. It has no one moving in and an average of 150 people moving away every month. In about how many months will the population of the towns be equal? Write an equation that represents this situation and solve.

14. Veronica is choosing between two health clubs. After how many months will the total cost for each health club be the same?

15. Higher Order Thinking The price of Stock A at 9 A.M. was $12.73. Since then, the price has been increasing at the rate of $0.06 per hour. At noon, the price of Stock B was $13.48. It begins to decrease at the rate of $0.14 per hour. If the stocks continue to increase and decrease at the same rates, in how many hours will the prices of the stocks be the same?

✓ Assessment Practice

16. In an academic contest, correct answers earn 12 points and incorrect answers lose 5 points. In the final round, School A starts with 165 points and gives the same number of correct and incorrect answers. School B starts with 65 points and gives no incorrect answers and the same number of correct answers as School A. The game ends with the two schools tied.

PART A

Which equation models the scoring in the final round and the outcome of the contest?

Ⓐ $12x + 5x - 165 = -12x + 65$

Ⓑ $12x - 5x + 165 = 12x + 65$

Ⓒ $5x - 12x + 165 = 12x + 65$

Ⓓ $12x - 5x - 165 = 12x + 65$

PART B

How many answers did each school get correct in the final round?

Solve & Discuss It!

ACTIVITY

A water tank fills through two pipes. Water flows through one pipe at a rate of 25,000 gallons an hour and through the other pipe at 45,000 gallons an hour. Water leaves the system at a rate of 60,000 gallons an hour.

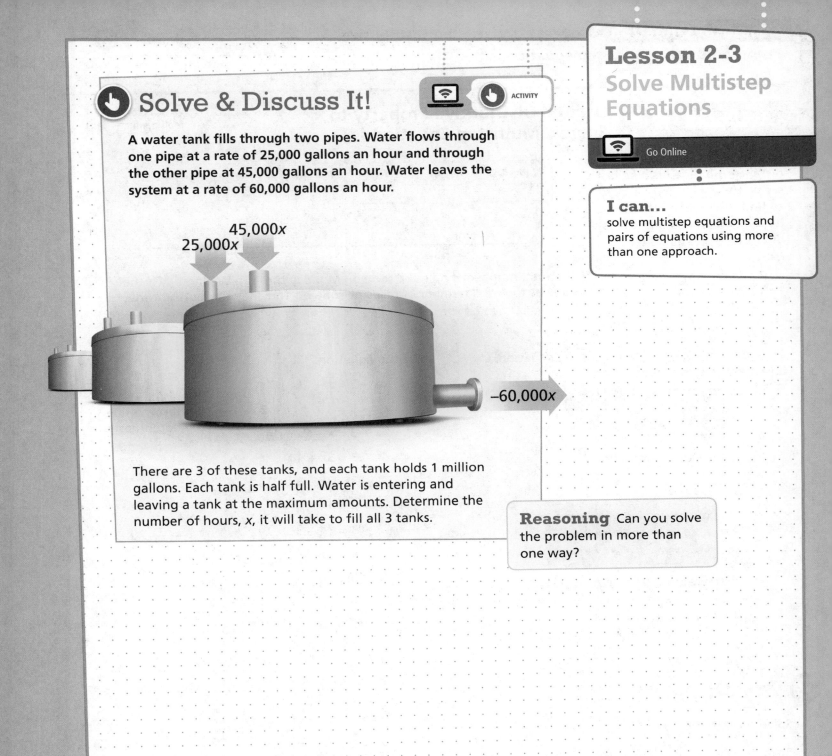

$45,000x$

$25,000x$

$-60,000x$

There are 3 of these tanks, and each tank holds 1 million gallons. Each tank is half full. Water is entering and leaving a tank at the maximum amounts. Determine the number of hours, x, it will take to fill all 3 tanks.

I can... solve multistep equations and pairs of equations using more than one approach.

Reasoning Can you solve the problem in more than one way?

Focus on math practices

Use Structure What are two different ways to simplify the expression $4(3x + 7x + 5)$ so that it equals $40x - 20$? Explain.

VISUAL LEARNING ASSESS

Scan for Multimedia

EXAMPLE 1 👁 **Use the Distributive Property to Solve a Multistep Equation**

A math teacher recorded the distances he rode his bike last week. He challenged his class to find the number of miles he rode on Thursday. How far did he ride on Thursday?

Monday	Tuesday	Wednesday	Thursday	Friday	Saturday
←	$4x + 3$	→	x	$x + 7$	$x + 7$

The total number of miles he rode on Monday through Wednesday is the same as the total number of miles he rode on Thursday through Saturday.

Draw a bar diagram to represent the situation, and use it to write an equation

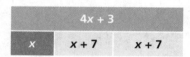

$$4x + 3 = x + 2(x + 7)$$

The quantity $x + 7$ appears twice, so you can write $2(x + 7)$.

Model with Math How can you find the solution of the equation using the bar diagram?

Solve the equation.

$$4x + 3 = x + 2(x + 7)$$

$$4x + 3 = x + 2 \cdot x + 2 \cdot 7$$

Distribute the 2 to the terms inside the parentheses.

$$4x + 3 = x + 2x + 14$$

$$4x + 3 = 3x + 14$$

$$4x - 3x + 3 = 3x - 3x + 14$$

$$x + 3 = 14$$

$$x + 3 - 3 = 14 - 3$$

$$x = 11$$

Check your answer.

$$4(11) + 3 \overset{?}{=} 11 + 2(11 + 7) \longrightarrow 47 = 47 ✔$$

The teacher rode 11 miles on Thursday.

✅ **Try It!**

Solve the equation $3(x - 5) - 5x = -25 + 6x$.

$$3\boxed{} + 3 \cdot \boxed{} - 5x = -25 + 6x$$

$$\boxed{} - 5x = -25 + 6x$$

$$\boxed{}x - 15 = -25 + 6x$$

$$-15 = -25 + \boxed{}x$$

$$\boxed{} = \boxed{}x$$

$$x = \boxed{} \text{ or } \boxed{}$$

Convince Me! Can you add x to $-5x$ on the left side of the equation as the first step? Explain.

EXAMPLE **2**

Distribute a Negative Coefficient to Solve Equations

Solve each equation.

A. $-5(x - 2) = -25$

$-5 \cdot x + -5 \cdot -2 = -25$

$-5x + 10 = -25$

$-5x + 10 - 10 = -25 - 10$

$-5x = -35$

$\dfrac{-5x}{-5} = \dfrac{-35}{-5}$

$x = 7$

> Distribute the -5 to the terms inside the parentheses.

B. $3 - (x - 3) = 25$

$3 + -1 \cdot x + -1 \cdot -3 = 25$

$3 - x + 3 = 25$

$-x + 6 = 25$

$-x + 6 - 6 = 25 - 6$

$-x = 19$

$\dfrac{-x}{-1} = \dfrac{19}{-1}$

$x = -19$

> Distribute the -1 to the terms inside the parentheses.

EXAMPLE **3**

Use the Distributive Property on Both Sides of an Equation

Solve the equation $\frac{1}{4}(x + 3) = \frac{1}{2}(x + 2)$.

$\frac{1}{4}(x + 3) = \frac{1}{2}(x + 2)$

$\frac{1}{4} \cdot x + \frac{1}{4} \cdot 3 = \frac{1}{2} \cdot x + \frac{1}{2} \cdot 2$

$\frac{x}{4} + \frac{3}{4} = \frac{x}{2} + 1$

$\frac{x}{4} - \frac{x}{2} + \frac{3}{4} = \frac{x}{2} - \frac{x}{2} + 1$

$-\frac{x}{4} + \frac{3}{4} = 1$

$-\frac{x}{4} + \frac{3}{4} - \frac{3}{4} = 1 - \frac{3}{4}$

$-\frac{x}{4} = \frac{1}{4}$

$-4 \cdot -\frac{x}{4} = -4 \cdot \frac{1}{4}$

$x = -1$

> Use the Distributive Property on both sides.

> **Use Structure** Be sure to use the Distributive Property on both sides of the equation.

☑ Try It!

Solve the equation $-3(-7 - x) = \frac{1}{2}(x + 2)$.

When solving multistep equations, sometimes you distribute first, and then combine like terms.

$$7(5 + 2x) + x = 65$$

$$35 + 14x + x = 65$$

Sometimes you combine like terms first, and then distribute.

$$8(5x + 9x + 6) = 160$$

$$8(14x + 6) = 160$$

Do You Understand?

1. **? Essential Question** How can you use the Distributive Property to solve multistep equations?

2. **Reasoning** What is the first step when solving the equation $3(3x - 5x) + 2 = -8$?

3. **Use Structure** How can you use the order of operations to explain why you cannot combine the the variable terms before using the Distributive Property when solving the equation $7(x + 5) - x = 42$?

Do You Know How?

4. Solve the equation $3x + 2 = x + 4(x + 2)$.

5. Solve the equation $-3(x - 1) + 7x = 27$.

6. Solve the equation $\frac{1}{3}(x + 6) = \frac{1}{2}(x - 3)$.

7. Solve the equation $0.25(x + 4) - 3 = 28$.

Practice & Problem Solving

Leveled Practice In 8–10, find the value of x.

8. Lori bought sunglasses and flip-flops at a half-off sale. If she spent a total of $21 on the two items, what was the original price of the sunglasses?

$$\frac{1}{2}(\boxed{} + 24) = 21$$

$$\frac{1}{2}x + \boxed{} = 21$$

$$\frac{1}{2}x = \boxed{}$$

$$x = \boxed{}$$

The original price of the sunglasses was $\boxed{}$.

SALE
$\frac{1}{2}$ OFF

Original Price
$24

9. Use the Distributive Property to solve the equation $28 - (3x + 4) = 2(x + 6) + x$.

$$28 - \boxed{}x - \boxed{} = 2x + \boxed{} + x$$

$$24 - \boxed{}x = \boxed{}x + \boxed{}$$

$$24 - \boxed{}x = \boxed{}$$

$$\boxed{}x = \boxed{}$$

$$x = \boxed{}$$

10. Use the Distributive Property to solve the equation $3(x - 6) + 6 = 5x - 6$.

$$\boxed{}x - \boxed{} + 6 = 5x - \boxed{}$$

$$\boxed{}x - \boxed{} = 5x - \boxed{}$$

$$\boxed{}x - \boxed{} = \boxed{}$$

$$\boxed{}x = \boxed{}$$

$$x = \boxed{}$$

11. What is the solution to $-2.5(4x - 4) = -6$?

12. What is the solution to the equation $3(x + 2) = 2(x + 5)$?

13. Solve the equation $\frac{1}{6}(x - 5) = \frac{1}{2}(x + 6)$.

14. Solve the equation $0.6(x + 2) = 0.55(2x + 3)$.

15. Solve the equation $4x - 2(x - 2) = -9 + 5x - 8$.

16. Use the Distributive Property to solve the equation $2(m + 2) = 22$. Describe what it means to distribute the 2 to each term inside the parentheses.

17. What is Peter's number?

If you subtract 12 from my number and multiply the difference by –3, the result is –54.

18. Higher Order Thinking Use the Distributive Property to solve the equation $\frac{4x}{5} - x = \frac{x}{10} - \frac{9}{2}$.

✓ Assessment Practice

19. How many solutions does the equation $-2(x + 4) = -2(x + 4) - 6$ have?

20. Solve the equation $3(x + 4) = 2x + 4x - 6$ for x.

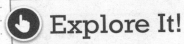

Explore It!

ACTIVITY

The Great Karlo called twins Jasmine and James onto the stage.

Jasmine, multiply your age by 3 and add 6. Then multiply this sum by 2. James, multiply your age by 2 and add 4. Then multiply this sum by 3. I predict you will both get the same number!

I can...
determine the number of solutions an equation has.

A. Write expressions to represent Great Karlo's instructions to each twin.

B. Choose 4 whole numbers for the twins' age and test each expression. Make a table to show the numbers you tried and the results.

C. What do you notice about your results?

Focus on math practices

Make Sense and Persevere Choose three more values and use them to evaluate each expression. What do you notice? Do you think this is true for all values? Explain.

Essential Question Will a one-variable equation always have only one solution?

EXAMPLE 1 Solve an Equation with Infinitely Many Solutions

Scan for Multimedia

For what values of x will the rectangle and triangle have the same perimeter?

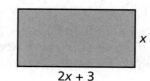

x

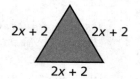

$2x + 3$

$2x + 2$ $2x + 2$

$2x + 2$

Model with Math How can you use bar diagrams to represent the equal perimeters?

ONE WAY Draw bar diagrams to represent the perimeters. Then decompose and reorder the bar diagrams to solve for x.

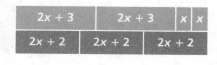

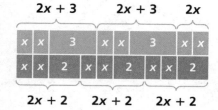

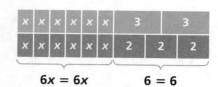

$6x = 6x$ $6 = 6$

The expressions $6x = 6x$ and $6 = 6$ are true for any value of x. This equation has infinitely many solutions.

ANOTHER WAY Write an equation to represent the equal perimeters. Then use inverse operations and properties of equality to solve.

$2x + 3 + 2x + 3 + x + x = 2x + 2 + 2x + 2 + 2x + 2$

$6x + 6 = 6x + 6$

$6x - 6x + 6 = 6x - 6x + 6$

$6 = 6$

For what values of x will $6x + 6 = 6x + 6$?

Because $6 = 6$ is always true, all values of x will make the equation true.

This equation has infinitely many solutions.

Try It!

How many solutions does the equation

$3x + 15 = 2x + 10 + x + 5$ have?

The equation has [ ] solutions.

$3x + 15 = 2x + 10 + x + 5$

$3x + 15 = $ [ ] $x + $ [ ]

$3x - $ [ ] $ + 15 = 3x - $ [ ] $ + 15$

[ ] $ = $ [ ]

Convince Me! If the value of x is negative, would the equation still be true? Explain.

EXAMPLE 2 — Solve an Equation with One Solution

Anna and Lee played soccer for the same number of hours one week. How many hours did Lee play on Sunday?

ONE WAY Use bar diagrams to solve.

	Sunday	Monday	Tuesday	Friday
soccer schedule				
Anna	A.M. x hours	A.M. x hours	A.M. x hours	A.M. x hours
	P.M. 1.2 hours	P.M. 1.2 hours	P.M. 1.2 hours	P.M. 1.2 hours
Lee	x hours	2.5 hours	2x hours	4.5 hours

Anna's Schedule: | x + 1.2 | x + 1.2 | x + 1.2 | x + 1.2 |

Lee's Schedule: | x | 2.5 | 2x | 4.5 |

| x | x | x | x | 4.8 |
| x | x | x | 2.2 | 4.8 |

$$x = 2.2$$

ANOTHER WAY Write and solve an equation.

$$4(x + 1.2) = x + 2.5 + 2x + 4.5$$
$$4x + 4.8 = x + 2.5 + 2x + 4.5$$
$$4x + 4.8 = 3x + 7.0$$
$$4x - 3x + 4.8 = 3x - 3x + 7.0$$
$$x + 4.8 - 4.8 = 7.0 - 4.8$$
$$x = 2.2$$

> This equation has one solution, $x = 2.2$.

Lee played soccer for 2.2 hours on Sunday.

EXAMPLE 3 — Solve an Equation with No Solution

Gil makes 3 bracelets and Mika makes 2 bracelets. They both use the same number of string colors. How many colors should they use to make the same amount of money?

Write an equation to represent this situation. Then solve.

Let x = the number of string colors.

$$3(2x + 5) = 2(3x + 3)$$
$$6x + 15 = 6x + 6$$
$$6x - 6x + 15 = 6x - 6x + 6$$
$$15 \neq 6$$

> Because 15 can never equal 6, this equation has no solution.

Because $15 \neq 6$, there is no number of string colors that results in Gil and Mika making the same amount of money.

Gil's Bracelets
$5 per bracelet
plus
$2 for each
string color

Bracelets by Mika
$3 per bracelet
and
$3 for each
string color

Try It!

How many solutions does the equation $4x + 8 = 0.1x + 3 + 3.9x$ have? Explain.

EXAMPLE 4 | Determine the Number of Solutions by Inspection

How can you determine the number of solutions each equation has without solving?

a. $x + 3 + 7 = 2x - 10 - x$

$x + 10 \neq x - 10$ — You can combine like terms mentally. The equivalent expressions $x + 10$ and $x - 10$ are not true for any values of x.

The equation $x + 3 + 7 = 2x - 10 - x$ has no solutions.

· ·

b. $3(x + 4) = 3x + 12$

$3x + 12 = 3x + 12$ — You can apply the Distributive Property on the left side of the equation mentally. It is easy to see that the equivalent equation $3x + 12 = 3x + 12$ is true for all values of x.

The equation $3(x + 4) = 3x + 12$ has infinitely many solutions.

· ·

c. $5x + 8 = 2x - 1$

$3x = -9$ — Notice that the coefficients of the variable terms are different. When like terms are collected and combined, the result will be a unique value of x.

The equation $5x + 8 = 2x - 1$ has one solution.

☑ Try It!

Determine the number of solutions each equation has without solving. Explain your reasoning.

a. $3x + 1.5 = 2.5x + 4.7$ **b.** $3(x + 2) = 3x - 6$ **c.** $9x - 4 = 5x - 4 + 4x$

A one-variable equation has **infinitely many solutions** when solving results in a true statement, such as 2 = 2.

A one-variable equation has **one solution** when solving results in one value for the variable, such as $x = 2$.

A one-variable equation has **no solution** when solving results in an untrue statement, such as 2 = 3.

Do You Understand?

1. ? **Essential Question** Will a one-variable equation always have only one solution?

2. **Use Structure** Kaylee writes the equation $6x + 12 = 2(3x + 6)$. Can you find the number of solutions this equation has without solving for x? Explain.

3. **Construct Arguments** The height of an experimental plant after x days can be represented by the formula $3(4x + 2)$. The height of a second plant can be represented by the formula $6(2x + 2)$. Is it possible that the two plants will ever be the same height? Explain.

Do You Know How?

4. How many solutions does the equation $3(2.4x + 4) = 4.1x + 7 + 3.1x$ have? Explain.

5. How many solutions does the equation $7x + 3x - 8 = 2(5x - 4)$ have? Explain.

6. Todd and Agnes are making desserts. Todd buys peaches and a carton of vanilla yogurt. Agnes buys apples and a jar of honey. They bought the same number of pieces of fruit. Is there a situation in which they pay the same amount for their purchases? Explain.

peaches $1.25 ea.

apples $1 ea.

$4

$6

Todd

Agnes

Practice & Problem Solving ✏️ ⏻

Leveled Practice In **7** and **8**, complete the equations to find the number of solutions.

7. Classify the equation $33x + 99 = 33x - 99$ as having one solution, no solution, or infinitely many solutions.

$$33x + 99 = 33x - 99$$

$$33x - \boxed{} + 99 = 33x - \boxed{} - 99$$

$$99 \boxed{} - 99$$

Since 99 is $\boxed{}$ equal to −99, the equation has $\boxed{}$ solution(s).

8. Solve $4(4x + 3) = 19x + 9 - 3x + 3$. Does the equation have one solution, no solution, or infinitely many solutions?

$$4(4x + 3) = 19x + 9 - 3x + 3$$

$$4 \cdot \boxed{} + 4 \cdot \boxed{} = 19x + 9 - 3x + 3$$

$$16x + 12 = \boxed{} + \boxed{}$$

$$16x - \boxed{} + 12 = 16x - \boxed{} + 12$$

$$12 \boxed{} 12$$

Since 12 is $\boxed{}$ equal to 12, the equation has $\boxed{}$ solution(s).

9. Generalize What does it mean if an equation is equivalent to $0 = 0$? Explain.

10. Solve $4x + x + 4 = 8x - 3x + 4$. Does the equation have one solution, no solution, or infinitely many solutions? If one solution, write the solution. Explain.

11. Reasoning Two rival dry cleaners both advertise their prices. Let x equal the number of items dry cleaned. Store A's prices are represented by the expression $15x - 2$. Store B's prices are represented by the expression $3(5x + 7)$. When do the two stores charge the same rate? Explain.

12. Reasoning How is solving an equation with no solution similar to solving an equation that has an infinite number of solutions?

13. Solve $0.9x + 5.1x - 7 = 2(2.5x - 3)$. How many solutions does the equation have?

14. Critique Reasoning Your friend solved the equation $4x + 12x - 6 = 4(4x + 7)$ and got $x = 34$.

What error did your friend make? What is the correct solution?

$$4x + 12x - 6 = 4(4x + 7)$$
$$16x - 6 = 16x + 28$$
$$16x - 16x - 6 = 16x - 16x + 28$$
$$x - 6 = 28$$
$$x - 6 + 6 = 28 + 6$$
$$x = 34$$

15. Solve $49x + 9 = 49x + 83$.

   a. Does the equation have one solution, no solution, or infinitely many solutions?

   b. Write two equations in one variable that have the same number of solutions as this equation.

16. Classify the equation $6(x + 2) = 5(x + 7)$ as having one solution, no solution, or infinitely many solutions.

17. Solve $6x + 14x + 5 = 5(4x + 1)$. Write a word problem that this equation, or any of its equivalent forms, represents.

18. Classify the equation $170x - 1,000 = 30(5x - 30)$ as having one solution, no solution, or infinitely many solutions.

19. **Higher Order Thinking** Write one equation that has one solution, one equation that has no solution, and one equation that has infinitely many solutions.

20. Solve $4(4x - 2) + 1 = 16x - 7$.

21. Solve $6x + 26x - 10 = 8(4x + 10)$.

22. Classify the equation $64x - 16 = 16(4x - 1)$ as having one solution, no solution, or infinitely many solutions.

23. Classify the equation $5(2x + 3) = 3(3x + 12)$ as having one solution, no solution, or infinitely many solutions.

Assessment Practice

24. Which of the following best describes the solution to the equation $4(2x + 3) = 16x + 12 - 8x$?

  Ⓐ The equation has one solution.

  Ⓑ The equation has infinitely many solutions.

  Ⓒ The equation has no solution.

  Ⓓ The equation has two solutions.

25. Which of the following statements are true about the equation $10x + 45x - 13 = 11(5x + 6)$?

  Select all that apply.

  ☐ The operations that can be used to solve the equation are addition and multiplication.

  ☐ The operations that can be used to solve the equation are multiplication and division.

  ☐ The equation has infinitely many solutions.

  ☐ The equation has a solution of $x = 53$.

  ☐ The equation has no solution.

1. **Vocabulary** How can you determine the number of solutions for an equation? *Lesson 2-4*

2. Solve the equation $-\frac{2}{3}d - \frac{1}{4}d = -22$ for d. *Lesson 2-1*

3. Edy has $450 in her savings account. She deposits $40 each month. Juan has $975 in his checking account. He writes a check for $45.45 each month for his cell phone bill. He also writes a check for $19.55 each month for his water bill. After how many months will Edy and Juan have the same amount of money in their accounts? *Lesson 2-2*

4. Which equation has infinitely many solutions? *Lesson 2-4*

   Ⓐ $\frac{3}{4}x + x - 5 = 10 + 2x$

   Ⓑ $3x - 2.7 = 2x + 2.7 + x$

   Ⓒ $9x + 4.5 - 2x = 2.3 + 7x + 2.2$

   Ⓓ $\frac{1}{5}x - 7 = \frac{3}{4} + 2x - 25\frac{3}{4}$

5. Solve the equation $-4(x - 1) + 6x = 2(17 - x)$ for x. *Lesson 2-3*

6. Hakeem subtracted 8 from a number, then multiplied the difference by $\frac{4}{5}$. The result was 20. Write and solve an equation to find the number, x. *Lesson 2-3*

How well did you do on the mid-topic checkpoint? Fill in the stars.

MID-TOPIC PERFORMANCE TASK

Hector is competing in a 42-mile bicycle race. He has already completed 18 miles of the race and is traveling at a constant speed of 12 miles per hour when Wanda starts the race. Wanda is traveling at a constant speed of 16 miles per hour.

PART A

Write and solve an equation to find when Wanda will catch up to Hector.

PART B

Will Wanda catch up to Hector before the race is complete? Explain.

PART C

At what constant speed could Wanda travel to catch up with Hector at the finish line? Explain.

3-ACT MATH ▷ ▷ ▷

ACT 1

1. After watching the video, what is the first question that comes to mind?

2. Write the Main Question you will answer.

3. Construct Arguments Predict an answer to this Main Question.
Explain your prediction.

4. On the number line below, write a time that is too early to be the answer.
Write a time that is too late.

Too early   **Too late**

5. Plot your prediction on the same number line.

6. What information in this situation would be helpful to know? How would you use that information?

7. Use Appropriate Tools What tools can you use to solve the problem? Explain how you would use them strategically.

8. Model with Math Represent the situation using mathematics. Use your representation to answer the Main Question.

9. What is your answer to the Main Question? Is it earlier or later than your prediction? Explain why.

10. Write the answer you saw in the video.

11. Reasoning Does your answer match the answer in the video? If not, what are some reasons that would explain the difference?

12. Make Sense and Persevere Would you change your model now that you know the answer? Explain.

Reflect

13. Model with Math Explain how you used a mathematical model to represent the situation. How did the model help you answer the Main Question?

14. Look for Relationships What pattern did you notice in the situation? How did you use that pattern?

15. Be Precise After 35 minutes, he started charging his phone. 21 minutes later, the battery is at 23%. Explain how you would determine when the phone will be charged to 100%.

👆 Solve & Discuss It!

📶 👆 ACTIVITY

Mei Li is going apple picking. She is choosing between two places. The cost of a crate of apples at each place is shown.

Where should Mei Li go to pick her apples? Explain.

☺ Pick your own.
20 lb $7.25
Annie's Apple Orchard

🍎 Pick your own.
12 lb $5.00
Franklin's Fruit Orchard

I can...
compare proportional relationships represented in different ways.

Construct Arguments
What information provided can be used to support your answer?

Focus on math practices

Model with Math Which representation did you use to compare prices? Explain why.

VISUAL LEARNING

ASSESS

Scan for Multimedia

EXAMPLE 1 Compare Proportional Relationships Represented by Tables and Graphs

Meera is researching cruising speeds of different planes. Which airplane has a greater cruising speed?

Cessna 310

Time (min)	5	15	30	45	60
Distance (km)	40	120	240	360	480

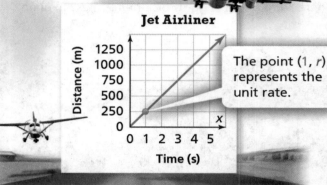

Jet Airliner

The point $(1, r)$ represents the unit rate.

STEP 1 Find the cruising speed of the Cessna.

Distance (km)	40	120	240	360	480
Time (min)	5	15	30	45	60
Distance (km) / Time (min)	$\frac{40}{5} = 8$	$\frac{120}{15} = 8$	$\frac{240}{30} = 8$	$\frac{360}{45} = 8$	$\frac{480}{60} = 8$

Find the constant of proportionality.

The Cessna has a cruising speed of 8 kilometers per minute.

STEP 2 Find the cruising speed of the Boeing 747.

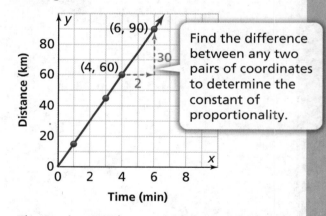

Find the difference between any two pairs of coordinates to determine the constant of proportionality.

The Boeing 747 has a cruising speed of 15 kilometers per minute. The Boeing 747 has a greater cruising speed than the Cessna.

✓ Try It!

The graph represents the rate at which Marlo makes origami birds for a craft fair. The equation $y = 2.5x$ represents the number of birds, y, Josh makes in x minutes. Who makes birds at a faster rate?

Convince Me! If you were to graph the data for Josh and Marlo on the same coordinate plane, how would the two lines compare?

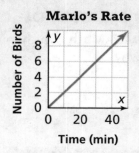

Marlo's Rate

EXAMPLE 2 — Compare Proportional Relationships Represented by Graphs and Equations

The graph on the right represents the rate at which Daniel earns points in his video game. The rate at which Brianna earns points in her video game is represented by the equation $y = 2x$, where y is the number of points and x is the time in minutes. At these rates, who will earn 100 points first?

Find Brianna's rate.

$y = 2x$

$y = 2(1)$ — Substitute 1 for x to find the unit rate.

$y = 2$

Brianna earns 2 points per minute.

Daniel earns 3 points per minute.
Daniel will earn 100 points first.

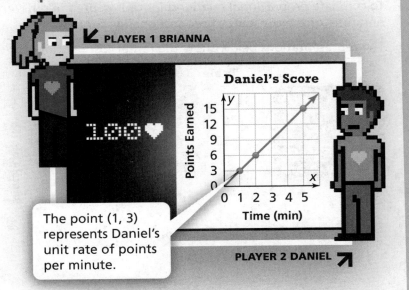

PLAYER 1 BRIANNA

Daniel's Score

The point (1, 3) represents Daniel's unit rate of points per minute.

PLAYER 2 DANIEL

EXAMPLE 3 — Compare Proportional Relationships Represented by Graphs and Verbal Descriptions

The graph represents the cost per ounce of a granola cereal. A 15-ounce box of a raisin cereal costs $3.90. Which cereal costs more per ounce?

Use an equivalent ratio to find the cost per ounce of the raisin cereal.

$$\frac{\$3.90}{15 \text{ oz}} = \frac{\$0.26}{1 \text{ oz}}$$

The raisin cereal costs $0.26 per ounce.
The granola cereal costs $0.25 per ounce.

The raisin cereal costs more per ounce.

Find the difference between the coordinates of two sets of ordered pairs to determine the constant of proportionality:

$$\frac{5-2.5}{20-10} = \frac{\$2.50}{10 \text{ oz}}$$
$$= \frac{\$0.25}{1 \text{ oz}}.$$

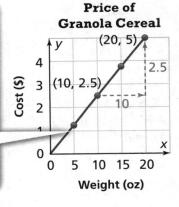

Price of Granola Cereal

✓ Try It!

The distance covered by the fastest high-speed train in Japan traveling at maximum speed is represented on the graph. The fastest high-speed train in the United States traveling at maximum speed covers 600 kilometers in $2\frac{1}{2}$ hours. Which train has a greater maximum speed? Explain.

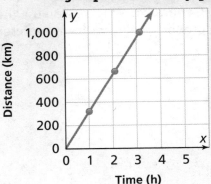

Distance Travelled at Maximum Speed by Fastest High-Speed Train in Japan

To compare proportional relationships represented in different ways, find the unit rate, or the constant of proportionality, for each representation.

The representations below show the rental cost per hour for canoes at three different shops.

Table

Rental Cost ($)	18	27	36	54
Time (hr)	$\frac{1}{2}$	$\frac{3}{4}$	1	$1\frac{1}{2}$
Rental Cost ($) / Time (hr)	$\frac{18}{0.5} = 36$	$\frac{27}{0.75} = 36$	$\frac{36}{1}$	$\frac{54}{1.5} = 36$

Graph

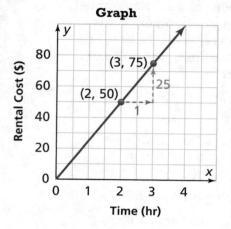

Equation

$c = 28t$

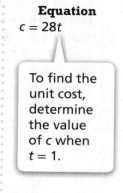

To find the unit cost, determine the value of c when $t = 1$.

Do You Understand?

1. **Essential Question** How can you compare proportional relationships represented in different ways?

2. How can you find the unit rate or constant of proportionality for a relationship represented in a graph?

3. **Generalize** Why can you use the constant of proportionality with any representation?

Do You Know How?

4. Amanda babysits and Petra does yard work on weekends. The graph relating Amanda's earnings to the number of hours she babysits passes through the points (0, 0) and (4, 24). The table below relates Petra's earnings to the number of hours she does yard work.

Petra's Earnings

Hours	3	6	9
Earnings ($)	15	30	45

Who earns more per hour?

5. Milo pays $3 per pound for dog food at Pat's Pet Palace. The graph below represents the cost per pound of food at Mark's Mutt Market. At which store will Milo pay a lower price per pound for dog food?

Dog Food at Mark's Mutt Market

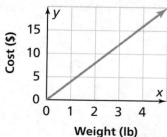

Practice & Problem Solving

Leveled Practice For **6** and **7**, complete the information to compare the rates.

6. Sam and Bobby want to know who cycled faster. The table shows the total miles Sam traveled over time. The graph shows the same relationship for Bobby. Who cycled faster?

Sam
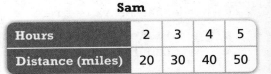

Hours	2	3	4	5
Distance (miles)	20	30	40	50

Find the unit rate (constant of proportionality) for Sam.

$$\frac{\text{distance}}{\text{time}} = \frac{20}{2} = \boxed{} \frac{\text{miles}}{\text{hour}}$$

Find the unit rate (constant of proportionality) for Bobby.

Use ($\boxed{}$, $\boxed{}$) and ($\boxed{}$, $\boxed{}$) to find the constant of proportionality.

The unit rate (constant of proportionality) is $\boxed{}$ $\frac{\text{miles}}{\text{hour}}$.

So $\boxed{}$ cycled faster.

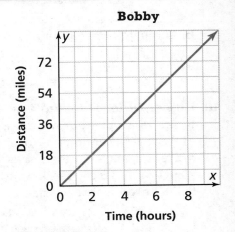

Bobby

7. **Model with Math** The equation $y = 15x$ can be used to determine the amount of money, y, Pauli's Pizzeria makes by selling x pizzas. The graph shows the money Leo's Pizzeria takes in for different numbers of pizzas sold. Which pizzeria makes more money per pizza?

Pauli's Pizzeria takes in $\boxed{}$ per pizza.

Leo's Pizzeria takes in $\boxed{}$ per pizza.

$\boxed{}$'s Pizzeria takes in more money per pizza.

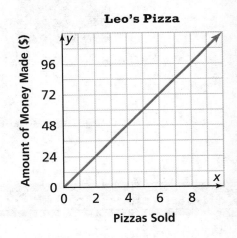

Leo's Pizza

8. The graph shows the amount of savings over time in Eliana's account. Lana, meanwhile, puts $50 each week into her savings account. If they both begin with $0, who is saving at the greater rate?

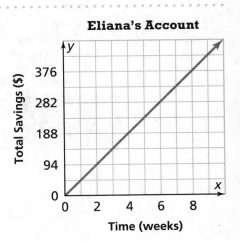

Eliana's Account

9. **Make Sense and Persevere** Beth, Manuel, and Petra are collecting sponsors for a walk-a-thon. The equation $y = 20x$ represents the amount of money Beth raises for walking x miles. The table shows the relationship between the number of miles Manuel walks and the amount of money he will raise. Petra will earn $15 for each mile that she walks.

WALK-A-THON RUN OR WALK
SPONSOR SHEET
NAME **Manuel**

MILES WALKED	MONEY RAISED
3	$45
5	$75
7	$105
9	$135

a. In order to compare the proportional relationships, what quantities should you use to find the unit rate?

b. Compare the amount of money raised per mile by the three people.

10. **Higher Order Thinking** Winston compares the heights of two plants to see which plant grows more per day. The table shows the height of Plant 1, in centimeters, over 5 days. The graph shows the height of Plant 2, in centimeters, over 10 days. Winston says that since Plant 1 grows 6 cm per day and Plant 2 grows 4 cm per day, Plant 1 grows more per day.

Plant 1

Days	2	3	4	5
Height (cm)	6	9	12	15

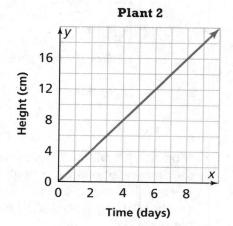

Plant 2

a. Do you agree with Winston? Explain your response.

b. What error might Winston have made?

Assessment Practice

11. Ashton, Alexa, and Clara want to know who types the fastest. The equation $y = 39x$ models the rate at which Ashton can type, where y is the number of words typed and x is the time in minutes. The table shows the relationship between words typed and minutes for Alexa. The graph shows the same relationship for Clara. Who types the fastest?

Alexa's Typing Rate

Minutes	2	3	4	5
Words Typed	78	117	156	195

Clara's Typing Rate

Solve & Discuss It!  ACTIVITY

In the fall, Rashida earns money as a soccer referee for her town's under-10 soccer league. So far, she has worked 5 games and has been paid $98.50. She will work a total of 14 games this fall. How can Rashida determine how much she will earn refereeing soccer games this fall?

Look for Relationships
How is the number of games Rashida works related to her earnings?

I can...
understand the slope of a line.

Focus on math practices

Reasoning How would Rashida's earnings change if she were paid by the hour instead of by the game?

VISUAL LEARNING   ASSESS

Scan for
Multimedia

EXAMPLE 1 **Understand Slope**

Maya and her father are building a tree house. The roof will have a 9:12 pitch; that is, for every 12 inches of horizontal distance, the roof rises 9 inches. How can Maya determine the height of the roof at its peak?

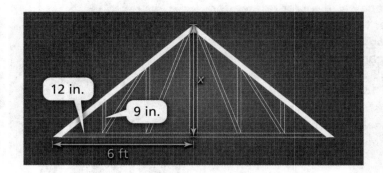

STEP 1 Make a table of values that show the 9 : 12 pitch.

Find the constant of proportionality.

Vertical distance	9	18	27	45
Horizontal distance	12	24	36	60
$\dfrac{\text{vertical distance}}{\text{horizontal distance}}$	$\dfrac{9}{12}=\dfrac{3}{4}$	$\dfrac{18}{24}=\dfrac{3}{4}$	$\dfrac{27}{36}=\dfrac{3}{4}$	$\dfrac{45}{60}=\dfrac{3}{4}$

STEP 2 Graph the ordered pairs from the table and draw a line to connect them. The line shows the steepness of the roof. The steepness is also called the slope of the line.

The **slope** of the line is the ratio $\frac{\text{rise}}{\text{run}}$.

Maya can use a graph to find that the roof is 54 inches in height at its peak.

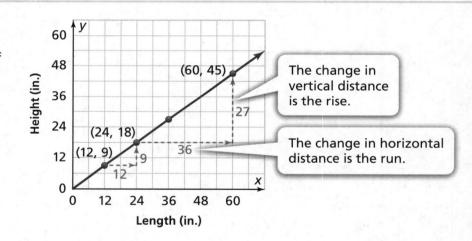

The change in vertical distance is the rise.

The change in horizontal distance is the run.

☑ **Try It!**

Jack graphs how far he plans to bike over a 3-day charity ride. Find the slope of the line.

slope: $\frac{\text{rise}}{\text{run}} = \dfrac{\boxed{}}{\boxed{}}$. The slope of the line is $\boxed{}$.

Convince Me! How do the unit rate and constant of proportionality relate to the slope of a line?

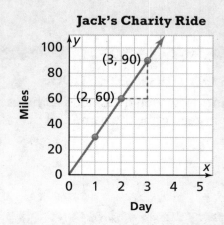

Jack's Charity Ride

EXAMPLE **2** **Find the Slope from Two Points**

  ACTIVITY ASSESS

The graph represents the depth of a diving submarine over time. At what speed is the submarine descending?

Find the slope of the line.

slope: $\frac{rise}{run} = \frac{y_2 - y_1}{x_2 - x_1}$

Find the rise and run using the x- and y-coordinates from two points on the line.

$= \frac{-800 - (-400)}{10 - 5}$

$= \frac{-400}{5}$

$= -80$

The slope of the line is -80. The submarine is decending at a rate of 80 feet per minute.

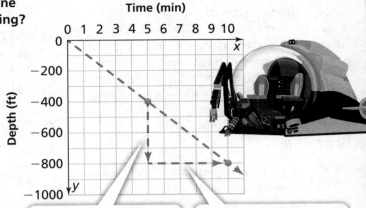

The rise is the change in the y-coordinates or $y_2 - y_1$.

The run is the change in the x-coordinates or $x_2 - x_1$.

Reasoning How do the x- and y-coordinates relate when the slope is negative?

EXAMPLE **3** **Interpret Slope**

The graph shows the distance a car travels over time. Find the slope of the line. What does it mean in the problem situation?

slope: $\frac{rise}{run} = \frac{y_2 - y_1}{x_2 - x_1}$

$= \frac{220 - 110}{4 - 2}$

$= 55$

The slope of the line is 55.

The car travels 55 miles per hour.

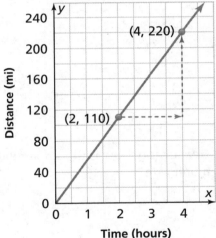

Distance Travelled

 Try It!

The graph shows the proportions of red and blue food coloring that Taylor mixes to make purple frosting. What is the slope of the line? Tell what it means in the problem situation.

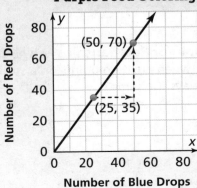

Purple Food Coloring

Slope is the measure of the steepness of a line. It represents the ratio of the rise (that is, the vertical distance) to the run (the horizontal distance) between two points on the line. In proportional relationships, slope is the same as the unit rate and constant of proportionality.

$$\text{slope} = \frac{\text{rise}}{\text{run}}$$

$$= \frac{\text{change in } y\text{-coordinates}}{\text{change in } x\text{-coordinates}}$$

$$= \frac{y_2 - y_1}{x_2 - x_1}$$

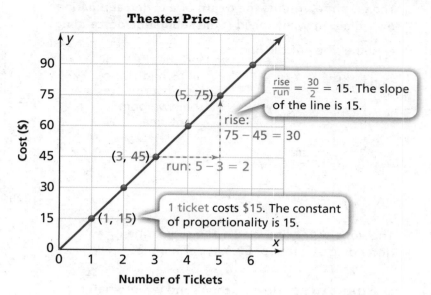

Theater Price

$\frac{\text{rise}}{\text{run}} = \frac{30}{2} = 15$. The slope of the line is 15.

rise: $75 - 45 = 30$

run: $5 - 3 = 2$

1 ticket costs $15. The constant of proportionality is 15.

Do You Understand?

1. **Essential Question** What is slope?

2. **Reasoning** How is the slope related to a unit rate?

3. **Look for Relationships** Why is the slope between any two points on a straight line always the same?

Do You Know How?

4. What is the slope of the line?

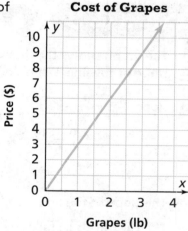

Cost of Grapes

5. The scale of a model airplane is shown in the graph.

   a. Find the slope of the line using $\frac{y_2 - y_1}{x_2 - x_1}$.

   b. What does the slope mean in the problem situation?

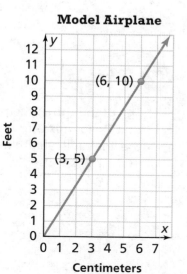

Model Airplane

Practice & Problem Solving

Leveled Practice In **6** and **7**, find the slope of each line.

6. The graph shows the number of soda bottles a machine can make over time. Use the two points shown to find the number of soda bottles the machine can make per minute.

slope: $\dfrac{\boxed{} - 50}{6 - \boxed{}} = \dfrac{\boxed{}}{4}$, or $\boxed{}$

The machine can make $\boxed{}$ soda bottles each minute.

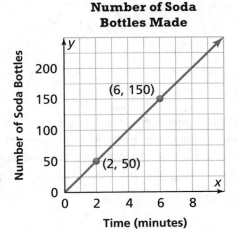

Number of Soda Bottles Made

Number of Soda Bottles

(6, 150)

(2, 50)

Time (minutes)

7. Find the slope of the line.

slope $= \dfrac{\text{rise}}{\text{run}}$

$= \dfrac{\boxed{}}{\boxed{}}$, or $\boxed{}$

The slope is $\boxed{}$.

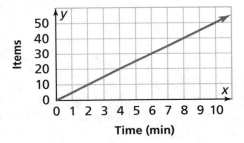

Items

Time (min)

8. Reasoning How can you find the slope of the line that passes through the points (0, 0) and (2, 4)? Explain.

9. The points (2.1, −4.2) and (2.5, −5) form a proportional relationship. What is the slope of the line that passes through these two points?

10. Find the slope of the line.

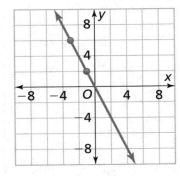

11. The graph shows the number of Calories Natalia burned while running.

   a. What is the slope of the line?

   b. What does the slope tell you?

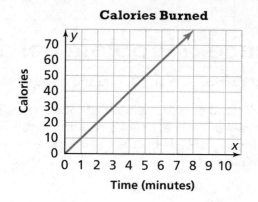

Calories Burned

12. **Critique Reasoning** A question on a test provides this graph and asks students to find the speed at which the car travels. Anna incorrectly says that the speed of the car is $\frac{1}{64}$ mile per hour.

   a. What is the speed of the car?

   b. What error might Anna have made?

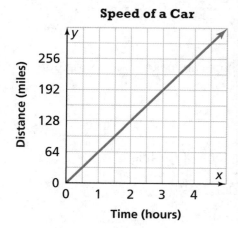

Speed of a Car

13. **Higher Order Thinking** You use a garden hose to fill a wading pool. If the water level rises 11 centimeters every 5 minutes and you record the data point of (10, y), what is the value of y? Use slope to justify your answer.

Rises 11 cm every 5 min

14. The points (15, 21) and (25, 35) form a proportional relationship.

   a. Find the slope of the line that passes through these points.

   b. Which graph represents this relationship?

Ⓐ
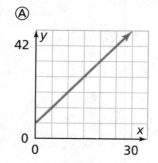

Ⓑ
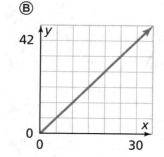

Ⓒ
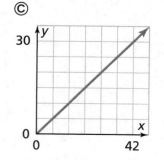

Ⓓ
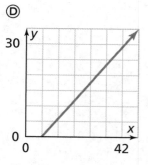

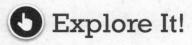 Explore It!

A group of college students developed a solar-powered car and entered it in a race. The car travels at a constant speed of 100 meters per 4 seconds.

I can...
write equations to describe linear relationships.

A. What representation can show the distance the car will travel over time?

B. What expression can show the distance the car will travel over time?

C. Compare the representation and the expression. Which shows the distance traveled over time more clearly? Explain.

Focus on math practices

Be Precise How would the representation or expression change if the speed was converted to miles per minute?

ASSESS

EXAMPLE 1 **Relate Constant of Proportionality to Slope**

Scan for Multimedia

The students in Meg's class are building a fence around the class garden. How can they use the pricing for the different lengths of fencing to determine the cost for 50 feet of fencing?

Look for Relationships What is the relationship between the length of fencing and the cost?

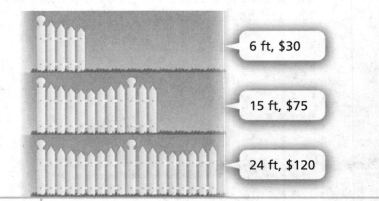

6 ft, $30

15 ft, $75

24 ft, $120

STEP 1 Write the length and cost as an ordered pair. Graph the ordered pairs and find the rise and run using any two ordered pairs.

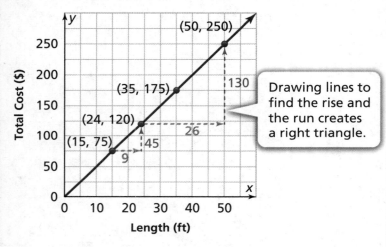

Drawing lines to find the rise and the run creates a right triangle.

STEP 2 Analyze the two right triangles. Notice that the ratios of the $\frac{rise}{run}$ are equivalent, so the slope of the line is constant.

For any ordered pair (x, y) on the line the slope, m, is constant. That is, $\frac{y}{x} = m$ or $y = mx$.

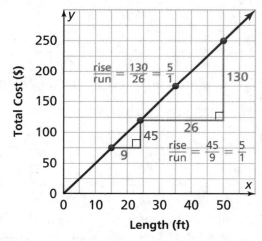

$$\frac{rise}{run} = \frac{130}{26} = \frac{5}{1}$$

$$\frac{rise}{run} = \frac{45}{9} = \frac{5}{1}$$

Meg and her classmates can use the equation $y = 5x$ to find the cost.

$5(50) = 250$, so 50 feet of fencing costs $250.

☑ Try It!

Write an equation to describe the relationship shown in the graph.

$\frac{rise}{run} : \dfrac{80 - \boxed{}}{\boxed{} - 3} = \dfrac{\boxed{}}{\boxed{}}$. The equation of the line is $y = \boxed{} x$.

Convince Me! How do the equations $y = mx$ and $y = kx$ compare?

Distance per Gallon

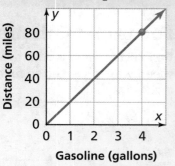

EXAMPLE 2 Write a Linear Equation from Two Points

A drone descends into a mining cave. The graph relates its distance below ground to time. Write an equation that describes the relationship.

Drone's Descent

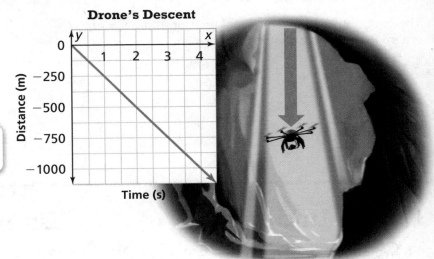

STEP 1 Find the slope of the line.

$$m = \frac{y_2 - y_1}{x_2 - x_1}$$

$$= \frac{-750 - (-500)}{3 - 2}$$ Substitute the coordinates.

$$= \frac{-250}{1}$$

The slope is −250. The drone descends 250 meters per second.

STEP 2 Write the equation of the line.

$$y = mx$$ Substitute −250 for m.

$$y = -250x$$

The equation of the line describing the drone's distance over time is $y = -250x$.

Generalize Lines that slant upward from left to right have **positive** slopes. Lines that slant downward from left to right have **negative** slopes.

EXAMPLE 3 Graph an Equation of the Form y = mx

A recipe for trail mix calls for 1 cup of raisins for every 2 cups of granola. Write an equation that describes the relationship between raisins and granola. Graph the line.

STEP 1 Find the equation of the line.

$$y = mx$$ Substitute $\frac{1}{2}$ for m.

$$y = \frac{1}{2}x$$

STEP 2 Graph the line by plotting the point (0, 0) and using the slope to plot another point.

Trail Mix Recipe

Try It!

a. Write the equation of the line.

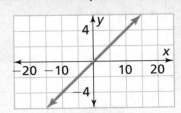

b. Graph the line $y = -3x$.

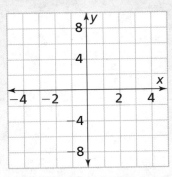

The equation for a proportional relationship is $y = mx$ where m represents the slope of the line.

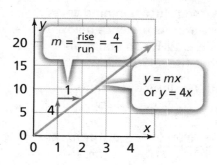

$m = \dfrac{rise}{run} = \dfrac{4}{1}$

$y = mx$ or $y = 4x$

Do You Understand?

1. **Essential Question** How does slope relate to the equation for a proportional relationship?

2. Look for Relationships What do the graphs of lines in the form $y = mx$ have in common? How might they differ?

3. Use Structure The table below shows the distance a train traveled over time. How can you determine the equation that represents this relationship?

Time (s)	Distance (m)
2	25
4	50
6	75
8	100

Do You Know How?

4. The relationship between a hiker's elevation and time is shown in the graph.

Hiking Elevation

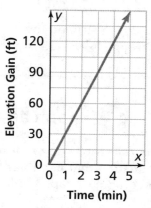

a. Find the constant of proportionality of the line. Then find the slope of the line.

b. Write the equation of the line.

5. Graph the equation $y = -\dfrac{1}{2}x$.

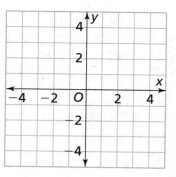

Practice & Problem Solving

Scan for
Multimedia

6. Leveled Practice Resting heart rate is a measure of how fast the heart beats when a person is not performing physical activity. The graph shows the number of heartbeats over time for a given person.

a. Use two sets of coordinates to write an equation to describe the relationship.

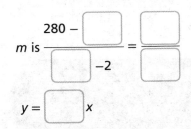

m is $\dfrac{280 - \boxed{}}{\boxed{} - 2} = \dfrac{\boxed{}}{\boxed{}}$

$y = \boxed{}\, x$

b. Interpret the equation in words.

The heart's resting heart rate is $\boxed{}$ beats each minute.

Resting Heart Rate

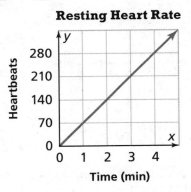

7. Model with Math The graph relates the number of gallons of white paint to the number of gallons of red paint Jess used to make the perfect pink. Write an equation that describes the relationship.

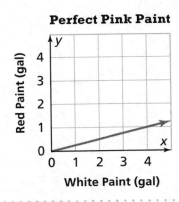

8. Critique Reasoning Franco made this graph to show the equation $y = -x$. Is the graph correct? Explain.

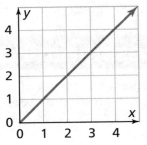

9. The graph shows a proportional relationship between the variables x and y.

a. Write an equation to model the relationship.

b. Reasoning Explain how you know if an equation or a graph represents a proportional relationship.

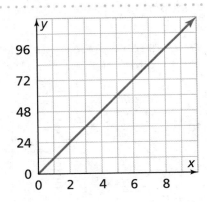

10. Model with Math Graph the equation $y = -5x$ on the coordinate plane.

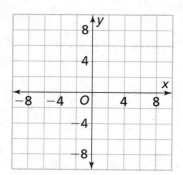

11. Graph the equation $y = \frac{3}{5}x$ on the coordinate plane.

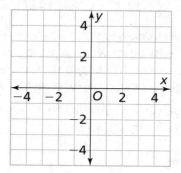

12. Higher Order Thinking A movie theater sends out a coupon for 70% off the price of a ticket.

a. Write an equation for the situation, where y is the price of the ticket with the coupon and x is the original price.

b. Graph the equation and explain why the line should only be in the first quadrant.

Original Price ($)

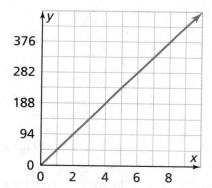

70% OFF
One Regular Movie Ticket

Assessment Practice

13. An equation and a graph of proportional relationships are shown. Which has the greater unit rate?

$y = \frac{47}{2}x$

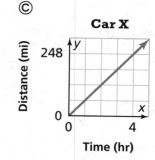

14. Car X travels 186 miles in 3 hours.

PART A Write the equation of the line that describes the relationship between distance and time.

PART B Which graph represents the relationship between distance and time for Car X?

Ⓐ
Car X
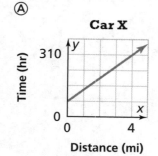
Distance (mi)

Ⓑ
Car X
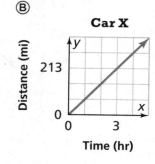
Time (hr)

Ⓒ
Car X
Time (hr)

Ⓓ
Car X
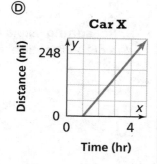
Time (hr)

Solve and Discuss It!

🛜 | 👆 ACTIVITY

Eight year-old Alex is learning to ride a horse. The trainer says that a horse ages 5 years for every 2 human years. The horse is now 50 years old in human years. How can you determine the age of the horse, in human years, when Alex was born?

Focus on math practices

Use Structure A veterinarian says that a cat ages 8 years for every 2 human years. If a cat is now 64 years old in cat years, how old is the cat in human years?

VISUAL LEARNING   ASSESS

EXAMPLE 1 **Determine the *y*-Intercept of a Relationship**

Scan for Multimedia

Mathilde and her friend are going bowling. She can rent shoes at the bowling alley or use her mother's old bowling shoes. How can she determine how much money she will save if she brings her mother's old bowling shoes?

Bowling Prices (includes shoe rental)	
One game	$4.00
Three games	$8.00
Five games	$12.00
Ten Games	$22.00

Look for Relationships What pattern can you see in the costs of different numbers of games?

STEP 1 Write the number of games and the cost as ordered pairs. Graph the ordered pairs and then find the slope to determine the cost of each game.

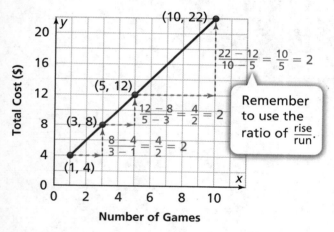

Remember to use the ratio of $\frac{rise}{run}$.

The slope is 2. That means the cost of each game is $2.

STEP 2 Extend the line to show where the line crosses the *y*-axis. The *y*-coordinate of the point where the line crosses the *y*-axis is the **y-intercept**.

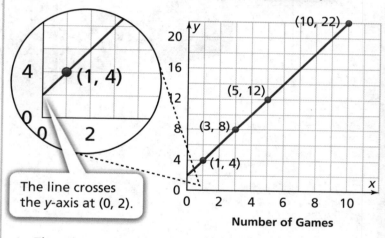

The line crosses the *y*-axis at (0, 2).

The *y*-intercept is 2. That means that the cost of shoe rental is $2. Mathilde saves $2 if she brings her mother's old bowling shoes.

✓ **Try It!**

Prices for a different bowling alley are shown in the graph. How much does this bowling alley charge for shoe rental?

The line crosses the *y*-axis as (☐ , ☐).

The *y*-intercept is ☐ .

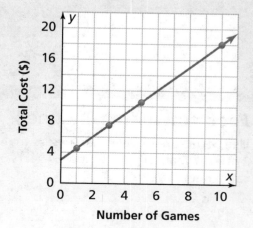

Convince Me! In these examples, why does the *y*-intercept represent the cost to rent bowling shoes?

EXAMPLE **2**  The *y*-Intercept of a Proportional Relationship

  ACTIVITY   ASSESS

A robotic assembly line manufactures a set number of parts per minute. Use a graph to verify how many parts the assembly line manufactures when it is first turned on.

STEP 1 Predict the number of parts.

The machine has not made any parts when it is first turned on, so the answer should be 0.

STEP 2 Determine the number of parts manufactured at different intervals.

Parts Manufactured	12	36	60	96
Time (minutes)	1	3	5	8

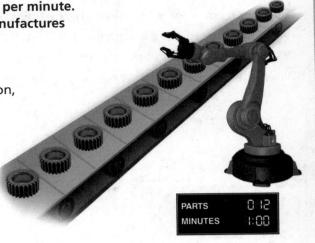

PARTS   0 12
MINUTES   1:00

STEP 3 Plot the points. Then draw a line to connect the points.

The *y*-intercept is 0. That agrees with the prediction. No parts are manufactured when the robotic assembly line is first turned on.

The line passes through the origin (0, 0).

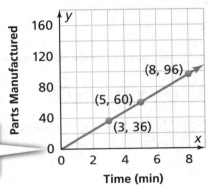

EXAMPLE **3**   Identify the *y*-Intercept

What is the *y*-intercept for each of the linear relationships shown?

The line crosses the *y*-axis at (0, 2). The *y*-intercept is 2.

The line crosses the *y*-axis at (0, −1). The *y*-intercept is −1.

The line crosses the *y*-axis at (0, 0). The *y*-intercept is 0.

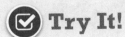 **Try It!**

What is the *y*-intercept of each graph? Explain.

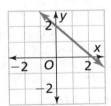   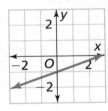   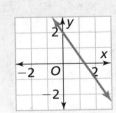   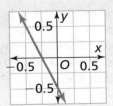   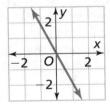

The *y*-intercept is the *y*-coordinate of the point on a graph where the line crosses the *y*-axis.

When the line crosses through the origin, the *y*-intercept is 0.

When the line crosses above the origin, the *y*-intercept is positive.

When the line crosses below the origin, the *y*-intercept is negative.

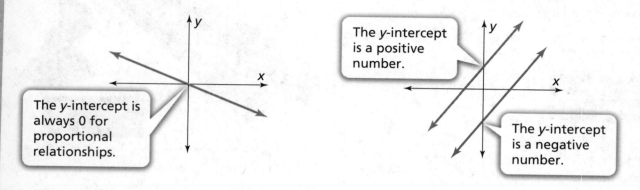

The *y*-intercept is always 0 for proportional relationships.

The *y*-intercept is a positive number.

The *y*-intercept is a negative number.

Do You Understand?

1. **Essential Question** What is the *y*-intercept and what does it indicate?

2. Look for Relationships Chelsea graphs a proportional relationship. Bradyn graphs a line that passes through the origin. What do you know about the *y*-intercept of each student's graph? Explain your answer.

3. Generalize When the *y*-intercept is positive, where does the line cross the *y*-axis on the graph? When it is negative?

Do You Know How?

4. What is the *y*-intercept shown in the graph?

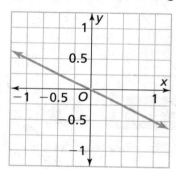

5. The graph shows the relationship between the remaining time of a movie and the amount of time since Kelly hit "play." What is the *y*-intercept of the graph and what does it represent?

Kelly's Movie

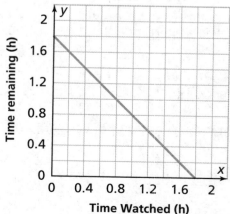

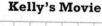

Practice & Problem Solving

6. Leveled Practice Find the *y*-intercept of the line.
The *y*-intercept is the point where the graph crosses

the ☐ -axis.

The line crosses the *y*-axis at the point (☐ , ☐).

The *y*-intercept is ☐ .

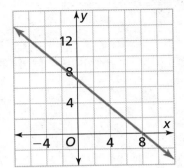

---

7. Find the *y*-intercept of the graph.

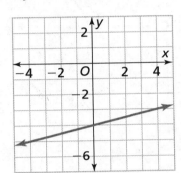

8. Find the *y*-intercept of the graph.

$y = kx$

---

9. The graph represents the height *y*, in meters, of a hot air balloon *x* minutes after beginning to descend. How high was the balloon when it began its descent?

Height of a Hot Air Balloon

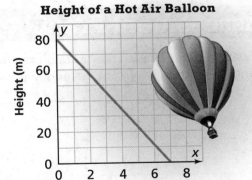

---

10. Model with Math The graph represents the amount of gasoline in a canister after Joshua begins to fill it at a gas station pump. What is the *y*-intercept of the graph and what does it represent?

Joshua's Gas Canister

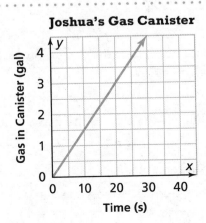

11. The line models the temperature on a certain winter day since sunrise.

a. What is the y-intercept of the line?

b. What does the y-intercept represent?

Temperature Since Sunrise

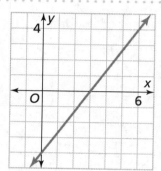

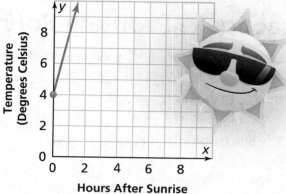

Hours After Sunrise

12. Higher Order Thinking Your friend incorrectly makes this graph as an example of a line with a y-intercept of 3.

a. Explain your friend's possible error.

b. Draw a line on the graph that does represent a y-intercept of 3.

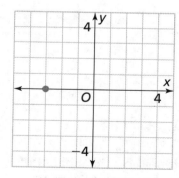

✓ Assessment Practice

13. For each graph, draw a line through the point such that the values of the x-intercept and y-intercept are additive inverses.

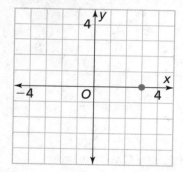

14. Which statements describe the graph of a proportional relationship? Select all that apply.

☐ The y-intercept is always at the point (0, 1).

☐ The line always crosses the y-axis at (0, 0).

☐ The y-intercept is 0.

☐ The y-intercept is 1.

☐ The line does NOT cross the y-axis.

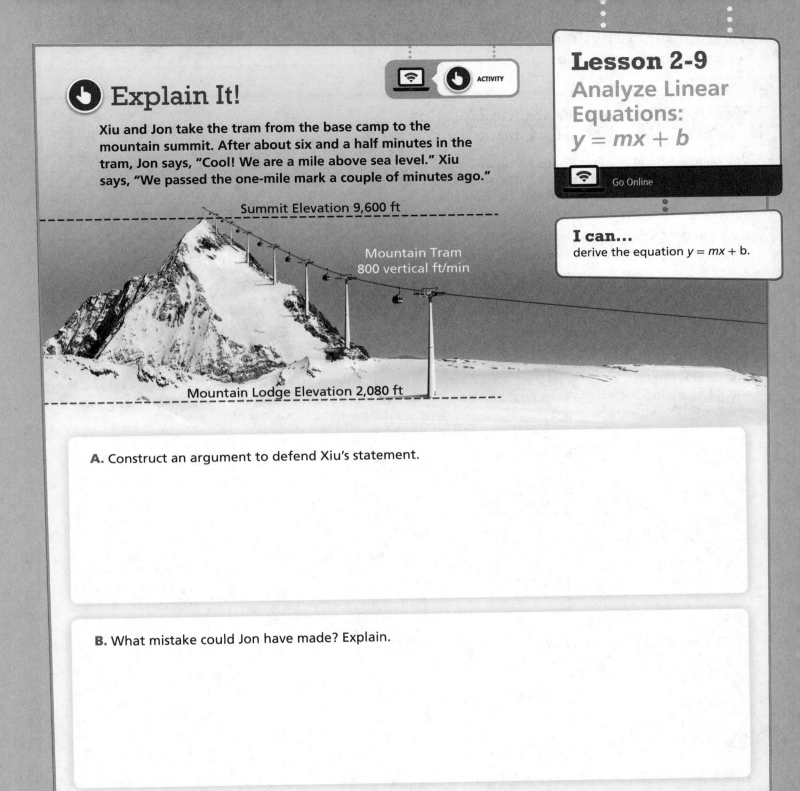

Explain It!

Lesson 2-9
Analyze Linear Equations:
$y = mx + b$

Go Online

I can...
derive the equation $y = mx + b$.

Xiu and Jon take the tram from the base camp to the mountain summit. After about six and a half minutes in the tram, Jon says, "Cool! We are a mile above sea level." Xiu says, "We passed the one-mile mark a couple of minutes ago."

Summit Elevation 9,600 ft

Mountain Tram
800 vertical ft/min

Mountain Lodge Elevation 2,080 ft

A. Construct an argument to defend Xiu's statement.

B. What mistake could Jon have made? Explain.

Focus on math practices

Reasoning Can you use the equation $y = mx$ to represent the path of the tram? Is there a proportional relationship between x and y? Explain.

VISUAL LEARNING ASSESS

EXAMPLE 1 Write the Equation of a Line

Scan for Multimedia

The Middle School Student Council is organizing a dance and has $500 to pay for a DJ. DJ Dave will charge $200 for a set-up fee and the first hour, or $425 for a set-up fee and four hours.

How can the Student Council determine whether they can afford to have DJ Dave play for 5 hours?

DJ DAVE
RATES
Set-Up Fee $125
Hourly Rate $75

STEP 1 Plot the total costs for DJ Dave for 1 hour and 4 hours. Find the initial value, or y-intercept, and the rate of change, or slope.

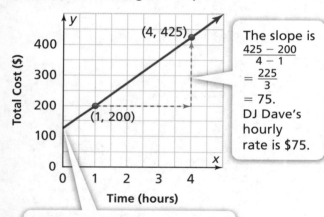

The slope is
$\frac{425 - 200}{4 - 1}$
$= \frac{225}{3}$
$= 75$.
DJ Dave's hourly rate is $75.

The initial value, or y-intercept, is 125. DJ Dave charges a $125 initial fee.

STEP 2 Write an equation to represent the total cost for DJ Dave for any number of hours.

Total Cost	=	Hourly Rate	+	Initial Fee
y	=	$75x$	+	125

This equation is in **slope-intercept form**, $y = mx + b$, where m is the rate of change, or slope, and b is the initial value, or y-intercept.

STEP 3 Evaluate the equation to find the total cost for 5 hours.

$y = 75x + 125$
$y = 75(5) + 125$
$= 375 + 125$
$= 500$

The total cost is $500. The student council can afford DJ Dave.

✓ Try It!

Write a linear equation in slope-intercept form for the graph shown.

The y-intercept of the line is ▢.

The slope is $\frac{▢}{▢}$. The equation in slope-intercept form is ▢ = ▢x + ▢.

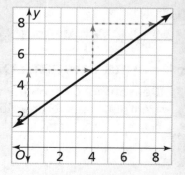

Convince Me! What two values do you need to know to write an equation of a line, and how are they used to represent a line?

EXAMPLE 2 — Write a Linear Equation Given Its Graph

A salt water solution is cooled to −6° C. During an experiment, the mixture is heated at a steady rate. Write an equation to represent the temperature, y, after x minutes.

Identify the slope and the y-intercept from the graph.

$y = mx + b$ — The slope $m = \frac{6}{3}$ or 2.

$y = 2x - 6$ — The y-intercept $b = -6$.

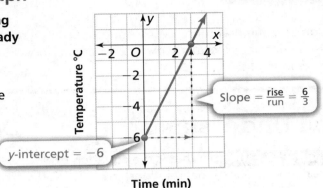

Slope $= \frac{rise}{run} = \frac{6}{3}$

y-intercept $= -6$

Temperature °C

Time (min)

The equation of the line is $y = 2x - 6$.

EXAMPLE 3 — Graph a Given Linear Equation

Graph the equation $y = -4x + 3$.

STEP 1 The y-intercept is 3. Plot a point at (0, 3).

STEP 2 The slope is −4 or $-\frac{4}{1}$. To locate another point on the line, start at (0, 3) and go down 4 and right 1.

STEP 3 Draw a line through the points.

Try It!

a. What is an equation for the line shown?

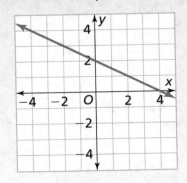

b. Graph the line with equation $y = \frac{1}{3}x - 5$.

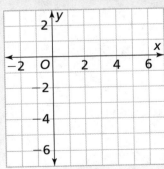

The equation of a line that represents a nonproportional relationship can be written in slope-intercept form, $y = mx + b$, where m is the slope of the line and b is the y-intercept.

Do You Understand?

1. **Essential Question** What is the equation of a line for a nonproportional relationship?

2. **Use Structure** The donations by a restaurant to a certain charity, y, will be two-fifths of its profits, x, plus $50. How can you determine the equation in slope-intercept form that shows the relationship between x and y without graphing the line?

3. **Be Precise** Priya will graph a line with the equation $y = \frac{3}{4}x - 4$. She wants to know what the line will look like before she graphs the line. Describe the line Priya will draw, including the quadrants the line will pass through.

Do You Know How?

4. Chrissie says the equation of the line shown on the graph is $y = \frac{1}{2}x - 5$. George says that the equation of the line is $y = \frac{1}{2}x + 5$. Which student is correct? Explain.

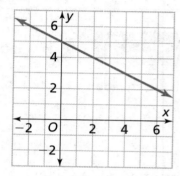

5. Fara wants to rent a tent for an outdoor celebration. The cost of the tent is $500 per hour, plus an additional $100 set-up fee.

   a. Draw a line to show the relationship between the number of hours the tent is rented, x, and the total cost of the tent, y.

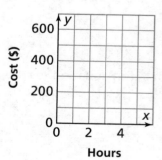

   b. What is the equation of the line in slope-intercept form?

Practice & Problem Solving

6. **Leveled Practice** What is the graph of the equation $y = 2x + 4$?

The y-intercept is ⬚, which means the line crosses the y-axis at the point (⬚, ⬚). Plot this point.

The slope of the line is positive, so it goes ⬚ from left to right.

Start at the y-intercept. Move up ⬚, and then move right ⬚.

You are now at the point (⬚, ⬚). Plot this point.

Draw a line to connect the two points.

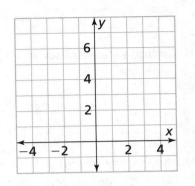

7. Write an equation for the line in slope-intercept form.

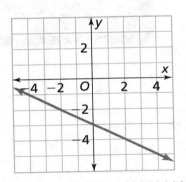

8. Write an equation for the line in slope-intercept form.

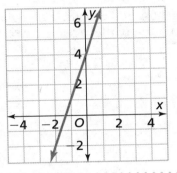

9. The line models the cost of renting a kayak. Write an equation in slope-intercept form for the line, where x is the number of hours the kayak is rented and y is the total cost of renting the kayak.

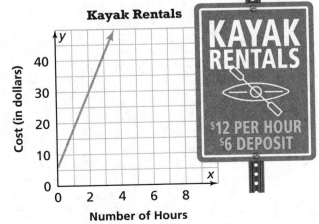

10. Graph the equation $y = 3x - 5$.

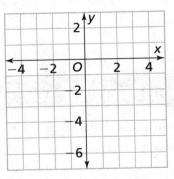

11. Amy began with $25 in her bank account and spent $5 each day. The line shows the amount of money in her bank account. She incorrectly wrote an equation for the line in slope-intercept form as $y = -5x + 5$.

Amy's Bank Account

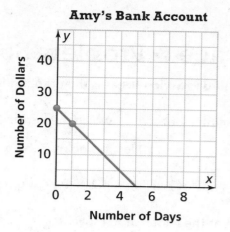

a. What is the correct equation for the line in slope-intercept form?

b. **Critique Reasoning** What mistake might Amy have made?

12. Higher Order Thinking The line represents the cost of ordering concert tickets online.

a. Write an equation for the line in slope-intercept form, where x is the number of tickets and y is the total cost.

b. Explain how you can write an equation for this situation without using a graph.

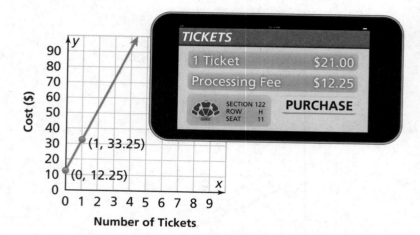

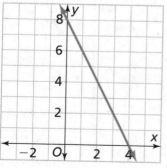

c. Is this graph a good representation of the situation? Explain.

Assessment Practice

13. What should you do first to graph the equation $y = \frac{2}{5}x - 1$?

Ⓐ Plot the point (0, 0).

Ⓑ Plot the point (2, 5).

Ⓒ Plot a point at the x-intercept.

Ⓓ Plot a point at the y-intercept.

14. Write an equation for the line in slope-intercept form.

? Topic Essential Question

How can you analyze connections between linear equations and use them to solve problems?

Vocabulary Review

Complete each definition and provide an example of each vocabulary word.

Vocabulary   slope of a line y-intercept   slope-intercept form x-intercept

Definition	Example
1. The change in y divided by the change in x is the _____.	
2. The point on the graph where the line crosses the y-axis is the _____ of a line.	
3. The _____ of a line is $y = mx + b$. The variable m in the equation stands for the _____. The variable b in the equation stands for the _____.	

Use Vocabulary in Writing

Paddle boats rent for a fee of $25, plus an additional $12 per hour. What equation, in $y = mx + b$ form, represents the cost to rent a paddle boat for x hours? Explain how you write the equation. Use vocabulary words in your explanation.

Concepts and Skills Review

Combine Like Terms to Solve Equations

Quick Review

You can use variables to represent unknown quantities. To solve an equation, collect like terms to get one variable on one side of the equation. Then use inverse operations and properties of equality to solve the equation.

Example

Solve $5x + 0.45x = 49.05$ for x.

$$5x + 0.45x = 49.05$$
$$5.45x = 49.05$$
$$\frac{5.45x}{5.45} = \frac{49.05}{5.45}$$
$$x = 9$$

Practice

Solve each equation for x.

1. $2x + 6x = 1,000$

2. $2\frac{1}{4}x + \frac{1}{2}x = 44$

3. $-2.3x - 4.2x = -66.3$

4. Javier bought a microwave for $105. The cost was 30% off the original price. What was the price of the microwave before the sale?

Solve Equations with Variables on Both Sides

Quick Review

If two quantities represent equal amounts and have the same variables, you can set the expressions equal to each other. Collect all the variables on one side of the equation and all the constants on the other side. Then use inverse operations and properties of equality to solve the equation.

Example

Solve $2x + 21 = 7x + 6$ for x.

$$2x + 21 = 7x + 6$$
$$21 = 5x + 6$$
$$15 = 5x$$
$$x = 3$$

Practice

Solve each equation for x.

1. $3x + 9x = 6x + 42$

2. $\frac{4}{3}x + \frac{2}{3}x = \frac{1}{3}x + 5$

3. $9x - 5x + 18 = 2x + 34$

4. Megan has $50 and saves $5.50 each week. Connor has $18.50 and saves $7.75 each week. After how many weeks will Megan and Connor have saved the same amount?

Solve Multistep Equations

Quick Review

When solving multistep equations, sometimes the Distributive Property is used before you collect like terms. Sometimes like terms are collected, and then you use the Distributive Property.

Example

Solve $8x + 2 = 2x + 4(x + 3)$ for x.

First, distribute the 4. Then, combine like terms. Finally, use properties of equality to solve for x.

$8x + 2 = 2x + 4x + 12$

$8x + 2 = 6x + 12$

$8x = 6x + 10$

$2x = 10$

$x = 5$

Practice

Solve each equation for x.

1. $4(x + 4) + 2x = 52$

2. $8(2x + 3x + 2) = -4x + 148$

3. Justin bought a calculator and a binder that were both 15% off the original price. The original price of the binder was $6.20. Justin spent a total of $107.27. What was the original price of the calculator?

Equations with No Solutions or Infinitely Many Solutions

Quick Review

When solving an equation results in a statement that is always true, there are infinitely many solutions. When solving an equation produces a false statement, there are no solutions. When solving an equation gives one value for a variable, there is one solution.

Example

How many solutions does the equation $6x + 9 = 2x + 4 + 4x + 5$ have?

First, solve the equation.

$6x + 9 = 2x + 4 + 4x + 5$

$6x + 9 = 6x + 9$

$9 = 9$

Because $9 = 9$ is alwyas a true statement, the equation has infinitely many solutions.

Practice

How many solutions does each equation have?

1. $x + 5.5 + 8 = 5x - 13.5 - 4x$

2. $4\left(\frac{1}{2}x + 3\right) = 3x + 12 - x$

3. $2(6x + 9 - 3x) = 5x + 21$

4. The weight of Abe's dog can be found using the expression $2(x + 3)$, where x is the number of weeks. The weight of Karen's dog can be found using the expression $3(x + 1)$, where x is the number of weeks. Will the dogs ever be the same weight? Explain.

Quick Review

To compare proportional relationships, compare the rate of change or find the unit rate.

Example

The graph shows the rate at which Rob jogs. Emily's jogging rate is represented by the equation $y = 8x$, where x is the number of miles and y is the number of minutes. At these rates, who will finish an 8-mile race first?

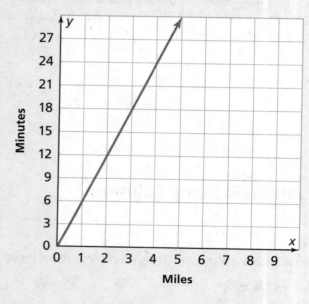

Emily's unit rate is $y = 8(1) = 8$ minutes per mile.

The point (1, 6) represents Rob's unit rate of 6 minutes per mile.

Rob's unit rate is less than Emily's rate, so Rob will finish an 8-mile race first.

Practice

1. Two trains are traveling at a constant rate. Find the rate of each train. Which train is traveling at the faster rate?

Train A

Time (h)	2	3	4	5	6
Distance (mi)	50	75	100	125	150

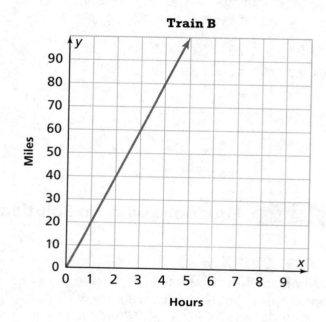

2. A 16-ounce bottle of water from Store A costs $1.28. The cost in dollars, y, of a bottle of water from Store B is represented by the equation $y = 0.07x$, where x is the number of ounces. What is the cost per ounce of water at each store? Which store's bottle of water costs less per ounce?

Quick Review

The **slope** of a line in a proportional relationship is the same as the unit rate and the constant of proportionality.

Example

The graph shows the number of miles a person walked at a constant speed. Find the slope of the line.

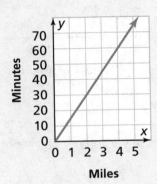

Miles

$$\text{slope} = \frac{y_2 - y_1}{x_2 - x_1} = \frac{60 - 30}{4 - 2} = \frac{30}{2} = 15$$

Practice

1. The graph shows the proportions of blue paint and yellow paint that Briana mixes to make green paint. What is the slope of the line? Tell what it means in the problem situation.

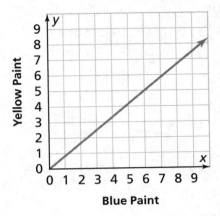

Blue Paint

Quick Review

A proportional relationship can be represented by an equation in the form $y = mx$, where m is the slope.

Example

Graph the line $y = 2x$.

Plot a point at $(0, 0)$. Then use the slope to plot the next point.

Practice

A mixture of nuts contains 1 cup of walnuts for every 3 cups of peanuts.

1. Write a linear equation that represents the relationship between peanuts, x, and walnuts, y.

2. Graph the line.

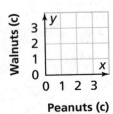

Peanuts (c)

LESSON 2-8 Understand the y-Intercept of a Line

Quick Review

The **y-intercept** is the y-coordinate of the point where a line crosses the y-axis. The y-intercept of a proportional relationship is 0.

Example

What is the y-intercept of the line?

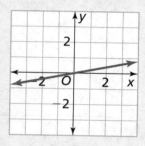

The y-intercept is 0.

Practice

The equation $y = 5 + 0.5x$ represents the cost of getting a car wash and using the vacuum for x minutes.

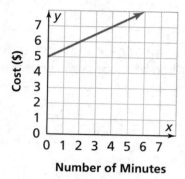

1. What is the y-intercept?

2. What does the y-intercept represent?

LESSON 2-9 Analyze Linear Equations: $y = mx + b$

Quick Review

An equation in the form $y = mx + b$, where $b \neq 0$, has a slope of m and a y-intercept of b. This form is called the **slope-intercept form**. There is not a proportional relationship between x and y in these cases.

Example

What is the equation of the line?

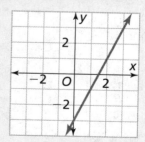

Since $m = 2$ and $b = -3$, the equation is $y = 2x - 3$.

Practice

1. Graph the line with the equation $y = \frac{1}{2}x - 1$.

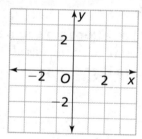

2. What is the equation of the line?

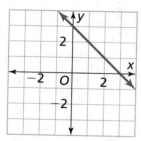

Pathfinder

Each block below shows an equation and a possible solution. Shade a path from START to FINISH. Follow the equations that are solved correctly. You can only move up, down, right, or left.

START

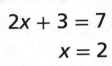

$2x + 3 = 7$ $x = 2$	$9y - 1 = -10$ $y = -1$	$5t + 1 = 9$ $t = 2$	$-11x + 12 = 1$ $x = -1$
$6h - 1 = 25$ $h = 4$	$14 + 3m = 35$ $m = 7$	$30 - j = 90$ $j = 60$	$19 - 4p = 9$ $p = -7$
$20t - 1 = 95$ $t = 5$	$20 - q = 17$ $q = 3$	$-4w + 7 = 11$ $w = -1$	$-a + 15 = 13$ $a = 2$
$100 - 4x = 0$ $x = -25$	$-9r - 4 = -85$ $r = -9$	$23 = 1 + 4y$ $y = 6$	$7y + 4 = 32$ $y = 4$
$-6b + 27 = 3$ $b = -4$	$2z + 1 = 0$ $z = \frac{1}{2}$	$47 - 2x = 45$ $x = -1$	$-12 + 9k = 42$ $k = 6$

FINISH

USE FUNCTIONS TO MODEL RELATIONSHIPS

? Topic Essential Question

How can you use functions to model linear relationships?

Topic Overview

3-1 Understand Relations and Functions

3-2 Connect Representations of Functions

3-3 Compare Linear and Nonlinear Functions

3-Act Mathematical Modeling: Every Drop Counts

3-4 Construct Functions to Model Linear Relationships

3-5 Intervals of Increase and Decrease

3-6 Sketch Functions from Verbal Descriptions

Topic Vocabulary

- constant rate of change
- function
- initial value
- interval
- linear function
- nonlinear function
- qualitative graph
- relation

Lesson Digital Resources

 INTERACTIVE STUDENT EDITION
Access online or offline.

 VISUAL LEARNING ANIMATION
Interact with visual learning animations.

 ACTIVITY Use with *Solve & Discuss It, Explore It,* and *Explain It* activities, and to explore Examples.

 VIDEOS Watch clips to support *3-Act Mathematical Modeling Lessons* and *STEM Projects.*

Go online

Every Drop Counts

▶ Every Drop Counts

Brushing your teeth every day is important. Not only does brushing affect your dental health, it can also affect your overall health.

While brushing their teeth, some people let the water run from the faucet. Other people shut off the faucet to save water. Did you ever wonder how much water people waste brushing their teeth? Think about this during the 3-Act Mathematical Modeling lesson.

 **PRACTICE** Practice what you've learned.

 TUTORIALS Get help from *Virtual Nerd*, right when you need it.

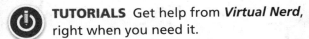 **MATH TOOLS** Explore math with digital tools.

 **GAMES** Play Math Games to help you learn.

 KEY CONCEPT Review important lesson content.

 GLOSSARY Read and listen to English/Spanish definitions.

A-Z

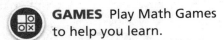 **ASSESSMENT** Show what you've learned.

enVision® STEM Project

Did You Know?

The world human population

1950: 2,500,000,000

2010: 7,300,000,000

2050: 9,400,000,000 (estimated)

The U.S. human population

1950: 151,000,000

2010: 320,000,000 and growing at an average rate of 1.1% per year

2050: 398,000,000 (estimated)

The human population in India

1950: 370,000,000

2010: 1,200,000,000 and growing at an average rate of 1.9% per year

2050: 1,620,000,000 (estimated)

Urbanization

1950: 30% of the world population lived in cities.

2010: More than 50% of the world population lived in cities.

2050: It is expected that 70% of the world population will live in cities.

U.S.
1950: 64% of the U.S. population lived in cities.

2010: 80% of the U.S. population lived in cities.

2050: It is expected that 91% of the U.S. population will live in cities.

India
1950: 17% of the Indian population lived in cities.

2010: 25% of the Indian population lived in cities.

2050: It is expected that 55% of the Indian population will live in cities.

As the population grows and moves to **urban** areas, the demand for food will grow. Demand for **cereals** is expected to grow from 2.1 billion tons in 2010 to 3 billion tons in 2050. Demand for **meat** is expected to grow from 250 million tons in 2010 to 470 million tons in 2050.

The demand on natural resources, such as **arable land**, **water**, and **energy**, will also increase.

Your Task: Modeling Population Growth

Population growth can affect availability of resources. You and your classmates will continue to explore your population model and make conjectures about the sustainability of the growth. You will also explore how the model can change if the demographic assumptions change.

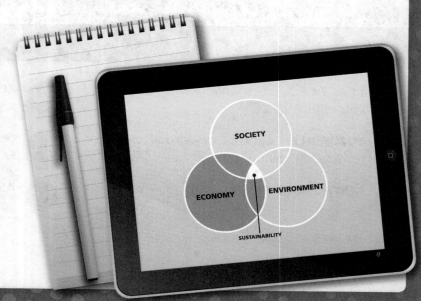

Review What You Know!

Vocabulary

Choose the best term from the box to complete each definition.

> linear equation
>
> proportional relationship
>
> slope
>
> slope-intercept form
>
> y-intercept

1. The _____ is the ratio of the vertical change to the horizontal change of a line.

2. A relationship that can be modeled by the equation $y = mx$ is a

_____ .

3. The y-value at which a line of a graph crosses the y-axis is called the

_____ .

4. An equation written in the form $y = mx + b$ is called the

_____ .

Slope and y-Intercept

Find the slope and y-intercept of a line that passes through these points.

5. (2, 2) and (3, 0)

6. (1, 5) and (4, 10)

7. (8, 2) and (−8, 6)

Compare Proportional Relationships

Jenna's mother is shopping for energy drinks in 12-ounce bottles for Jenna's soccer team. Store A sells a case of 18 bottles for $10. Store B sells a case of 12 bottles for $6. Which store sells the drinks for less? Use the graph to compare the unit costs of the drinks.

8.

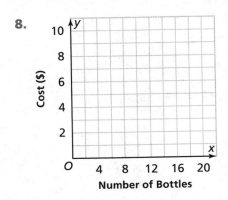

Linear Equations

9. Write the equation for the graph of the line shown.

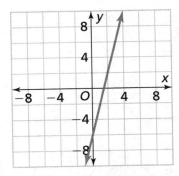

Language Development

Write key words or phrases associated with each representation.
Then write *function* or *not a function* on the given lines.

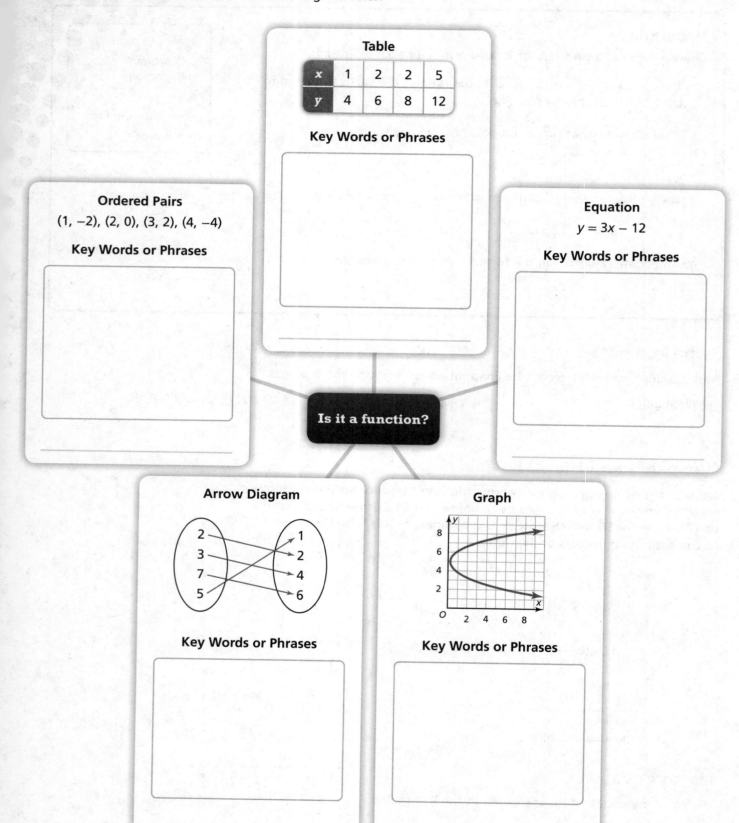

Table

x	1	2	2	5
y	4	6	8	12

Key Words or Phrases

Ordered Pairs

(1, −2), (2, 0), (3, 2), (4, −4)

Key Words or Phrases

Equation

$y = 3x - 12$

Key Words or Phrases

Is it a function?

Arrow Diagram

2 3 7 5 → 1 2 4 6

Key Words or Phrases

Graph

Key Words or Phrases

PROJECT
3A

What machine could be invented to make your life better?

PROJECT: BUILD A RUBE GOLDBERG MACHINE

PROJECT
3B

What games can you play indoors?

PROJECT: MAKE A MATH CARD GAME

PROJECT
3C

What are the steps for fixing a leaky pipe?

PROJECT: PLAN A MAINTENANCE ROUTE

PROJECT
3D

If you were to make a video game, what kind of game would it be?

PROJECT: DESIGN A VIDEO GAME ELEMENT

Solve & Discuss It!

 ACTIVITY

The 10 members of Photography Club want to raise $500, so they will hold a raffle with donated prizes. Jesse proposes that to reach their goal, each member should sell 50 raffle tickets. Alexis proposes that each member should raise $50.

Whose plan would you recommend? Explain.

RAFFLE TICKETS

$1   1 ticket
$5   6 tickets
$20   25 tickets

I can...
tell whether a relation is a function.

Focus on math practices

Reasoning How are the two plans different? How are they similar?

VISUAL LEARNING ASSESS

EXAMPLE 1 Identify Functions with Arrow Diagrams

Scan for Multimedia

Jonah is shipping five boxes for his uncle. Each box is the same size but a different weight. The cost to ship each box is shown. Should Jonah expect that the cost to ship a 15-pound box will be a unique cost?

Use Structure Is there a relationship between the weight of the box and the cost to ship the box?

STEP 1 Organize the data using ordered pairs.

$\left(\begin{matrix} \text{input} & \text{output} \\ \text{(weight),} & \text{(cost)} \end{matrix} \right)$

(8, 8.56)

(9, 8.72)

(10, 9.01)

(12, 9.55)

(14, 10.03)

Any set of ordered pairs is a **relation**.

STEP 2 Use an arrow diagram to match each input value to its output value.

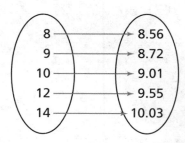

A relation is a **function** when each input is assigned exactly one output. For each input above, there is exactly one output. So, the relation is a function.

Jonah can expect that the cost to ship a 15-pound box will be a unique cost.

✓ Try It!

Joe needs to advertise his company. He considers several different brochures of different side lengths and areas. He presents the data as ordered pairs (*side length, area*).

(4, 24), (5, 35), (8, 24), (2, 20), (9, 27)

Complete the arrow diagram. Is the area of a brochure a function of the side length? Explain.

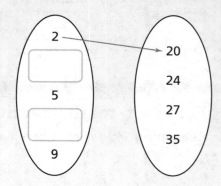

Convince Me! There are two outputs of 24. Does this help you determine whether the relation is a function? Explain.

EXAMPLE **2** Use Tables to Identify Functions

Frank uses a table to record the ages and heights of the six students he tutors. **Is the relation a function? Explain.**

Determine whether each input has exactly one output.

Two 9-year-olds have different heights.

Two 8-year-olds have different heights.

Age, x	Height, y
9	54
10	54
9	61
8	45
12	65
8	50

Look for Relationships
How might the two quantities be related?

No, this relation is not a function because two inputs have more than one output.

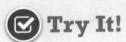 **Try It!**

Frank reverses the ordered pairs to show the heights and ages of the same six students. Is age a function of height? Explain.

Height (in.)	54	54	61	45	65	50
Age (years)	9	10	9	8	12	8

EXAMPLE **3** **Interpreting Functions**

Heather and her parents are going to an art museum for the day. The parking garage near the museum charges the rates shown in the sign.

A. Is the cost to park a function of time? Explain.

Each hour of parking time has a different cost. So the cost to park is a function of time.

B. If they stay at the museum for 6 hours, should they expect to pay more than $25?

Yes, they should expect to pay more than $25.

Art Museum Parking Rates

Time (hours)	Cost ($)
Up to **1** hour	$5
Up to **2** hours	$10
Up to **3** hours	$15
Up to **4** hours	$20
Up to **5** hours	$25

 **Try It!**

Heather claims that she can tell exactly how long a family was at the museum by how much the family pays for parking. Is Heather correct? Explain.

A relation is a function if each input corresponds to exactly one output.
You can use an arrow diagram or a table to determine whether
a relation is a function.

This relation is a function.

Each input corresponds
to exactly one output.

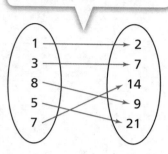

This relation is not a function.

Input	Output
2	4
5	10
4	8
2	6

One input is assigned
two different outputs.

Do You Understand?

1. **Essential Question** When is a relation a function?

2. Model with Math How can you use different representations of a relation to determine whether the relation is a function?

3. Generalize Is a relation always a function? Is a function always a relation? Explain.

Do You Know How?

4. Is the relation shown below a function? Explain.

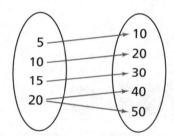

5. Is the relation shown below a function? Explain.

Input	3	4	1	5	2
Output	4	6	2	8	5

6. Is the relation shown below a function? Explain.

(4, 16), (5, 25), (3, 9), (6, 36), (2, 4), (1, 1)

Practice & Problem Solving

7. The set of ordered pairs (1, 19), (2, 23), (3, 23), (4, 29), (5, 31) represents the number of tickets sold for a fundraiser. The input values represent the day and the output values represent the number of tickets sold on that day.

   a. Make an arrow diagram that represents the relation.

   b. Is the relation a function? Explain.

8. Does the relation shown below represent a function? Explain.

   (−2, 2), (−7, 1), (−3, 9), (3, 4), (−9, 5), (−6, 8)

9. Is the relation shown in the table a function? Explain.

Input	Output
4	1
8	3
4	5
8	4

10. **Construct Arguments** During a chemistry experiment, Sam records how the temperature changes over time using ordered pairs (*time in minutes, temperature in*).

    (0, 15), (5, 20), (10, 50), (15, 80), (20, 100), (25, 100)

    Is the relation a function? Explain.

11. **Reasoning** Taylor has tracked the number of students in his grade since third grade. He records his data in the table below. Is the relation a function? Explain.

Grade	3	4	5	6	7	8
# People	726	759	748	792	804	835

12. James raises chickens. He tracks the number of eggs his chickens lay at the end of each week. Is this relation a function? Explain.

Week	1	2	3	4	5	6
Eggs	7	13	13	22	26	30

13. Relations P and Q are shown below.

Relation P

Input	Output
3	6
7	14
15	6
16	14

Relation Q

Input	Output
6	7
6	16
14	3
14	15

a. Make an arrow diagram to represent Relation P.

b. Make an arrow diagram to represent Relation Q.

c. Which relation is a function? Explain.

14. Higher Order Thinking On a recent test, students had to determine whether the relation represented by the ordered pairs (1, 2), (6, 12), (12, 24), (18, 36) is a function. Bobby drew the arrow diagram on the right and said the relation was not a function. What error did Bobby most likely make?

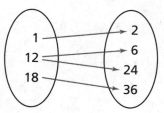

Assessment Practice

15. Write the set of ordered pairs that is represented by the arrow diagram at the right. Is the relation a function? Explain.

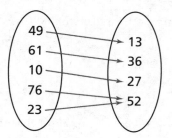

16. Which of these relations are functions? Select all that apply.

☐ **Relation 1**

x	y
3	3
4	5
5	7
5	9
6	11

☐ **Relation 2**

x	y
5	31
6	28
7	25
8	22
9	19

☐ **Relation 3**

x	y
2	3
3	3
4	3
5	3
6	3

☐ **Relation 4**

x	y
7	10
8	20
9	30
9	40
10	50

☐ **Relation 5**

x	y
3	2
3	3
3	4
3	5
3	6

Go Online

I can...
identify functions by their equations, tables, and graphs.

Solve & Discuss It!

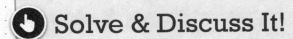 ACTIVITY

Eliza volunteers at a nearby aquarium, where she tracks the migratory patterns of humpback whales from their feeding grounds to their breeding grounds. She recorded the distance, in miles, traveled by the whales each day for the first 7-day period of their migration. Based on Eliza's data, about how long will it take the humpback whales to travel the 3,100 miles to their breeding grounds?

Day	1	2	3	4	5	6	7
Distance (miles)	30	28	30	27	30	24	36

Focus on math practices

Construct Arguments How does finding an average distance the whales travel in miles help with finding a solution to this problem?

EXAMPLE 1 > Represent a Linear Function with an Equation and a Graph

Scan for Multimedia

A 10,000-gallon swimming pool needs to be emptied. Exactly 2,000 gallons have already been pumped out of the pool and into the tanker. How can you determine how long it will take to pump all of the water into the tanker?

Generalize How can you use what you know about linear equations to solve the problem?

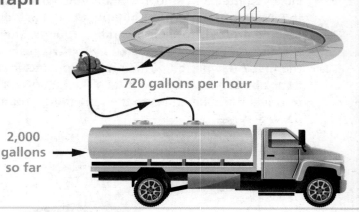

720 gallons per hour

2,000 gallons so far

ONE WAY Use the information given to draw a diagram that represents the situation, and then write an equation.

The total amount of water to be pumped

10,000

2,000   720

h hours

The amount of water already pumped is the **initial value**, or *y*-intercept.

The amount of water pumped every hour is the constant **rate of change**, or slope.

$$10,000 = 720h + 2,000$$

ANOTHER WAY Use the information given to make a graph.

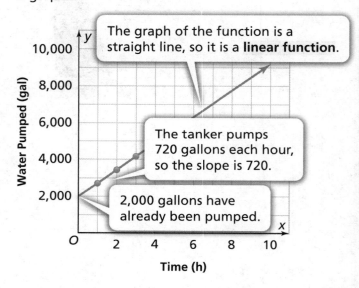

The graph of the function is a straight line, so it is a **linear function**.

The tanker pumps 720 gallons each hour, so the slope is 720.

2,000 gallons have already been pumped.

Water Pumped (gal) / Time (h)

✓ Try It!

As the pump is pumping water, the amount of water in the pool decreases at a constant rate. Complete the statements below. Then graph the function.

The amount of water remaining in the pool is ☐ gallons.

The amount of water pumped each hour is ☐ gallons.

The equation is ☐.

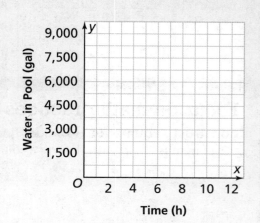

Water in Pool (gal) / Time (h)

Convince Me! How is the rate of change of this function different from that in Example 1? Explain.

EXAMPLE 2 — Represent a Nonlinear Function with a Graph

$$A = s^2$$

How can you determine whether the relationship between side length and area is a function?

STEP 1 Make a table that relates different side lengths and areas.

Length, s (in.)	Area, A (in.^{2})
0	0
1	1
2	4
3	9
4	16
5	25

Each input value has a unique output value, so the relationship is a function.

STEP 2 Graph the ordered pairs from the table.

Because each x-value corresponds to exactly one y-value, the graph represents a function.

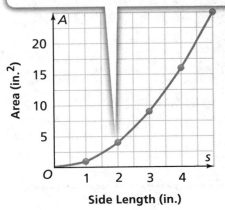

The graph of this function is not a straight line, so it is a **nonlinear function**.

EXAMPLE 3 — Identify Functions from Graphs

Determine whether each graph represents a function.

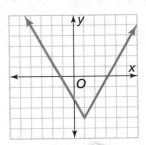
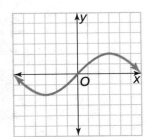
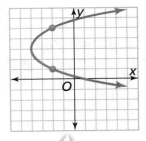

Each of these graphs represents a function because each x-value corresponds to exactly one y-value.

This graph does not represent a function because each x-value does not correspond to exactly one y-value. For example, the x-value, -2, corresponds to two y-values, 1 and 5.

✓ Try It!

Draw a graph that represents a linear function. What equation represents the function?

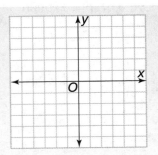

You can represent a function in different ways: in a table, in a graph, or as an equation.

A day at the amusement park costs $10 for an entrance fee and $2.50 for each ride ticket.

Table

Number of Tickets	0	1	2	3	4
Cost ($)	10	12.5	15	17.5	20

Equation in the form of $y = mx + b$:
$y = 2.5x + 10$

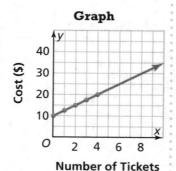

Graph

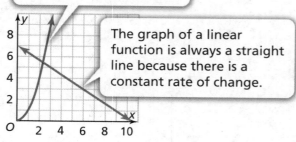

The graph of a nonlinear function is not a straight line because there is no constant rate of change.

The graph of a linear function is always a straight line because there is a constant rate of change.

Do You Understand?

1. **? Essential Question** What are different representations of a function?

2. **Use Appropriate Tools** How can you use a graph to determine that a relationship is **NOT** a function?

3. **Construct Arguments** Must the ordered pairs of a function be connected by a straight line or a curve on a graph? Explain.

Do You Know How?

4. Each week, Darlene tracks the number of party hats her company has in stock. The table shows the weekly stock. Is the relationship a linear function? Use the graph below to support your answer.

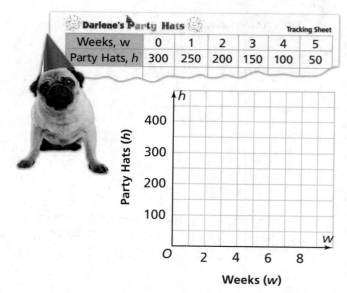

Darlene's Party Hats						Tracking Sheet
Weeks, w	0	1	2	3	4	5
Party Hats, h	300	250	200	150	100	50

5. How can Darlene use the graph above to know when to order more party hats?

Practice & Problem Solving

Leveled Practice In **6–7**, explain whether each graph represents a function.

6.

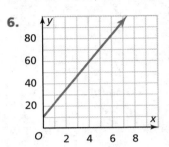

7.

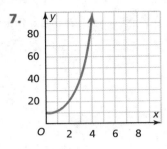

8. Hannah approximates the areas of circles using the equation $A = 3r^2$, and records areas of circles with different radius lengths in a table.

Radius (in.)	1	2	3	4	5
Area (in.²)	3	12	27	48	75

a. Graph the ordered pairs from the table.

b. Is the relation a function? Explain.

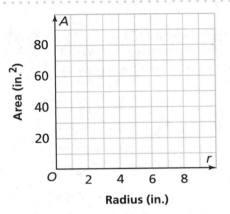

9. Model with Math The relationship between the number of hexagons, x, and the perimeter of the figure they form, y, is shown in the graph. Is the perimeter of the figure a function of the number of hexagons? Explain.

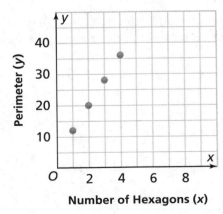

10. Construct Arguments Do the ordered pairs plotted in the graph below represent a function? Explain.

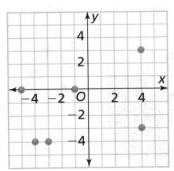

11. A train leaves the station at time $t = 0$. Traveling at a constant speed, the train travels 360 kilometers in 3 hours.

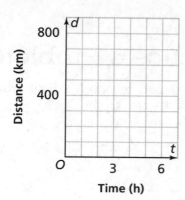

a. Write a function that relates the distance traveled, d, to the time, t.

b. Graph the function and tell whether it is a linear function or a nonlinear function.

The function is a [ ] function.

12. **Higher Order Thinking** Tell whether each graph is a function and justify your answer. Which graph is not a good representation of a real-world situation? Explain.

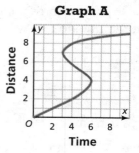

Graph A

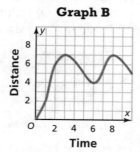

Graph B

Assessment Practice

13. You have an ant farm with 22 ants. The population of ants in your farm doubles every 3 months.

PART A

Complete the table.

Number of Months	0	3	6	9
Ant Population	22			

PART B

Is the relation a function? If so, is it a linear function or a nonlinear function? Explain.

14. Use the function $y = \frac{3}{2}x + 3$ to complete the table of values.

x				
y	9	6	0	−3

Solve & Discuss It!

ACTIVITY

Two streaming video subscription services offer family plans with different monthly costs, as shown in the ads below. What do the two plans have in common? How are they different? When is Movies4You a better deal than Family Stream?

MOVIES4YOU

$10 for the first device

$2 for each additional device

NEW

FAMILY STREAM

$12 FLAT RATE FOR UP TO 4 DEVICES

ADDITIONAL FEE OF $1 PER DEVICE FOR 5 OR MORE DEVICES

Model with Math How can you represent the relationship between cost and number of devices?

I can...
compare linear and nonlinear functions.

Focus on math practices

Look for Relationships Describe the relationship between the cost and the number of devices for each service. What do you notice about each relationship?

EXAMPLE 1 Compare Two Linear Functions

Scan for Multimedia

An auto assembly factory needs to purchase new welding robots. The factory manager has information on two different models of welding robots. The welding rates for each model are shown below. How do the welding rates for the two robots compare?

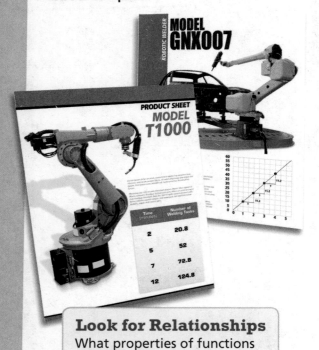

Look for Relationships
What properties of functions can be used to compare functions?

STEP 1 Find the welding rate, or the constant rate of change, for each robot.

Model T1000

Time (minutes)	Number of Welding Tasks
2	20.8
5	52
7	72.8
12	124.8

Model GNX007

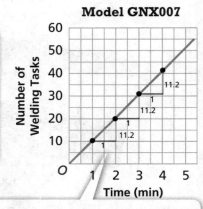

Number of Welding Tasks vs. Time (min)

$$\frac{52 - 20.8}{5 - 2} = \frac{31.2}{3} = 10.4$$

The constant rate of change is 11.2.

The constant rate of change is 10.4.

STEP 2 Find the initial value for each robot.

At 0 minutes, each robot has performed 0 tasks, so the initial value is 0.

The data for the model GXN007 robot has a greater constant rate of change, or welding rate, so it can complete more welding tasks per minute than the Model T1000 robot.

Try It!

The welding rate of a third robot is represented by the equation $t = 10.8w$, where t represents the time in minutes and w represents the number of welding tasks. How does it compare to the other two?

Convince Me! How can linear equations help you compare linear functions?

EXAMPLE 2 Compare a Linear and a Nonlinear Function

A square with side length *s* is shown. The table shows the relationship between the side length and perimeter as the side length increases. The graph shows the relationship between the side length and area. How do the two relationships compare?

Side Length, s (in.)	Perimeter, P (in.)
0	0
1	4
2	8
3	12
4	16

+1 ... +4 (between each row)

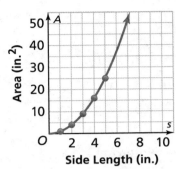

This relation is a function. It has a constant rate of change. It is a *linear* function.

This relation is a function, but it does not have a constant rate of change. It is a *nonlinear* function.

Both relationships are functions. Both perimeter and area are functions of side length.

EXAMPLE 3 Compare Properties of Linear Functions

Two linear functions are represented below. Compare the properties of the two functions.

Function A

The constant rate of change is 2.

$y = 2x - 3$

The initial value is −3.

Function B

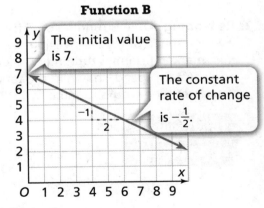

The initial value is 7.

The constant rate of change is $-\frac{1}{2}$.

Function A has a greater rate of change. Function B has a greater initial value.

✓ Try It!

Compare the properties of these two linear functions.

Function 1

x	2	5	9	11	14
y	1	5.5	11.5	14.5	19

Function 2

$y = 2x - 4$

You can compare functions in different representations by using the properties of functions.

Compare the constant rate of change and the initial value.

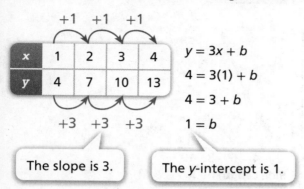

$y = 3x + b$

$4 = 3(1) + b$

$4 = 3 + b$

$1 = b$

The slope is 3.

The y-intercept is 1.

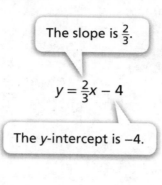

The slope is $\frac{2}{3}$.

$y = \frac{2}{3}x - 4$

The y-intercept is −4.

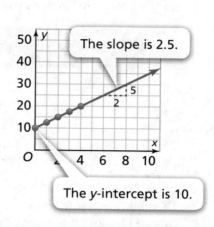

The slope is 2.5.

The y-intercept is 10.

Do You Understand?

1. **? Essential Question** How can you compare two functions?

2. Reasoning Anne is running on a trail at an average speed of 6 miles per hour beginning at mile marker 4. John is running on the same trail at a constant speed, shown in the table. How can you determine who is running faster?

Time (hours), x	0	0.5	1	1.5
Mile Marker, y	1	4.5	8	11.5

3. Reasoning In Item 2, how do Anne and John's starting positions compare? Explain.

Do You Know How?

Felipe and Samantha use a payment plan to buy musical instruments. Felipe writes the equation $y = -30x + 290$ to represent the amount owed, y, after x payments. The graph shows how much Samantha owes after each payment.

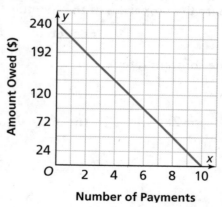

Number of Payments

4. Whose musical instrument costs more, Felipe's or Samantha's? Explain.

5. Who will pay more each month? Explain.

Practice & Problem Solving

PRACTICE   TUTORIAL

Scan for
Multimedia

6. Two linear functions are shown below. Which function has the greater rate of change?

Function A

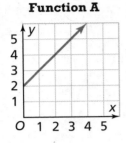

Function B

x	y
0	0
2	3
4	6
6	9

7. Two linear functions are shown below. Which function has the greater initial value?

Function A

x	y
−1	6
0	4
1	2
2	0

Function B

$y = 7x + 3$

8. Tell whether each function is *linear* or *nonlinear*.

Function A

x	y
0	1
1	2
2	5
3	10

Function B

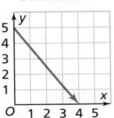

9. Tell whether each function is *linear* or *nonlinear*.

Function A

Function B

$y = x$

10. Determine whether each function is *linear* or *nonlinear* from its graph.

Function I

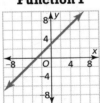

Function II

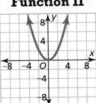

11. Look for Relationships Justin opens a savings account with $4. He saves $2 each week. Does a linear function or a nonlinear function represent this situation? Explain.

Justin's Savings Account

Week	0	1	2	3	4	5
Money in Account	4	6	8	10	12	14

12. Reasoning The function $y = 4x + 3$ describes Player A's scores in a game of trivia, where x is the number of questions answered correctly and y is the score. The function represented in the table shows Player B's scores. What do the rates of change tell you about how each player earns points?

Player B's Trivia Scores

Correct Answers	Score
1	4
2	5
3	6
4	7

13. Two athletes are training over a two-week period to increase the number of push-ups each can do consecutively. Athlete A can do 16 push-ups to start, and increases his total by 2 each day. Athlete B's progress is charted in the table. Compare the initial values for each. What does the initial value mean in this situation?

Athlete B Push-up Progress

Day	Number of Push-ups
0	12
1	15
2	18
3	21

14. Higher Order Thinking The equation $y = 4x - 2$ and the table and graph shown at the right describe three different linear functions. Which function has the greatest rate of change? Which has the least? Explain.

x	y
1	5
2	10
3	15
4	20

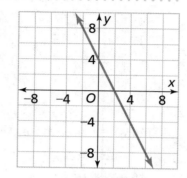

✅ Assessment Practice

15. The students in the After-School Club ate 12 grapes per minute. After 9 minutes, there were 32 grapes remaining. The table shows the number of carrots remaining after different amounts of time. Which snack did the students eat at a faster rate? Explain.

Carrot Consumption

Time Elapsed	Carrots Remaining
6 minutes	136
8 minutes	118
9 minutes	109
11 minutes	91

16. The height of a burning candle can be modeled by a linear function. Candle A has an initial height of 201 millimeters, and its height decreases to 177 millimeters after 4 hours of burning. The height, h, in millimeters, of Candle B can be modeled by the function $h = 290 - 5t$, where t is the time in hours. Which of the following statements are true?

☐ The initial height of Candle A is greater than the initial height of Candle B.

☐ The height of Candle A decreases at a faster rate than the height of Candle B.

☐ Candle B will burn out in 58 hours.

☐ After 10 hours, the height of Candle A is 110 millimeters.

☐ Candle A will burn out before Candle B.

1. **Vocabulary** How can you determine whether a relation is a function? *Lesson 3-1*

2. Can an arrow or arrows be drawn from 10.3 so the relation in the diagram is a function? Explain your answer. *Lesson 3-1*

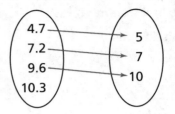

3. Two linear functions are shown below. Which function has the greater rate of change? Justify your response. *Lesson 3-3*

Function A

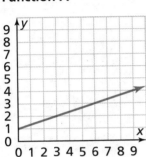

Function B

$y = \frac{1}{2}x - 1$

4. Neil took 3 math tests this year. The number of hours he spent studying for each test and the corresponding grades he earned are shown in the table. Is the relation of hours of study time to grade earned on a test a function? Explain why. Use the graph to justify your answer. *Lesson 3-2*

Hours	4	6	6
Grade	75	75	82

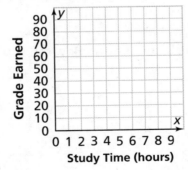

5. Is the function shown linear or nonlinear? Explain your answer. *Lesson 3-3*

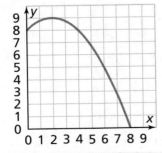

How well did you do on the mid-topic checkpoint? Fill in the stars.

MID-TOPIC PERFORMANCE TASK

Sarah, Gene, and Paul are proposing plans for a class fundraiser. Each presents his or her proposal for the amount of money raised, *y*, for *x* number of hours worked, in different ways.

Sarah's Proposal

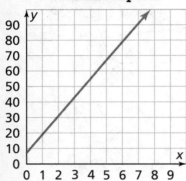

Gene's Proposal

Hours Worked	Money Raised
5	42
10	77
15	112
20	147

Paul's Proposal

$y = 10x + 7$

PART A

Are each of the proposals represented by linear functions? Explain.

PART B

Does the class have any money in the account now? How can you tell?

PART C

Which fundraising proposal raises money at the fastest rate? Explain.

PART D

If Sarah and her classmates are hoping to raise $200, which proposal do you recommend that Sarah and her classmates choose? Explain why you recommend that proposal.

3-ACT MATH ▷ ▷ ▷

Every Drop Counts

ACT 1

1. After watching the video, what is the first question that comes to mind?

2. Write the Main Question you will answer.

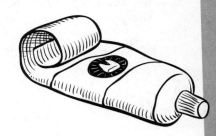

3. Construct Arguments Predict an answer to this Main Question. Explain your prediction.

4. On the number line below, write a number that is too small to be the answer. Write a number that is too large.

Too small   Too large

5. Plot your prediction on the same number line.

6. What information in this situation would be helpful to know?
   How would you use that information?

7. **Use Appropriate Tools** What tools can you use to solve the problem?
   Explain how you would use them strategically.

8. **Model with Math** Represent the situation using mathematics.
   Use your representation to answer the Main Question.

9. What is your answer to the Main Question? Is it higher or lower than your
   prediction? Explain why.

10. Write the answer you saw in the video.

11. Reasoning Does your answer match the answer in the video? If not, what are some reasons that would explain the difference?

12. Make Sense and Persevere Would you change your model now that you know the answer? Explain.

Reflect

13. Model with Math Explain how you used a mathematical model to represent the situation. How did the model help you answer the Main Question?

14. Be Precise How do the units you chose and the method you used help you communicate your answer?

15. Use Structure How much water will he save in a year?

Explore It!

Erick wants to buy a new mountain bike that costs $250. He has already saved $120 and plans to save $20 each week from the money he earns for mowing lawns. He thinks he will have saved enough money after seven weeks.

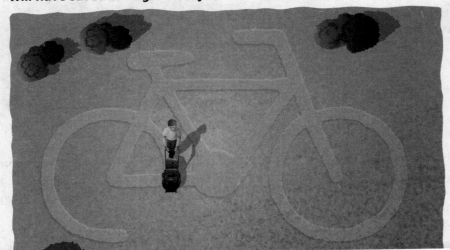

I can...
write an equation in the form $y = mx + b$ to describe a linear function.

A. Complete the table. Then graph the data.

Time (weeks)	0	1	2	3
Money Saved ($)	120			

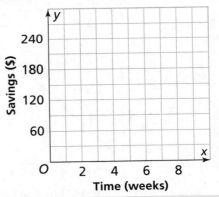

B. How can you tell that the relationship is a linear function from the table? How can you tell from the graph?

Focus on math practices

Generalize How can the different representations help you determine properties of functions?

? Essential Question How can you use a function to represent a linear relationship?

 VISUAL LEARNING   ASSESS

EXAMPLE 1 **Write a Function from a Graph**

Scan for Multimedia

A plan for a skateboard ramp shows that the plywood for the triangular sides of the ramp should be cut such that for every 9 inches of height, the triangle should have a base that is 33 inches long. What is the height of the skateboard ramp shown?

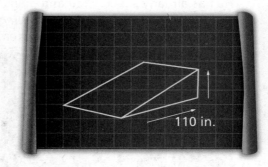

110 in.

STEP 1 Use a graph to represent the situation and to determine the slope.

For every 9 in. of height, the base is 33 in. long

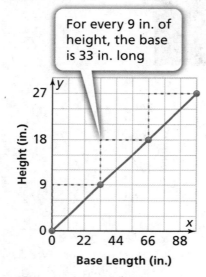

Base Length (in.)

The slope of the line is the change in height (y) divided by the change in base length (x), which is $\frac{9}{33} = \frac{3}{11}$.

STEP 2 Use the slope to write an equation that represents the function shown in the graph. Then use the equation to find the height for a base length of 110 inches.

Height   Slope

Base length

The equation is $y = \frac{3}{11}x$.

$y = \frac{3}{11}(110)$

$y = 30$

The height of the ramp is 30 inches.

☑ **Try It!**

How will the height of the ramp change if the plan shows that for every 3 inches of height, the triangle should have a base that is 15 inches long?

Graph the function. The slope of the function shown in the graph

is ☐ . The equation of the function is $y = $ ☐ x. If the base length

is 110 inches, then the height of the ramp will be ☐ inches.

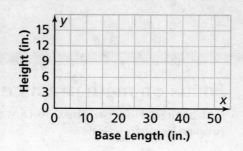

Base Length (in.)

Convince Me! Explain why the initial value and the y-intercept are equivalent.

EXAMPLE 2 Write a Function from Two Values

The cost to manufacture 5 toys is $17.50; the cost to manufacture 10 toys is $30. Construct a linear function in the form $y = mx + b$ that represents the relationship between the number of toys produced and the cost of producing them.

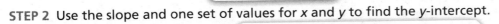

10 toys cost $30.00.

5 toys cost $17.50.

STEP 1 Determine the constant rate of change.

$$\frac{30 - 17.5}{10 - 5} = \frac{12.5}{5} = \frac{2.5}{1}$$

The constant rate of change is 2.5.

STEP 2 Use the slope and one set of values for x and y to find the y-intercept.

$$30 = 2.5(10) + b \qquad 5 = b$$

The initial value, or y-intercept, is 5.

The linear function that models this relationship is $y = 2.5x + 5$.

 Try It!

Jin is tracking how much food he feeds his dogs each week. After 2 weeks, he has used $8\frac{1}{2}$ cups of dog food. After 5 weeks, he has used $21\frac{1}{4}$ cups. Construct a function in the form $y = mx + b$ to represent the amount of dog food used, y, after x weeks.

EXAMPLE 3 Interpret a Function from a Graph

The graph shows the relationship of the height of a burning candle over time. What function represents the relationship?

The function $y = -1x + 10$ represents the relationship.

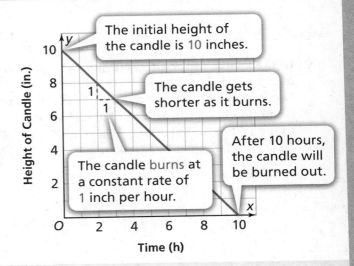

The initial height of the candle is 10 inches.

The candle gets shorter as it burns.

The candle burns at a constant rate of 1 inch per hour.

After 10 hours, the candle will be burned out.

 Try It!

The graph shows the relationship between the number of pages printed by a printer and the warm-up time before each printing. What function in the form $y = mx + b$ represents this relationship?

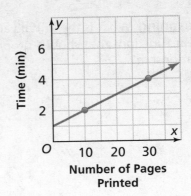

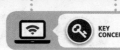

A function in the form $y = mx + b$ represents a linear relationship between two quantities, x and y.

Slope or constant rate of change

$$y = mx + b$$

y-Intercept or initial value

Do You Understand?

1. **Essential Question** How can you use a function to represent a linear relationship?

2. **Make Sense and Persevere** Tonya is looking at a graph that shows a line drawn between two points with a slope of −5. One of the points is smudged and she cannot read it. The points as far as she can tell are (3, 5) and (x, 10). What must the value of x be? Explain.

3. **Reasoning** What is the initial value of all linear functions that show a proportional relationship?

Do You Know How?

4. Write a function in the form $y = mx + b$ for the line that contains the points (−8.3, −5.2) and (6.4, 9.5).

5. The data in the table below represent a linear relationship. Fill in the missing data.

x	10	20		40
y	10	15	20	

6. What is an equation that represents the linear function described by the data in Item 5?

Practice & Problem Solving

7. A line passes through the points (4, 19) and (9, 24). Write a linear function in the form $y = mx + b$ for this line.

8. What is a linear function in the form $y = mx + b$ for the line passing through (4.5, −4.25) with y-intercept 2.5?

9. A car moving at a constant speed passes a timing device at $t = 0$. After 8 seconds, the car has traveled 840 feet. What linear function in the form $y = mx + b$ represents the distance in feet, d, the car has traveled any number of seconds, t, after passing the timing device?

10. At time $t = 0$, water begins to drip out of a pipe into an empty bucket. After 56 minutes, 8 inches of water are in the bucket. What linear function in the form $y = mx + b$ represents the amount of water in inches, w, in the bucket after t minutes?

11. The graph of the line represents the cost of renting a kayak. Write a linear function in the form $y = mx + b$ to represent the relationship of the total cost, c, of renting a kayak for t hours.

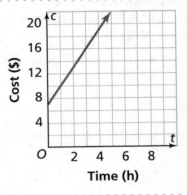

12. An online clothing company sells custom sweatshirts. The company charges $6.50 for each sweatshirt and a flat fee of $3.99 for shipping.

   a. Write a linear function in the form $y = mx + b$ that represents the total cost, y, in dollars, for a single order of x sweatshirts.

   b. Describe how the linear function would change if the shipping charge applied to each sweatshirt.

13. A store sells packages of comic books with a poster.

   a. Model with Math Write a linear function in the form $y = mx + b$ that represents the cost, y, of a package containing any number of comic books, x.

   b. Construct Arguments Suppose another store sells a similar package, modeled by a linear function with initial value $7.99. Which store has the better deal? Explain.

14. Higher Order Thinking Recommendations for safely thawing a frozen turkey are provided on the packaging.

a. What is the thaw rate of the turkey in hours per pound for refrigerator thawing? For cold water thawing?

b. Write a linear function in the form $y = mx + b$ to represent the time, t, in hours it takes to thaw a turkey in the refrigerator as a function of the weight, w, in pounds of the turkey.

refrigerator thawing
1 day for every 4 pounds

cold water thawing
30 minutes per pound

15. Reasoning The graph shows the relationship between the number of cubic yards of mulch ordered and the total cost of the mulch delivered.

a. What is the constant rate of change? What does it represent?

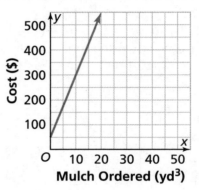

b. What is the initial value? What might that represent?

✅ Assessment Practice

16. An international food festival charges for admission and for each sample of food. Admission and 3 samples cost $5.75. Admission and 6 samples cost $8.75.

Which linear function represents the cost, y, for any number of samples, x?

Ⓐ $y = x + 2.75$ Ⓒ $y = 3x + 2.75$

Ⓑ $y = x + 3$ Ⓓ $y = 3x + 3$

17. Some eighth-graders are making muffins for a fundraiser. They have already made 200 muffins and figure they can make 40 muffins in an hour.

PART A

Write a linear function in the form $y = mx + b$ that represents the total number of muffins the students will make, y, and the number of additional hours spent making the muffins, x.

PART B

How many additional hours would the students spend to make 640 muffins?

Solve & Discuss It!  ACTIVITY

Martin will ride his bike from his house to his aunt's house. He has two different routes he can take. One route goes up and down a hill. The other route avoids the hill by going around the edge of the hill. How do you think the routes will differ? What do you think about the relationship of speed and time?

I can...
describe the behavior of a function and write a description to go with its graph.

Focus on math practices

Reasoning How do the characteristics of each route affect Martin's travel time and speed?

Essential Question How does a qualitative graph describe the relationship between quantities?

EXAMPLE 1  Interpret a Qualitative Graph

Scan for Multimedia

An express train reaches its travel speed of 150 miles per hour a short time after leaving the station and travels at this speed for an extended period of time. What does a qualitative graph of the distance the train travels over time look like once it reaches its travel speed?

Make Sense and Persevere
What is the relationship between time and distance?

STEP 1 Draw a *qualitative graph*. A **qualitative graph** represents the relationship between quantities without numbers. Identify the input variable, the output variable, and the intervals.

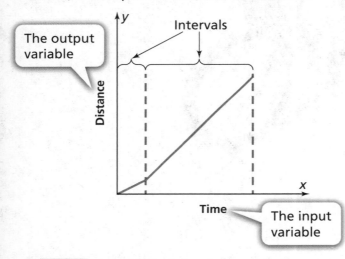

The output variable

Intervals

Distance

Time

The input variable

An **interval** is a period of time between two events or points in time. The second interval starts when the train reaches its travel speed.

STEP 2 Determine the relationship between the two variables during the second interval.

As time increases, the distance the train has traveled increases.

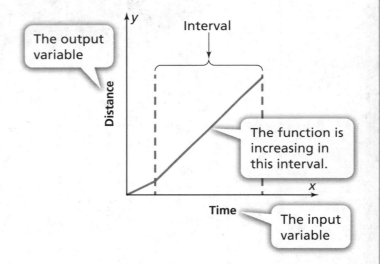

The output variable

Interval

Distance

The function is increasing in this interval.

Time

The input variable

✓ Try It!

The graph at the right shows another interval in the train's travel. Which best describes the behavior of the train in the interval shown?

As time ⬚, the speed of the train ⬚.

The function is ⬚.

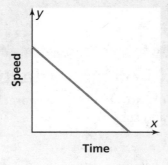

Speed

Time

Convince Me! How would the graph of the function change if the speed of the train was increasing?

EXAMPLE 2 **Interpret the Graph of a Nonlinear Function**

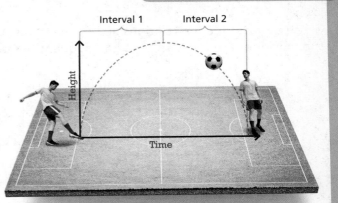

The graph shows the behavior of a ball that a soccer player kicks to a teammate. Describe how the height of the ball and time are related in each interval.

Determine whether the function is increasing, decreasing, or constant in each interval.

The function is **increasing** in interval 1 because as time increases, so does the height of the ball.

The function is **decreasing** in interval 2 because as time increases, the height of the ball decreases.

 Try It!

The graph shows the behavior of Skylla skateboarding at a skateboard park. In which intervals is the function increasing, decreasing, and constant?

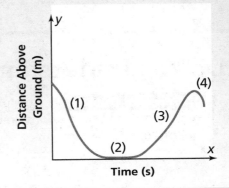

EXAMPLE 3 **Describe the Relationship of Quantities**

In which intervals is the function increasing, decreasing, or constant?

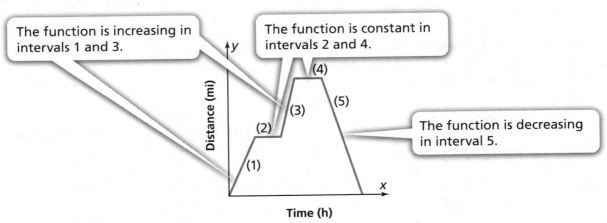

The function is increasing in intervals 1 and 3.

The function is constant in intervals 2 and 4.

The function is decreasing in interval 5.

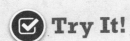 **Try It!**

Write a scenario that the graph above could represent.

You can describe the relationship between two quantities by analyzing the behavior of the function relating the quantities in different intervals on a graph.

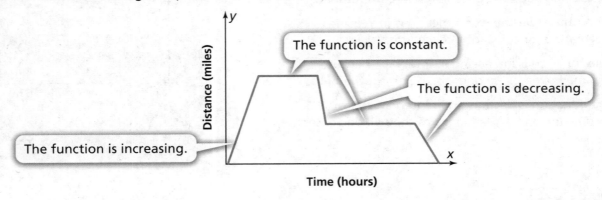

The function is constant.

The function is decreasing.

The function is increasing.

Do You Understand?

1. **Essential Question** How does a qualitative graph describe the relationship between quantities?

2. **Look for Relationships** How would knowing the slope of a linear function help determine whether a function is increasing or decreasing?

3. **Use Structure** What kind of graph of a function shows the same output values, or *y*-values, for each input value, or *x*-value?

Do You Know How?

4. What does the graph of the function at each interval represent?

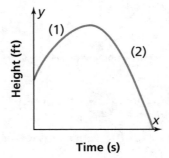

5. In which intervals is the function increasing, decreasing, or constant?

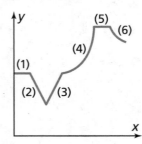

Practice & Problem Solving

6. Use the graph to complete the statements.

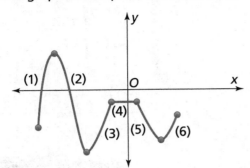

The function is [_____] in intervals 1, 3, and 6.

The function is [_____] in intervals 2 and 5.

The function is constant in interval [___].

7. The graph below shows the temperature in Paula's house over time after her mother turned on the air conditioner. Describe the relationship between the two quantities.

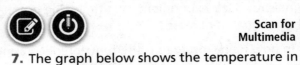

Temperature in Paula's House

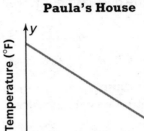

8. You have a device that monitors the voltage across a lamp over time. The results are shown in the graph. Describe the behavior of the function in each interval.

In interval (a), the function is [_____].

In interval (b), the function is [_____].

In interval (c), the function is [_____].

In interval (d), the function is [_____].

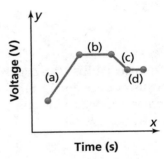

9. The graph below shows the height of a roller coaster over time during a single ride. Circle the intervals in which the function is increasing. In which interval is the increase the greatest?

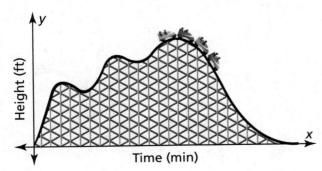

10. Reasoning The graph shows the speed of a car over time. What might the constant intervals in the function represent?

Speed of a Car

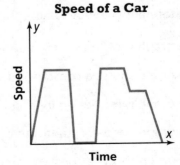

11. Higher Order Thinking A signal generator is used to generate signals for a lab experiment over time. The graph shows the frequency of the signal generated.

Frequency of a Signal Generated

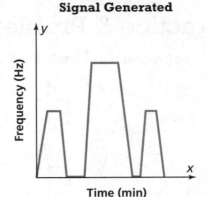

a. In how many intervals is the function decreasing?

b. How are the decreasing intervals alike?

c. How are the decreasing intervals different?

12. Critique Reasoning The graph shows the speed of a person riding his stationary exercise bicycle over time.

a. A student claims that the function is constant in two intervals. Do you agree? Explain.

b. What error might the student have made?

13. Look for Relationships The graph shows the speed of a roller coaster over time. Describe the relationship of the speed as a function of time.

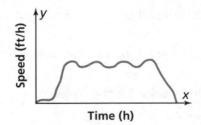

Assessment Practice

14. Which statements about the graph are true? Select all that apply.

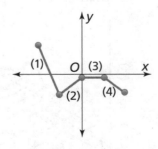

☐ The graph is decreasing in intervals (1) and (4).

☐ The graph shows a constant function in interval (2).

☐ The graph is increasing in intervals (2) and (4).

☐ The graph has a constant rate of change.

☐ The graph shows a constant function in interval (3).

 ACTIVITY

👆 Explain It!

The Environmental Club is learning about oil consumption and energy conservation around the world. Jack says oil consumption in the United States has dropped a lot. Ashley says oil consumption in China is the biggest problem facing the world environment.

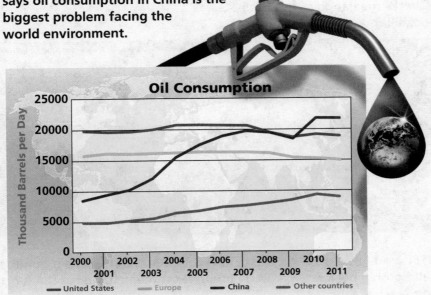

Oil Consumption

I can...
sketch the graph of a function that has been described verbally.

A. Do you agree or disagree with Jack's statement? Construct an argument based on the graph to support your position.

B. Do you agree or disagree with Ashley's statement? Construct an argument based on the graph to support your position.

Focus on math practices

Look for Relationships What trend do you see in oil consumption in the United States and in Europe?

VISUAL LEARNING ASSESS

EXAMPLE 1 **Sketch the Graph of a Linear Function**

Scan for Multimedia

A scuba diver starts a dive with a full tank of oxygen. While diving, she breathes at a constant rate. She checks the gauge after 22 minutes. What does a graph of the function look like?

Look for Relationships
What happens to the oxygen level in the tank over time?

STEP 1 Identify the two variables.

Input variable: *t* (time)

Output variable: *l* (oxygen level in the tank)

STEP 2 Analyze the relationship between the two variables.

The oxygen level in the tank decreases at a constant rate over time.

STEP 3 Sketch and label a graph that represents the behavior of the function.

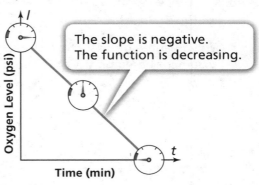

The slope is negative. The function is decreasing.

Try It!

The weight of the water exerts pressure on a diver. At a depth of 10 feet, the water pressure is 19.1 pounds per square inch (psi) and at a depth of 14 feet, the water pressure is 20.9 psi. Complete the statements, and then sketch the qualitative graph of this function.

The input, or *x*-variable, is [   ].

The output, or *y*-variable, is [   ].

Convince Me!
Generalize How are the sketches of the two functions similar? How are they different?

EXAMPLE 2 — Analyze the Sketch of a Nonlinear Function

Danika sketched the relationship between altitude and time for one of her parasailing flights. Describe the behavior of the function in each interval based on her sketch.

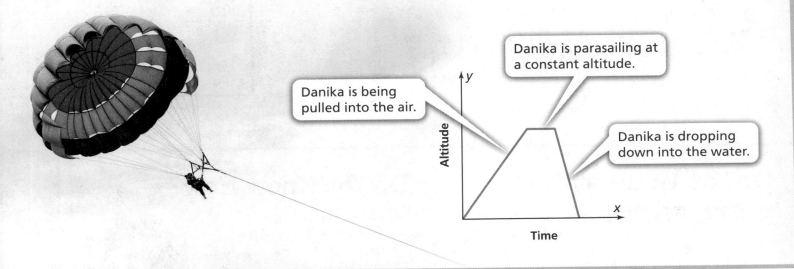

Danika is being pulled into the air.

Danika is parasailing at a constant altitude.

Danika is dropping down into the water.

EXAMPLE 3 — Sketch the Graph of a Nonlinear Function

José is practicing javelin throws. What is the relationship between the height of the javelin and time? What would the graph of this function look like?

STEP 1 Identify the two variables in the relationship.

Input variable: time (t)

Output variable: height (h) of the javelin

STEP 2 Analyze the relationship between the two variables.

When José first throws the javelin, it increases in height, reaches a maximum height, and then decreases in height until it hits the ground.

STEP 3 Sketch the graph.

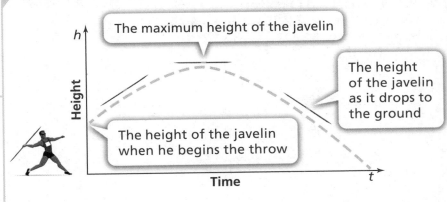

The maximum height of the javelin

The height of the javelin as it drops to the ground

The height of the javelin when he begins the throw

✅ Try It!

Haru rides his bike from his home for 30 minutes at a fast pace. He stops to rest for 20 minutes, and then continues in the same direction at a slower pace for 30 more minutes. Sketch a graph of the relationship of Haru's distance from home over time.

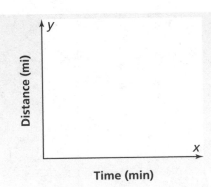

You can sketch a graph of a function to describe its behavior. When sketching a function, follow these steps:

1. Identify the two variables (input, output) that have a relationship.

2. Analyze the situation. Look for key words that indicate that the function is increasing, decreasing, or constant.

3. Sketch the graph.

Do You Understand?

1. **? Essential Question** How does the sketch of a graph of a function help describe its behavior?

2. **Make Sense and Persevere** How do you know which variable goes with which axis when you graph?

3. **Reasoning** How can you determine the shape of a graph?

Do You Know How?

4. A class plants a tree. Sketch the graph of the height of the tree over time.

a. Identify the two variables.

b. How can you describe the relationship between the two variables?

c. Sketch the graph.

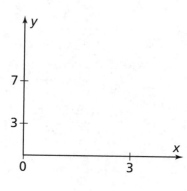

5. An airplane takes 15 minutes to reach its cruising altitude. The plane cruises at that altitude for 90 minutes, and then descends for 20 minutes before it lands. Sketch the graph of the height of the plane over time.

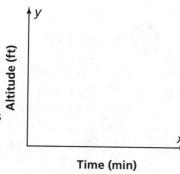

Practice & Problem Solving

Scan for
Multimedia

6. What relationship between money (in dollars) and time (in months) does this graph show? Write a description of the given graph.

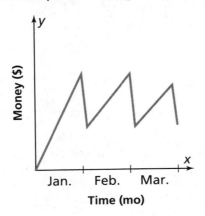

7. When a new laptop became available in a store, the number sold in the first week was high. Sales decreased over the next two weeks and then they remained steady over the next two weeks. The following week, the total number sold by the store increased slightly. Sketch the graph that represents this function over the six weeks.

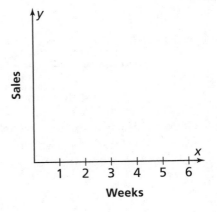

8. Aaron's mother drives to the gas station and fills up her tank. Then she drives to the market. Sketch the graph that shows the relationship between the amount of fuel in the gas tank of her car and time.

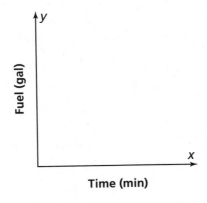

9. Melody starts at her house and rides her bike for 10 minutes to a friend's house. She stays at her friend's house for 60 minutes. Sketch a graph that represents this description.

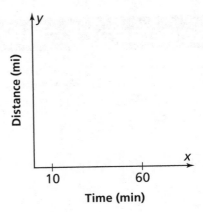

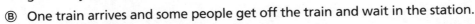

10. Which description best represents the graph shown?

Ⓐ People are waiting for a train. A train comes and some people get on. The other people wait for the next train. As time goes by, people gradually leave the station.

Ⓑ One train arrives and some people get off the train and wait in the station.

Ⓒ People are waiting for a train. Everyone gets on the first train that comes.

Ⓓ People are waiting for a train. A train comes and some people get on the train. The other people wait for the next train. Another train arrives and all of the remaining people get on.

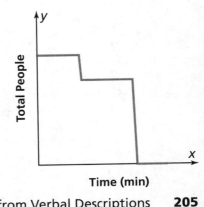

11. A baker has already made 10 cakes. She can make the same number of cakes each hour, which she does for 5 hours. Sketch the graph of the relationship between the number of cakes made and time.

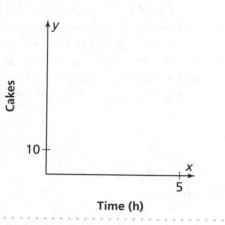

12. Model with Math An air cannon launches a T-shirt upward toward basketball fans. It reaches a maximum height and then descends for a couple seconds until a fan grabs it. Sketch the graph that represents this situation.

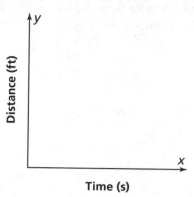

13. Higher Order Thinking Write a verbal description of how these two variables are related. The description must suggest at least two intervals. Sketch the graph that represents the verbal description.

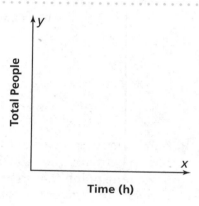

14. A baseball team scores the same number of runs in each of the first 4 innings. After that, the team did not score a run for the rest of the game, which lasts 9 innings. Let x represent the innings of the game, and y represent the total number of runs.

PART A

Sketch the graph of this situation below.

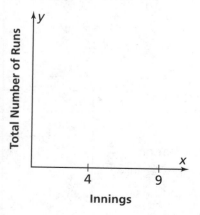

PART B

How would the graph change if the innings in which the team scores runs changes?

? Topic Essential Question

How can you use functions to model linear relationships?

Vocabulary Review

Match each vocabulary term with its definition.

Definition
1. A function whose graph is not a straight line
2. The slope of a line
3. A relation in which each input, or *x*-value, has exactly one output, or *y*-value
4. The value of the output when the input is 0, or the *y*-intercept of the graph of a line
5. A period of time between two points of time or events

Vocabulary Term
initial value
nonlinear function
constant rate of change
interval
function

Use Vocabulary in Writing

Explain how to write a linear function in the form $y = mx + b$ by using the two points given below. Use vocabulary words in your explanation. (0, −2), (2, 6)

Concepts and Skills Review

LESSON **3-1** **Understand Relations and Functions**

Quick Review

A **relation** is a set of ordered pairs. A relation is a **function** if each input, or *x*-value, has exactly one unique output, or *y*-value.

Example

This relation is a function. Each input, or *x*-value, aligns to only one output, or *y*-value.
(3, 2), (2, 4), (5, 6), (1, 3), (7, 4)

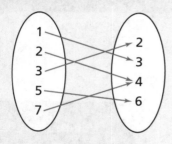

Practice

1. Is the relation shown in the table a function? Explain.

Input	2	4	6	8	10
Output	1	2	3	4	3

2. Does the relation {(−5, −3), (7, 2), (3, 8), (3, −8), (5, 10)} represent a function? Use the arrow diagram. Then explain your answer.

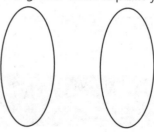

LESSON **3-2** **Connect Representations of Functions**

Quick Review

You can represent a function in a table, in a graph, or as an equation. The graph of a **linear function** is a straight line.

Example

Equation

$y = 10x + 8$

Table

x	1	2	3	4
y	18	28	38	48

Graph

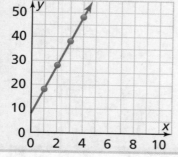

Practice

Mark has a $100 gift card to buy apps for his smartphone. Each week, he buys one new app for $4.99.

1. Write an equation that relates the amount left on the card, *y*, over time, *x*.

2. Make a graph of the function.

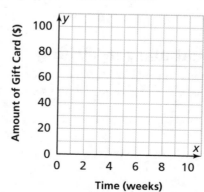

Compare Linear and Nonlinear Functions

Quick Review

You can compare functions in different representations by looking at the properties of functions: the **constant rate of change** and the **initial value.**

Function A

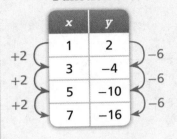

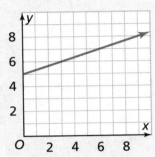

Practice

Two linear functions are shown.

Function A

$y = -3x + 2$

Function B

x	1	2	3	4
y	−1	1	3	5

1. Which function has the greater initial value? Explain.

2. Which function has the greater rate of change?

Construct Functions to Model Linear Relationships

Quick Review

A function in the form $y = mx + b$ represents a linear relationship between two quantities, x and y, where m represents the constant rate of change and b represents the initial value.

Example

-3 pizzas delivered cost $25.75⌐
+2 ⌡5 pizzas delivered cost $40.25 ⌐+14.5

STEP 1: Find the constant rate of change.

$$\frac{40.25 - 25.75}{5 - 3} = \frac{14.5}{2} = \frac{7.25}{1}$$

STEP 2: Find the initial value.

$$40.25 = 7.25(5) + b \qquad 4 = b$$

The linear function that models the relationship is $y = 7.25x + 4$.

Practice

1. What is the equation of a line that passes through (0.5, 4.25) and (2, 18.5) and has a y-intercept of −0.5?

2. The graph shows the relationship of the number of gallons being drained from an aquarium over time. What function models the relationship?

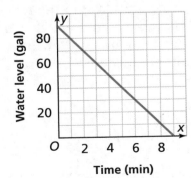

Quick Review

You can describe the relationship between two quantities by looking at the behavior of the line at different **intervals** on a qualitative graph. The function is **increasing** if both *x*- and *y*-values increase. The function is **decreasing** if the *y*-values decrease as the *x*-values increase.

Example

In interval 1, the function is decreasing.
In interval 2, the function is increasing.

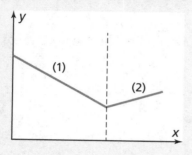

Practice

The graph shows the altitude of an airplane over time.

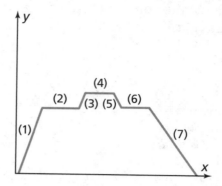

1. In which intervals is the graph of the function constant? Explain.

2. In which intervals is the graph of the function decreasing? Explain.

Quick Review

You can sketch a graph of a function to describe its behavior. When sketching a function, identify the variables (input, output) that have a relationship, analyze the situation, and then sketch the graph.

Example

Raina is running laps around the school track while her younger brother watches her in the stands. Sketch a graph that shows Raina's distance from her brother as she runs laps.

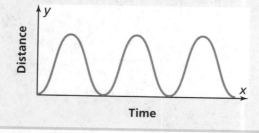

Practice

1. Jack's mother brings him a bowl of carrots as a snack. At first he does not eat any; then he eats one at a time until half of the carrots are gone. Then he does not eat any more. Sketch a graph that shows the number of carrots in the bowl over time.

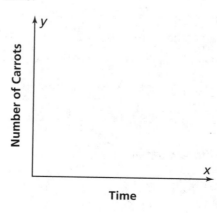

What's the Message?

In each row, determine which equation has the greater solution. Circle the letter next to the equation with the greater solution in each row.

$3x + 8 = 12$ **G** **N** $5x - 4 = 5$

$15 + 2n = 57$ **I** **R** $3d - 7 = 53$

$8x - 12 = 14$ **A** **C** $12 + 6p = 36$

$54 = 14 + 8c$ **W** **E** $8m - 14 = 50$

$12x + 16 = 100$ **B** **X** $6z - 24 = 12$

$59 + 81w = 68$ **E** **D** $40r + 67 = 71$

$31g - 15 = 47$ **R** **L** $99 = 22 + 35y$

$14r - 7 = 14$ **S** **T** $13 = 12t - 8$

What does the zero say to the eight?

◯ ◯ ◯ ◯   ◯ ◯ ◯ ◯ !

INVESTIGATE BIVARIATE DATA

? Topic Essential Question

How can you represent the relationship between paired data and use the representation to make predictions?

Topic Overview

4-1 Construct and Interpret Scatter Plots

4-2 Analyze Linear Associations

4-3 Use Linear Models to Make Predictions

4-4 Interpret Two-Way Frequency Tables

4-5 Interpret Two-Way Relative Frequency Tables

3-Act Mathematical Modeling: Reach Out

Topic Vocabulary

- categorical data
- cluster
- gap
- measurement data
- negative association
- outlier
- positive association
- relative frequency table
- scatter plot
- trend line

Lesson Digital Resources

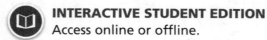

INTERACTIVE STUDENT EDITION
Access online or offline.

VISUAL LEARNING ANIMATION
Interact with visual learning animations.

ACTIVITY Use with *Solve & Discuss It, Explore It*, and *Explain It* activities, and to explore Examples.

VIDEOS Watch clips to support *3-Act Mathematical Modeling Lessons* and *STEM Projects*.

Go online

reach out

▶ Reach Out

Reach for the skies! Who in your class can reach the highest? That height depends on how tall each person is and the lengths of their arms.

Now stick your arms out to your sides. Sometimes this horizontal distance is called your *wingspan*. The wandering albatross can have a wingspan of up to 12 feet. How does your wingspan compare? Think about this during the 3-Act Mathematical Modeling lesson.

✏ **PRACTICE** Practice what you've learned.

⚷ **KEY CONCEPT** Review important lesson content.

⏻ **TUTORIALS** Get help from *Virtual Nerd*, right when you need it.

A-Z **GLOSSARY** Read and listen to English/Spanish definitions.

🔧 **MATH TOOLS** Explore math with digital tools.

☑ **ASSESSMENT** Show what you've learned.

🎮 **GAMES** Play Math Games to help you learn.

enVision® STEM Project

 VIDEO

Did You Know?

A fishery biologist collects data on fish, such as the size and health of the fish population in a particular body of water.

Largemouth bass and smallmouth bass are **the most popular game fish** in North America.

Biologists often **use tagging studies to estimate fish population,** as well as to estimate catch and harvest rates.

The average lifespan of a bass is about 16 years, but some **have lived more than 20 years.**

Research suggests that **bass can see red better** than any other color on the spectrum.

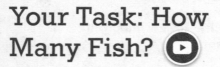

Your Task: How Many Fish?

Suppose a fishery biologist takes 500 bass from a lake, tags them, and then releases them back into the water. Several days later, the biologist nets a sample of 200 bass, of which 30 are tagged. How many bass are in the lake? You and your classmates will explore how the biologist can use sampling to describe patterns and to make generalizations about the entire population.

Review What You Know!

Vocabulary

Choose the best term from the box to complete each definition.

ratio
slope
x-axis
y-axis

1. _____ is the change in *y* divided by the change in *x*.

2. A relationship where for every *x* units of one quantity there

   are *y* units of another quantity is a _____.

3. The _____ is the horizontal line in a coordinate plane.

4. The _____ is the vertical line in a coordinate plane.

Graphing Points

Graph and label each point on the coordinate plane.

5. (−2, 4)

6. (0, 3)

7. (3, −1)

8. (−4, −3)

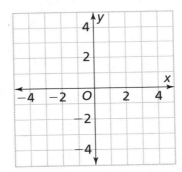

Finding Slope

Find the slope between each pair of points.

9. (4, 6) and (−2, 8)

10. (−1, 3) and (5, 9)

11. (5, −1) and (−3, −7)

Writing Fractions as Percents

12. Explain how to write $\frac{36}{60}$ as a percent.

Language Development

Complete the graphic organizer. Write the definitions of the terms in your own words.
Use words or a sketch to show an example.

Term	Definition	Example or Illustration
measurement data		
scatter plot		
cluster		
gap		
outlier		
trend line		
categorical data		
relative frequency table		

PROJECT
4A

What carnival games do you have a good chance of winning, and why?

PROJECT: BUILD A CARNIVAL GAME

x^x

%

π

PROJECT
4B

If you had a superpower, what would it be?

PROJECT: SUMMARIZE SUPERHERO DATA

PROJECT 4C

What makes a song's lyrics catchy?

PROJECT: WRITE A SONG

PROJECT 4D

How does your dream job use math?

PROJECT: RESEARCH A CAREER

Solve & Discuss It!

 ACTIVITY

Luciana is starting a two-week social media campaign to attract new subscribers to BlastOn, a music website for teens. She has the following data from her last campaign to help plan her strategy.

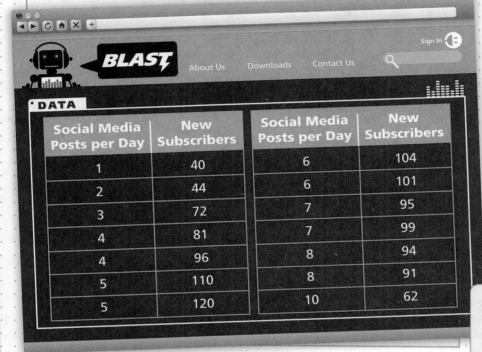

DATA

Social Media Posts per Day	New Subscribers	Social Media Posts per Day	New Subscribers
1	40	6	104
2	44	6	101
3	72	7	95
4	81	7	99
4	96	8	94
5	110	8	91
5	120	10	62

Based on this data, what should be Luciana's strategy for the new campaign?

Lesson 4-1
Construct and Interpret Scatter Plots

 Go Online

I can...
construct a scatter plot and use it to understand the relationship between paired data.

Look for Relationships
How are the number of media posts and the number of subscribers related?

Focus on math practices

Use Structure What patterns do you see in the data from Luciana's last social media campaign?

? **Essential Question** How does a scatter plot show the relationship between paired data?

EXAMPLE 1 Construct a Scatter Plot

Scan for Multimedia

Luciana analyzes the data collected to determine how long after posting a new blog her new home page received its maximum number of new views. Her data are presented in the table.

How can she determine whether there is a relationship between the time after posting and the number of new views?

Look for Relationships
Can you see a pattern between the time after posting and the number of new views?

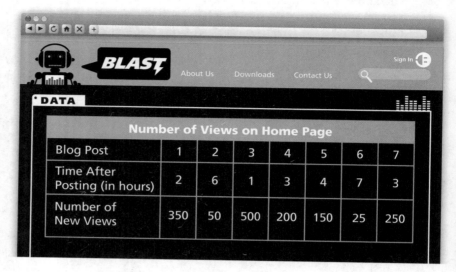

Number of Views on Home Page

Blog Post	1	2	3	4	5	6	7
Time After Posting (in hours)	2	6	1	3	4	7	3
Number of New Views	350	50	500	200	150	25	250

STEP 1 Draw a scatter plot. A **scatter plot** is a graph in the coordinate plane that shows the relationship between two sets of data.

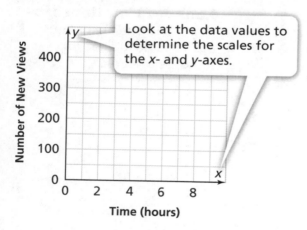

Look at the data values to determine the scales for the x- and y-axes.

STEP 2 Plot the ordered pairs (*time after posting*, *number of new views*) on the graph.

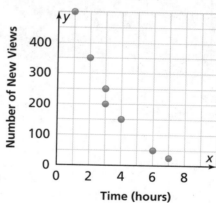

Luciana can use a scatter plot to determine whether there is a relationship between the two data sets.

✓ Try It!

Giveaway Entries

Age (years)	10	11	12	13	14	15
Number of Entries	8	8	9	9	10	10

Luciana collects data about the number of entries and the ages of the subscribers who enter the concert giveaway.

The point that represents the data in the fourth column has coordinates (☐ , ☐).

Convince Me! Explain how Luciana would choose scales for the x-axis and y-axis.

EXAMPLE 2 ▶ Interpret a Scatter Plot

Rochelle asked 10 friends how many hours of sleep they got the night before a math test and then matched that data with their scores. She plotted her data in the graph below. Did students who slept more get higher test scores?

Look at the way the data points are clustered. If the y-values tend to increase as the x-values increase, there is a **positive association** between the data sets. If the y-values tend to decrease as the x-values increase, there is a **negative association**.

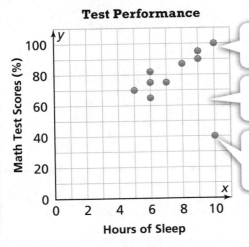

A **cluster** is a group of points that lie close together.

A **gap** is an area on the graph that contains no data.

This data point is set off from the other data points. It is an **outlier**.

The scatter plot shows a positive association between hours of sleep and math test scores.

EXAMPLE 3 ▶ Construct and Interpret a Scatter Plot

Avery is the middle school basketball statistician. She tracks the number of minutes a player plays and the number of fouls the player makes. Her data are shown in the scatter plot. Is there an association between the number of minutes played and the number of fouls made?

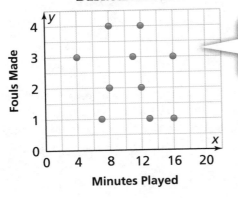

The y-values do not increase or decrease as the x-values increase.

The scatter plot shows no association between the number of minutes played and number of fouls made.

☑ Try It!

Avery also tracks the number of minutes a player plays and the number of points the player scored. Describe the association between the two data sets. Tell what the association suggests.

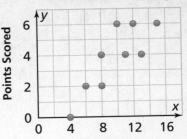

A scatter plot shows the relationship, or association, between two sets of data.

Positive Association	Negative Association	No Association
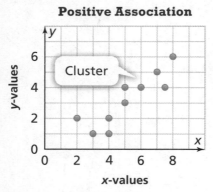	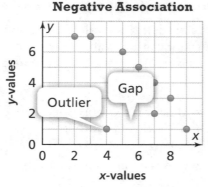	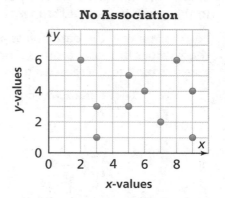
The y-values increase as the x-values increase.	The y-values decrease as the x-values increase.	There is no consistent pattern between the y-values and the x-values.

Do You Understand?

1. **? Essential Question** How does a scatter plot show the relationship between paired data?

2. **Model with Math** Marcy always sleeps fewer than 9 hours each night and has never scored more than 27 points in a basketball game. A scatter plot suggests that the more sleep she gets, the more she scores. What scales for the axes might be best for constructing the scatter plot?

3. **Construct Arguments** Kyle says that every scatter plot will have a cluster, gap, and outlier. Is he correct? Explain.

Do You Know How?

4. Phoebe constructs a scatter plot to show the data. What scales could she use for the x- and y-axes?

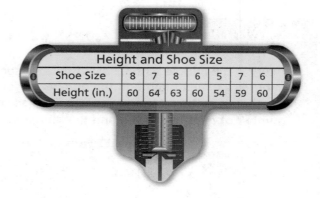

Height and Shoe Size						
Shoe Size	8	7	8	6	5	7	6
Height (in.)	60	64	63	60	54	59	60

5. Germaine constructs a scatter plot to show how many people visit different theme parks in a month. Why might clusters and outliers be present?

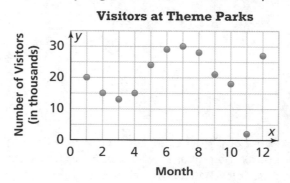

Practice & Problem Solving

6. Leveled Practice The table shows the racing times in minutes for the first two laps in a race. Complete the scatter plot.

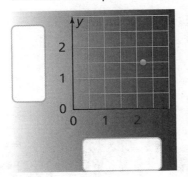

Racing Times (min)

LAP 1	2.4	1.4	1.6	2.4	2.5	1.8	2.2
LAP 2	2.3	1.6	1.3	2.7	2.6	1.6	1.5

7. The scatter plot represents the prices and number of books sold in a bookstore.

a. Identify the cluster in the scatter plot and explain what it means.

b. **Generalize** How does the scatter plot show the relationship between the data points? Explain.

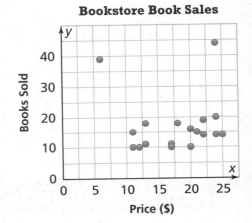

Bookstore Book Sales

8. The table shows the monthly attendance in thousands at museums in one country over a 12-month period.

Museum Attendance

Month	5	5	6	6	6	7	10	10	11	11	12	12	12
Number of People (in thousands)	6	9	6	12	36	3	21	27	18	24	24	18	3

a. Complete the scatter plot to represent the data.

b. Identify any outliers in the scatter plot.

c. What situation might have caused an outlier?

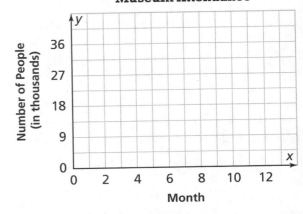

Museum Attendance

9. **Higher Order Thinking** The table shows the number of painters and sculptors enrolled in seven art schools. Jashar makes an incorrect scatter plot to represent the data.

Enrollment

Number of Painters	30	43	47	30	11	48	20
Number of Sculptors	25	33	50	27	6	58	45

Enrollment

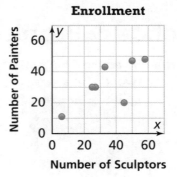

a. What error did Jashar likely make?

b. Explain the relationship between the number of painters and sculptors enrolled in the art schools.

c. **Reasoning** Jashar's scatter plot shows two possible outliers. Identify them and explain why they are outliers.

✓ **Assessment Practice**

Use the scatter plot to answer **10** and **11**.

10. Ten athletes in the Florida Running Club ran two races of the same length. The scatter plot shows their times. Select all statements that are true.

☐ Nine of the times for the first race were at least 16 seconds.

☐ Eight of the times for the second race were less than 17 seconds.

☐ There were seven athletes who were faster in the second race than in the first.

☐ There were three athletes who had the same time in both races.

☐ There were three athletes whose times in the two races differed by exactly 1 second.

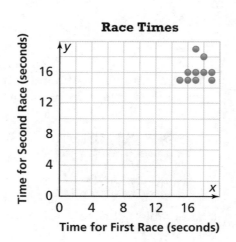

11. What was the greatest difference for a single runner in finishing times in the races?

Ⓐ 3 seconds   Ⓑ 4 seconds   Ⓒ 5 seconds   Ⓓ 7 seconds

 Solve & Discuss It!  ACTIVITY

Angus has a big test coming up. Should he stay up and study or go to bed early the night before the test? Defend your recommendation.

Test #1 - went to bed at 9:15, got 80%

Test #2 - studied until 10:30, got 75%

Test #3 - studied until 11:00, got 92%

Test #4 - went to bed at 8:30, got 89%

Test #5 - studied until 10:45, got 86%

Test #6 - went to bed at 9:00, got 93%

I can...
use a line to represent the relationship between paired data.

Generalize Can you make a general statement about which option leads to a better result?

Focus on math practices

Construct Arguments What other factors should Angus also take into consideration to make a decision? Defend your response.

? **Essential Question** How can you describe the association of two data sets?

 VISUAL LEARNING   ASSESS

Scan for Multimedia

EXAMPLE 1 **Linear Associations**

Georgia and her classmates are measuring their height and arm span. They record their data in a table.

> **Make Sense and Persevere** What relationship might there be between the two measurements?

Student	1	2	3	4	5	6	7	8	9	10	11
Height (in.)	66	67	62	64	59	62	65	64	62	61	58
Arm Span (in.)	64	65	64	62	61	59	67	66	62	62	62

How can they determine what relationship, if any, exists between the two sets of measurements?

STEP 1 Plot the data points in a scatter plot.

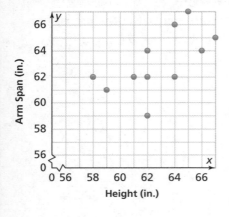

STEP 2 Use a pencil to find a line that passes through the middle of the plotted points. This line is called a **trend line**.

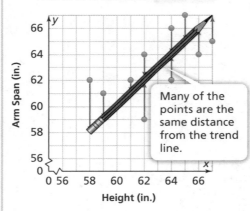

Many of the points are the same distance from the trend line.

STEP 3 Look at the slope of the line. The slope is positive.

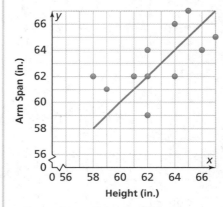

Georgia can draw a trend line on the scatter plot to determine that there is a positive relationship between height and arm span.

Try It!

Georgia and her classmates also measured their foot length. Use a pencil to find the trend line. Sketch the trend line for the scatter plot.

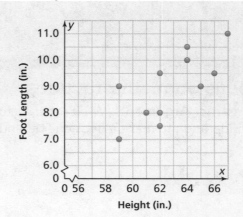

EXAMPLE **2** Strength of Linear Associations

The Johanssens own an ice cream shop near the beach. The scatter plots show their sales by daily high temperature. They compare their sales by daily high temperature to the number of beach-goers by daily high temperature. Describe the associations shown.

As the temperature increases, ice cream sales increase. The association is positive.

As the temperature increases, the number of beach-goers also increases. The association is positive.

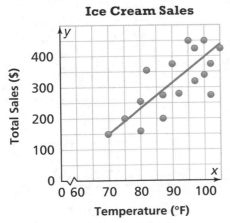

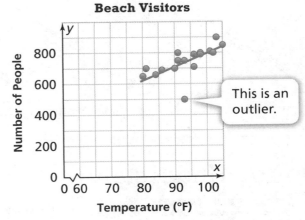

Some of the points are far from the trend line. This shows a **weak association**.

Nearly all of the points are close to the trend line. This shows a **strong association**.

EXAMPLE **3** Recognize Nonlinear Associations

Does the scatter plot show a linear or nonlinear association?

The points in the scatter plot form a curve so the scatter plot shows a nonlinear association between the data.

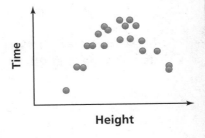

Try It!

For each scatter plot, identify the association between the data. If there is no association, state so.

a.

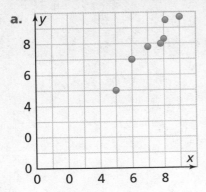

b.

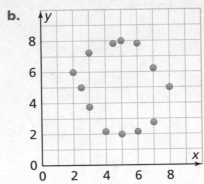

c.

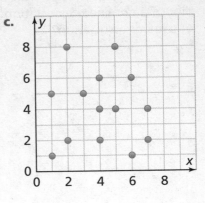

Scatter plots can show a linear association, a nonlinear association, or no association. For scatter plots that suggest a linear association, you can draw a trend line to show the association. You can assess the strength of the association by looking at the distances of plotted points from the trend line.

Linear Associations

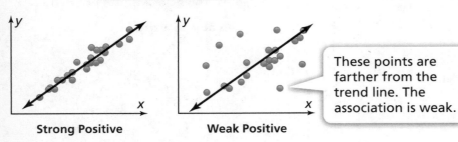

Strong Positive　　**Weak Positive**

These points are farther from the trend line. The association is weak.

Nonlinear Association

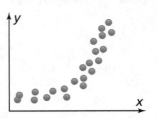

Do You Understand?

1. **Essential Question** How can you describe the relationship between the two sets of data?

2. **Look for Relationships** How does a trend line describe the strength of the association?

3. **Construct Arguments** How does the scatter plot of a nonlinear association differ from that of a linear association?

Do You Know How?

4. Describe the association between the two sets of data in the scatter plot.

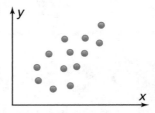

5. Describe the association between the two sets of data in the scatter plot.

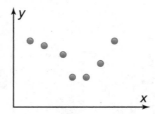

Practice & Problem Solving

6. The scatter plot shows the average heights of children ages 2–12 in a certain country. Which line is the best model of the data?

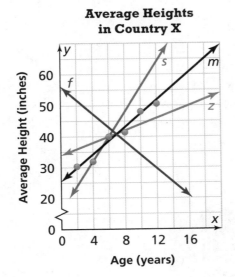

Average Heights in Country X

---

7. Does the scatter plot show a positive, a negative, or no association?

8. Determine whether the scatter plot of the data for the following situation would have a positive or negative linear association.

time working and amount of money earned

---

9. Describe the relationship between the data in the scatter plot.

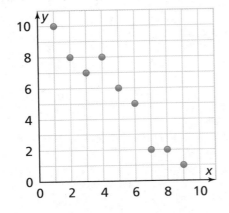

10. Describe the relationship between the data in the scatter plot.

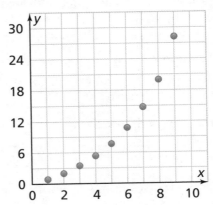

11. **Higher Order Thinking** Describe a real situation that would fit the relationship described.

   a. A strong, positive association

   b. A strong, negative association

12. A sociologist is studying how sleep affects the amount of money a person spends. The scatter plot shows the results of the study. What type of association does it show between the amount of sleep and money spent?

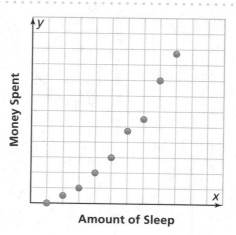

Amount of Sleep

(y-axis: Money Spent, x-axis: Amount of Sleep)

☑ Assessment Practice

13. Which paired data would likely show a positive association? Select all that apply.

   ☐ Population and the number of schools

   ☐ Hair length and shoe size

   ☐ Number of people who carpool to work and money spent on gas

   ☐ Hours worked and amount of money earned

   ☐ Time spent driving and amount of gas in the car

14. Which paired data would likely show a negative association? Select all that apply.

   ☐ Population and the number of schools

   ☐ Hair length and shoe size

   ☐ Number of people who carpool to work and money spent on gas

   ☐ Hours worked and amount of money earned

   ☐ Time spent driving and amount of gas in the car

Solve & Discuss It!  ACTIVITY

Bao has a new tracking device that he wears when he exercises. It sends data to his computer. How can Bao determine how long he should exercise each day if he wants to burn 5,000 Calories per week?

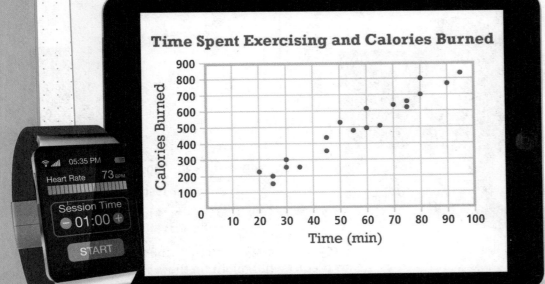

I can...
make a prediction by using the equation of a line that closely fits a set of data.

Focus on math practices

Reasoning Suppose another set of data were plotted with a trend line passing through (25, 100) and (80, 550). Would this indicate that more or fewer calories were burned per minute? Explain.

EXAMPLE 1 ▸ **Use the Slope to Make a Prediction**

Scan for Multimedia

Michaela is a speed skater and hopes to compete in future Olympic games. She researched the winning times of the past 50 years. If the trend in faster speeds continues at the same rate, how can she use the information to predict what might be the time to beat in 2026?

Make Sense and Persevere What relationship might there be between the two measurements?

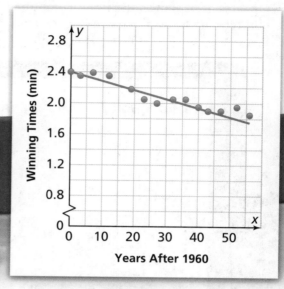

STEP 1 Write an equation for the trend line.

The y-intercept is about 2.4.

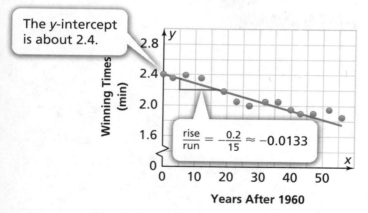

$$\frac{\text{rise}}{\text{run}} = -\frac{0.2}{15} \approx -0.0133$$

The equation of the trend line is $y = -0.0133x + 2.4$.

STEP 2 Use the equation of the trend line to predict what might be the winning time in 2026.

$$y = -0.0133x + 2.4$$
$$= -0.0133(66) + 2.4$$
$$= -0.8778 + 2.4$$
$$= 1.5222$$

If the trend in faster times continues at the same rate, Michaela should target about 1.5222 minutes, or 1 minute 30 seconds.

☑ Try It!

Assuming the trend shown in the graph continues, use the equation of the trend line to predict average fuel consumption in miles per gallon in 2025.

The equation of the trend line is $y = \boxed{} x + \boxed{}$. In 2025,

the average fuel consumption is predicted to be about _____ mpg.

Convince Me! Why can you use a linear model to predict the y-value for a given x-value?

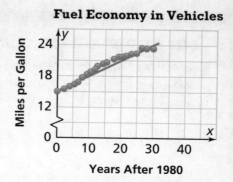

EXAMPLE 2 — Use a Scatter Plot to Make a Prediction

The scatter plot shows the relationship between the number of people at a water park and the temperature. About how many people should the owners of the park expect at the water park when the outside temperature is 90°F?

Find the y-value for an x-value of 90.

The park owners should expect about 800 people at the water park when the outside temperature is 90°F.

> You can approximate the y-value since this is an estimated value.

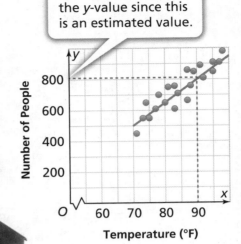

EXAMPLE 3 — Interpret the Slope and y-intercept

The scatter plot at the right suggests a linear relationship between the temperature and the number of smoothies purchased, in thousands.

A. What does the rate of change, or slope, represent in this situation?

The rate of change, or slope, describes the number of smoothies purchased for each 1 degree of temperature increase.

B. What does the y-intercept of the line represent in this situation?

The y-intercept represents the number of smoothies sold when the temperature is 0°F.

C. What equation relates the temperature, x, and the number of people who buy a smoothie, y?

Find the slope. Two points on the graph of the trend line are (40, 32) and (80, 56).

$$y = \frac{3}{5}x + 8$$

> Slope $= \frac{56 - 32}{80 - 40} = \frac{24}{40} = \frac{3}{5}$

> y-intercept = 8

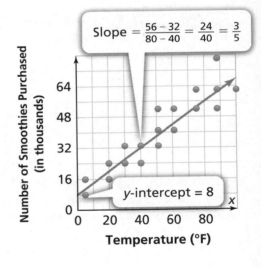

✓ Try It!

A smoothie café has the ingredients needed to make 50,000 smoothies on a day when the high temperature is expected to reach 90°F. Should the café employees expect to have enough ingredients for the day's smoothie sales? Explain.

Scatter plots can be used to make predictions about current or future trends.

Look for the corresponding y-value for a given x-value.

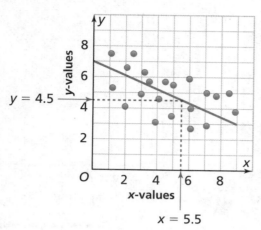

$y = 4.5$

$x = 5.5$

Find the equation of the trend line and find the y-value of a given x-value.

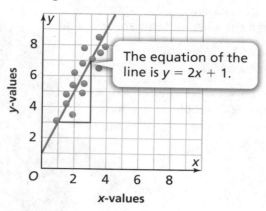

The equation of the line is $y = 2x + 1$.

Do You Understand?

1. **? Essential Question** How do linear models help you to make a prediction?

2. **Model with Math** How do you find the equation of a linear model when you are given the graph but not given the equation?

3. **Reasoning** Can the linear model for a set of data that is presented in a scatter plot always be used to make a prediction about any x-value? Explain.

Do You Know How?

4. The graph shows a family's grocery expenses based on the number of children in the family.

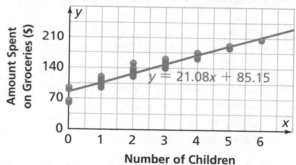

Family's Grocery Cost Per Week

$y = 21.08x + 85.15$

a. Using the slope, predict the difference in the amount spent on groceries between a family with five children and a family with two children.

b. How many children can you predict a family has if the amount spent on groceries per week is $169.47?

Practice & Problem Solving

5. Leveled Practice The scatter plot shows the number of people at a fair based on the outside temperature. How many fewer people would be predicted to be at the fair on a 100°F day than on a 75°F day?

The slope is [ ].

For each degree that the outside temperature increases, the fair attendance decreases by [ ] thousand people.

The difference between 75°F and 100°F is [ ] °F.

−0.16 · [ ] = [ ]

About [ ] thousand fewer people are predicted to be at the fair on a 100°F day than on a 75°F day.

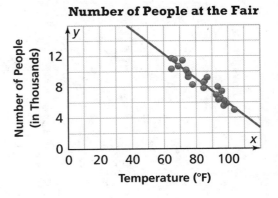

Number of People at the Fair

6. Make Sense and Persevere If x represents the number of years since 2000 and y represents the gas price, predict what the difference between the gas prices in 2013 and 2001 is? Round to the nearest hundredth.

2001   2013

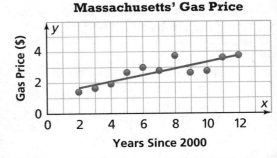

Massachusetts' Gas Price

7. Make Sense and Persevere If x represents the number of months since the beginning of 2016, and y represents the total precipitation to date, predict the amount of precipitation received between the end of March and the end of June.

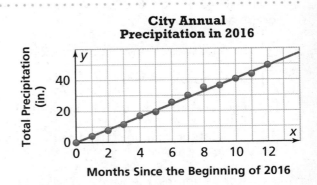

City Annual Precipitation in 2016

8. The scatter plot shows a hiker's elevation above sea level over time. The equation of the trend line shown is $y = 8.77x + 686$. To the nearest whole number, predict what the hiker's elevation will be after 145 minutes.

Hiker's Elevation

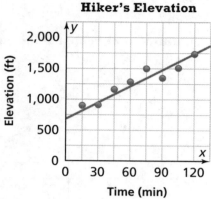

9. **Make Sense and Persevere** The graph shows the number of gallons of water in a large tank as it is being filled. Based on the trend line, predict how long it will take to fill the tank with 375 gallons of water.

Tank Volume

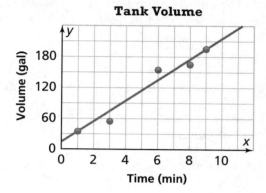

10. **Higher Order Thinking** The graph shows the temperature, y, in a freezer x minutes after it was turned on. Five minutes after being turned on, the temperature was actually three degrees from what the trend line shows. What values could the actual temperature be after the freezer was on for five minutes?

Freezer Temperature

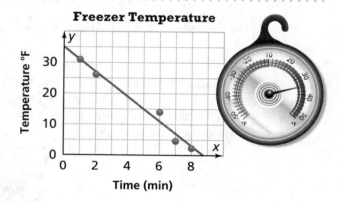

11. The graph shows the altitude above sea level of a weather balloon over time. The trend line passes through the points (0, 453) and (10, 359). Which statements about the graph are true?

☐ The data show a positive correlation.

☐ The trend line is $-9.4x - 453$.

☐ In general, the balloon is losing altitude.

☐ The weather balloon started its flight at about 455 feet above sea level.

☐ After 4 minutes, the weather balloon had an altitude of about 415 feet above sea level.

☐ After 395 minutes, the weather balloon had an altitude of about 8 feet above sea level.

Balloon Elevation

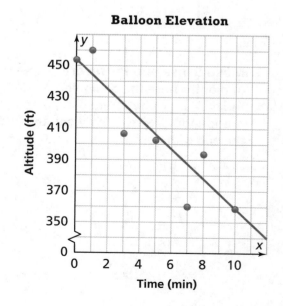

1. **Vocabulary** How can you use a trend line to determine the type of linear association for a scatter plot? *Lesson 4-2*

The scatter plot shows the amount of time Adam spent studying and his test scores. Use the scatter plot for Items 2–4.

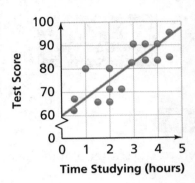

2. What relationship do you see between the amount of time spent studying and the test scores? Is the relationship linear? *Lesson 4-1*

   Ⓐ In general, Adam scores higher on a test when he spends more time studying. There is not a linear relationship.

   Ⓑ In general, Adam scores higher on a test when he spends more time studying. There is a positive linear relationship.

   Ⓒ In general, Adam scores lower on a test when he spends more time studying. There is a negative linear relationship.

   Ⓓ In general, Adam scores lower on a test when he spends more time studying. There is not a relationship.

3. Use the *y*-intercept and the point (4, 90) from the line on the scatter plot. What is the equation of the linear model? *Lesson 4-3*

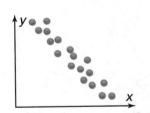

4. Predict Adam's test score when he studies for 6 hours. *Lesson 4-3*

5. Describe the relationship between the data in the scatter plot. *Lesson 4-2*

6. The scatter plot shows the mean annual temperature at different elevations. Select all the observations that are true about the scatter plot. *Lesson 4-1*

   ☐ The majority of the elevations are in a cluster between 1,250 meters and 2,250 meters.

   ☐ There is a gap in the data between 500 meters and 1,250 meters.

   ☐ There is an outlier at about (50, 21).

   ☐ In general, the mean annual temperature decreases as the elevation increases.

   ☐ Because there is a gap in the values, there is no association between the temperature and elevation.

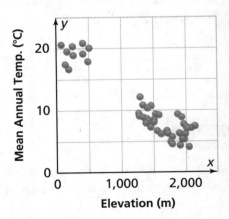

How well did you do on the mid-topic checkpoint? Fill in the stars.

☆ ☆ ☆

MID-TOPIC PERFORMANCE TASK

A pitcher's ERA (earned run average) is the average number of earned runs the pitcher allows every 9 innings pitched. The table shows the ERA and number of wins for starting pitchers in a baseball league.

ERA	1	1.5	2	2.5	3	3.5	4	5
Number of Wins	14	12	10	10	9	7	6	4

PART A

Construct a scatter plot of the data in the table.

PART B

Identify the association between the data. Explain the relationship between ERA and number of wins shown in the scatter plot.

PART C

Draw a trend line. Write an equation of the linear model. Predict the number of wins of a pitcher with an ERA of 6.

Explore It!

The owners of a ski resort want to know which is more popular, skiing or snowboarding. The resort conducts a poll, asking visitors their age and which activity they prefer. The results are shown in the table.

I can...
display and interpret relationships between paired categorical data.

		Skiing	Snowboarding	Total
Age	35 & Under	12	31	43
	Over 35	33	24	57
	Total	45	55	100

A. Use the table to describe the visitors polled.

B. What information can the owners of the resort determine from the data in the table?

C. Make a statement that is supported by the data.

Focus on math practices

Model with Math How else might you display the data to show the relationship between people's ages and which activity they prefer?

239

? **Essential Question** How does a two-way frequency table show the relationships between sets of paired data?

EXAMPLE 1 Construct a Two-Way Frequency Table

Scan for Multimedia

Jensen asked 100 people at his school whether they prefer digital or print textbooks. Construct a two-way frequency table that shows the relationship between the person's position and their textbook preference.

Model with Math A two-way frequency table is a way to show and interpret the relationships between paired categorical data.

Which type of textbook do you prefer?

	Digital	Print
Students	42	28
Teachers	6	24

These data are **categorical data**. Categorical data consist of data that fall into categories. They do not have an inherent order, like numerical data.

ONE WAY Construct a two-way frequency table.

The column category is People at School: Students or Teachers.

	People at School		
Textbooks	**Teachers**	**Students**	**Total**
Digital	6	42	48
Print	24	28	52
Total	30	70	100

The row category is Textbooks: Digital or Print.

ANOTHER WAY Construct a different two-way frequency table.

The rows and columns can be interchanged.

	Textbooks		
People at School	**Digital**	**Print**	**Total**
Students	42	28	70
Teachers	6	24	30
Total	48	52	100

The order of the categories does not matter here since these are not numerical.

✅ Try It!

A weatherman asks 75 people from two different cities if they own rain boots. Complete the two-way frequency table to show the results of the survey.

Convince Me! What pattern do you see in the two-way frequency table?

	Rain Boots		
City	**Yes**	**No**	**Total**
A	☐	19	32
B	28	☐	☐
Total	☐	34	☐

EXAMPLE 2 Interpret a Two-Way Frequency Table

The two-way frequency table shows the results of a media survey. People responded to the question, "Do you spend more time watching the winter or the summer Olympics on television?" Decide if the following statement is true or false. Explain.

More men than women to watch the winter Olympics more.

$\frac{45}{79} \approx 0.57$

$\frac{27}{71} \approx 0.38$

The statement is true because 45 of 79 men watched the winter Olympics, which is a greater ratio than 27 of 71 women.

Gender	Olympics		
	Winter	Summer	Total
Men	45	34	79
Women	27	44	71
Total	72	78	150

Look in the Winter and Total columns to compare the data.

EXAMPLE 3 Construct and Interpret a Two-Way Frequency Table

Two hundred people responded to a survey. Of those who had green eyes, 7 had blonde hair, 9 had brown hair, and 2 had red hair. Of those who had brown eyes, 76 had blonde hair, 89 had brown hair, and 17 had red hair. Construct a two-way table to display these data. Then identify the least common combination of eye and hair color. Explain.

		Hair Color		
		Blonde	Brown	Red	Total
Eye Color	Green	7	9	2	18
	Brown	76	89	17	182
	Total	83	98	19	200

Check that the sum of the row and column totals is 200.

Because 2 is in the Green row and the Red column, green-eyed people with red hair is the least common combination.

☑ Try It!

One hundred students were asked how they traveled to school. Of the girls, 19 rode in a car, 7 rode the bus, and 27 took the train. Of the boys, 12 took the train, 25 rode in a car, and 10 rode the bus. Construct a two-way frequency table. Then tell which mode of transportation is the most popular. Explain.

		Transportation			
		Car	Bus	Train	Total
Gender	Boys				
	Girls				
	Total				

A two-way frequency table displays the relationship between paired categorical data. You can interpret the data in the table to draw conclusions.

$19 + 24 + 9 + 12 + 15 + 26 = 105$

		Winter Activity			
		Ski	Sled	Ice Skate	Total
Gender	Boys	19	24	9	52
	Girls	12	15	26	53
	Total	31	39	35	105

$52 + 53 = 105$

$31 + 39 + 35 = 105$

Total population

Do You Understand?

1. **? Essential Question** How does a two-way frequency table show the relationship between sets of paired categorical data?

2. **Model with Math** How do you decide where to start filling in a two-way frequency table when some of the data are already there?

3. **Use Structure** How can you use the structure of a two-way frequency table to complete it?

Do You Know How?

4. A basketball coach closely watches the shots of 60 players during basketball tryouts. Complete the two-way frequency table to show her observations.

		Basketball Shots		
		Free Throws	3-Point Shots	Total
Grade Level	Underclassmen	18		28
	Upperclassmen		19	
	Total	31		

5. Do the data in the two-way frequency table support the following statement? Explain.

There are more middle school students who wear glasses than high school students who wear contacts.

		Vision		
		Glasses	Contacts	Total
Grade	Middle School	13	6	19
	High School	11	20	31
	Total	24	26	50

Practice & Problem Solving

Leveled Practice In 6–8, complete the two-way frequency tables.

6. You ask 70 of your classmates if they have any siblings. Complete the two-way frequency table to show the results of the survey.

Have Siblings?	Gender		
	Boys	**Girls**	**Total**
Yes	☐	25	45
No	15	☐	☐
Total	☐	35	70

7. A company surveyed 200 people and asked which car model they preferred. Complete the two-way frequency table to show the results of the survey.

Car Model	Gender		
	Male	**Female**	**Total**
2-door	81	☐	☐
4-door	☐	36	75
Total	120	☐	200

8. Make Sense and Persevere
You ask 203 of your classmates how they feel about the school year being made longer. Complete the two-way frequency table to show the results of the survey.

How Do You Feel About a Longer School Year?

Grade	😦	🙁	😐	🙂	😁	Total
6th	☐	25	14	☐	4	72
7th	1	2	☐	☐	8	☐
8th	☐	24	21	3	☐	73
Total	44	☐	47	42	☐	203

9. Students at a local school were asked, "About how many hours do you spend on homework each week?" The two-way frequency table shows the results of the survey. Classify the statement below as true or false. Explain.

More students study for 5 to 6 hours than for 1 to 2 hours.

Grade	Number of Hours of Homework					
	<1	**1–2**	**3–4**	**5–6**	**>6**	**Total**
6th	18	53	45	20	6	142
7th	21	48	42	27	12	150
8th	17	46	65	57	15	200
Total	56	147	152	104	33	492

10. **Higher Order Thinking** Demi and Margaret record the weather in their respective cities on weekend days over the summer.

a. Construct a single, two-way frequency table to show the results.

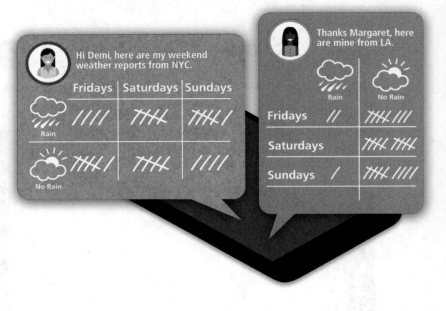

		Weather		
		Rain	No Rain	Total
Day	Friday			
	Saturday			
	Sunday			
	Total			

b. Which day saw the least rain? Explain.

11. At one point last year, the local animal shelter had only cats and dogs. There were 74 animals in all. Of the cats, 25 were male and 14 were female. Of the dogs, 23 were male and 12 were female.

PART A

Construct a two-way frequency table of the data.

		Type of Animal		
		Cat	Dog	Total
Gender	Male			
	Female			
	Total			

PART B

For which gender, male or female, is there a greater need for pet adoption? Explain.

Ⓐ There are almost twice as many female pets, so there is a greater need for people to adopt female dogs and cats.

Ⓑ There are almost twice as many male pets, so there is a greater need for people to adopt male dogs and cats.

Ⓒ There are almost twice as many female pets, so there is a greater need for people to adopt male dogs and cats.

Ⓓ There are almost twice as many male pets, so there is a greater need for people to adopt female dogs and cats.

Solve & Discuss It!

 ACTIVITY

Mr. Day's math class asked 200 cell phone owners which size phone they prefer. They presented the results in a two-way frequency table. How can you use the data to compare the percent of students who chose the small screen to the percent of adults who chose the small screen?

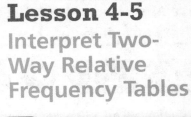

Screen Size Preference			
	Small	**Large**	**Total**
Students	48	52	100
Adults	18	82	100
Total	66	134	200

People Polled

Go Online

I can...
find the relative frequencies of two-way tables and interpret what they mean.

Make Sense and Persevere
Two-way frequency tables allow you to interpret relationships between categorical data using rows and columns.

Focus on math practices

Make Sense and Persevere How does knowing a percentage change the way you interpret the results?

Essential Question
What is the advantage of a two-way relative frequency table for showing relationships between sets of paired data?

EXAMPLE 1 Construct a Two-Way Relative Frequency Table

Scan for Multimedia

Caiden asked 150 parents and students about their preferred method of communication. What percent of people polled were students who preferred email?

Look for Relationships How is a two-way relative frequency table similar to a two-way frequency table?

Step 1 Make a two-way frequency table.

		Method of Communication		
		Email	Text	Total
People Polled	Parent	18	12	30
	Student	18	102	120
	Total	36	114	150

Step 2 Make a two-way *relative frequency table*.

A relative frequency table shows the ratio of the number of data in each category to the total number of data items. The ratio can be expressed as a fraction, decimal, or percent.

$\frac{18}{150} \cdot 100 = 12\%$

		Method of Communication		
		Email	Text	Total
People Polled	Parent	12%	8%	20%
	Student	12%	68%	80%
	Total	24%	76%	100%

Twelve percent of the people polled were students who preferred email.

Try It!

Asha asked 82 classmates whether they play sports on the weekend. The results are shown in the two-way frequency table below.

Two-Way Frequency Table

		Play Sports on the Weekend		
		Yes	No	Total
People Polled	Boys	21	18	39
	Girls	26	17	43
	Total	47	35	82

Convince Me! How is a two-way relative frequency table different from a two-way frequency table?

Use Asha's two-way frequency table to complete the two-way relative frequency table.

Two-Way Relative Frequency Table

		Play Sports on the Weekend		
		Yes	No	Total
People Polled	Boys	___%	___%	___%
	Girls	___%	___%	___%
	Total	___%	___%	100%

EXAMPLE 2 **Compare Relative Frequency by Rows**

Use the given data to make a two-way relative frequency table by rows.

According to the row relative frequency table, what percent of students polled attended the last home game compared to the percent of faculty polled who attended the last home game?

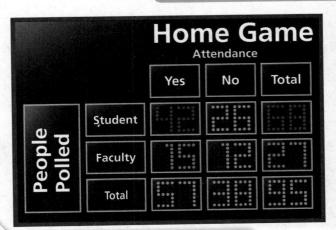

	Last Home Game Attendance		
People Polled		**Yes**	**No**	**Total**
Student	$\frac{42}{68} \cdot 100 \approx 61.8\%$	38.2%	100%
Faculty	$\frac{15}{27} \cdot 100 \approx 55.6\%$	44.4%	100%
Total	60%	40%	100%

The data you need to compare are in two different rows. Divide each frequency by the row total, not the table total.

61.8% of students polled attended the last home game, which is more than the 55.6% of faculty polled who attended the last home game.

EXAMPLE 3 **Compare Relative Frequency by Columns**

Use the given data to make a two-way relative frequency table by columns.

According to the column relative frequency table, do 8th graders check out a greater percentage of e-books than 7th graders? Explain.

		Grade		
Book Type		**7th**	**8th**	**Total**
E-books	85	125	210
Audio	122	72	194
Total	207	197	404

		Grade		
Book Type		**7th**	**8th**	**Total**
E-books	$\frac{85}{207} \cdot 100 \approx 41.1\%$	$\frac{125}{197} \cdot 100 \approx 63.5\%$	52%
Audio	58.9%	36.5%	48%
Total	100%	100%	100%

The data you need to compare are in two different columns. Divide each frequency by the column total, not the table total.

Yes; of the 8th graders, 63.5% have checked out an e-book, compared to 41.1% of the 7th graders.

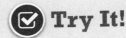 **Try It!**

Use the data in the table above.

a. How does the percent of students who choose e-books compare to the percent of students who choose audiobooks?

b. Is there evidence that 7th graders have a greater tendency to choose audiobooks? Explain.

Relative frequency is the ratio of a data value to the total of a row, a column, or the entire data set. It is expressed as a percent. A total two-way relative frequency table gives the percent of the population that is in each group.

In a row two-way relative frequency table, the percents in each row add up to 100%.

In a column two-way relative frequency table, the percents in each column add up to 100%.

Total Two-Way Relative Frequency Table

Totals 100%

		Garage Parking		
		Yes	No	Total
Type of Dwelling	House	42%	33%	75%
	Condo	18%	7%	25%
	Total	60%	40%	100%

Totals 100%

Totals 100%

Do You Understand?

1. **Essential Question** What is the advantage of a two-way relative frequency table for showing relationships between sets of paired data?

2. **Reasoning** When comparing relative frequency by rows or columns only, why do the percentages not total 100%? Explain.

3. **Critique Reasoning** Maryann says that if 100 people are surveyed, the frequency table will provide the same information as a total relative frequency table. Do you agree? Explain why or why not.

Do You Know How?

In 4–6, use the table. Round to the nearest percent.

		Artistic Ability		
		Yes	No	Total
Dominant Hand	Left	86	45	131
	Right	15	77	92
	Total	101	122	223

4. What percent of the people surveyed have artistic ability?

5. What percent of left-handed people surveyed have artistic ability?

6. What percent of the people who have artistic ability are left-handed?

Name: _____

Practice & Problem Solving

Leveled Practice In 7–8, complete the two-way relative frequency tables.

7. In a group of 120 people, each person has a dog, a cat, or a bird. The two-way frequency table shows how many people have each kind of pet. Complete the two-way relative frequency table to show the distribution of the data with respect to all 120 people. Round to the nearest tenth of a percent.

Two-Way Frequency Table

Pets		Gender		
		Men	**Women**	**Total**
	Dog	25	33	58
	Cat	20	15	35
	Bird	12	15	27
	Total	57	63	120

Total Two-Way Relative Frequency Table

Pets		Gender		
		Men	**Women**	**Total**
	Dog	⬚ %	⬚ %	⬚ %
	Cat	⬚ %	⬚ %	⬚ %
	Bird	⬚ %	⬚ %	⬚ %
	Total	⬚ %	⬚ %	100%

8. There are 55 vehicles in a parking lot. The two-way frequency table shows data about the types and colors of the vehicles. Complete the two-way relative frequency table to show the distribution of the data with respect to color. Round to the nearest tenth of a percent.

Two-Way Frequency Table

Color		Type of Vehicle		
		Car	**Truck**	**Total**
	Blue	15	10	25
	Red	13	17	30
	Total	28	27	55

Row Two-Way Relative Frequency Table

Color		Type of Vehicle		
		Car	**Truck**	**Total**
	Blue	⬚ %	⬚ %	100%
	Red	⬚ %	⬚ %	100%
	Total	⬚ %	⬚ %	100%

9. Men and women are asked what type of car they own. The table shows the relative frequencies with respect to the total population asked. Which type of car is more popular?

Total Two-Way Relative Frequency Table

Gender		Type of Car		
		2-Door	**4-Door**	**Total**
	Men	32%	18%	50%
	Women	15%	35%	50%
	Total	47%	53%	100%

10. **Make Sense and Persevere** Students were asked if they like raspberries. The two-way relative frequency table shows the relative frequencies with respect to the response.

a. What percent of students who do not like raspberries are girls?

b. Is there evidence of an association between the response and the gender? Explain.

Column Two-Way Relative Frequency Table

		Like Raspberries?		
		Yes	No	Total
Gender	Boys	49%	52%	50.5%
	Girls	51%	48%	49.5%
	Total	100%	100%	100%

11. **Higher Order Thinking** All the workers in a company were asked a survey question. The two-way frequency table shows the responses from the workers in the day shift and night shift.

a. Construct a two-way relative frequency table to show the relative frequencies with respect to the shift.

Two-Way Frequency Table

		Response		
		Yes	No	Total
Shift	Day	68	32	100
	Night	22	78	100
	Total	90	110	200

		Response		
		Yes	No	Total
Shift	Day	___ %	___ %	___ %
	Night	___ %	___ %	___ %
	Total	___ %	___ %	___ %

b. Is there evidence of an association between the response and the shift? Explain.

Assessment Practice

12. Patients in a blind study were given either Medicine A or Medicine B. The table shows the relative frequencies with respect to improvement.

Is there evidence that improvement was related to the type of medicine? Explain.

Column Two-Way Relative Frequency Table

		Improvement?		
		Yes	No	Total
Type	Medicine A	26%	64%	50%
	Medicine B	74%	36%	50%
	Total	100%	100%	100%

Ⓐ The same number of people took each medicine, but the percent of people who reported improvement after taking Medicine B was significantly greater than the percent for Medicine A.

Ⓑ The same number of people took each medicine, but the percent of people who reported improvement after taking Medicine A was significantly greater than the percent for Medicine B.

Ⓒ Different numbers of people took each medicine, but the percent of people who reported improvement after taking Medicine B was significantly greater than the percent for Medicine A.

Ⓓ Different numbers of people took each medicine, but the percent of people who reported improvement after taking Medicine A was significantly greater than the percent for Medicine B.

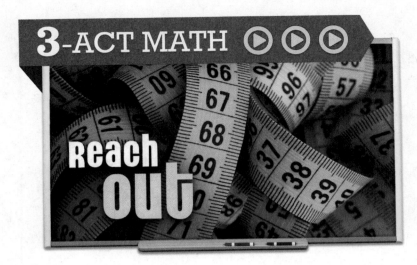

ACT 1

1. After watching the video, what is the first question that comes to mind?

2. Write the Main Question you will answer.

3. Construct Arguments Predict an answer to this Main Question. Explain your prediction.

4. On the number line below, write a number that is too small to be the answer. Write a number that is too large.

Too small   Too large

5. Plot your prediction on the same number line.

6. What information in this situation would be helpful to know? How would you use that information?

7. Use Appropriate Tools What tools can you use to solve the problem? Explain how you would use them strategically.

8. Model with Math Represent the situation using mathematics. Use your representation to answer the Main Question.

9. What is your answer to the Main Question? Is it higher or lower than your initial prediction? Explain why.

10. Write the answer you saw in the video.

11. Reasoning Does your answer match the answer in the video? If not, what are some reasons that would explain the difference?

12. Make Sense and Persevere Would you change your model now that you know the answer? Explain.

Reflect

13. Model with Math Explain how you used a mathematical model to represent the situation. How did the model help you answer the Main Question?

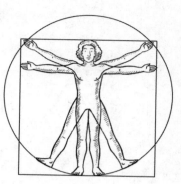

14. Critique Reasoning Choose a classmate's model. How would you adjust that model?

◣ SEQUEL ▶

15. Model with Math Measure a classmate's wingspan. Use your model to predict your classmate's height. How well did your model predict your classmate's actual height?

? Topic Essential Question

How can you represent the relationship between paired data and use the representation to make predictions?

Vocabulary Review

Match each example on the left with the correct word and then provide another example.

Vocabulary	categorical data	cluster(s)	measurement data
	outlier(s)	relative frequency	trend line

Example	Additional Example
1. Number of visits, age, months, and time are examples of _____.	
2. Colors, gender, and nationality are examples of _____.	
3. If 7 out of 20 people prefer reading a book to watching a movie, then saying that 35% of the people polled prefer reading a book is the _____.	

Use Vocabulary in Writing

Describe the scatter plot at the right. Use vocabulary terms in your description.

Employees at ABC Corp.

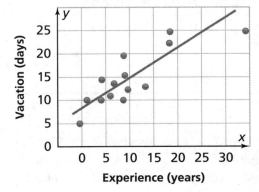

Concepts and Skills Review

Quick Review

A **scatter plot** shows the relationship between paired **measurement data**. Scatter plots can be used to interpret data by looking for **clusters**, **gaps**, and **outliers**.

Example

The table shows the temperature and number of tickets sold at a movie theater. Construct a scatter plot of the data. Is there a relationship between temperature and the number of tickets sold?

Temperature (°F)	Tickets Sold
40	120
45	100
50	125
55	105
60	90
65	105
80	60
85	55
90	60
95	50

Determine the scales and plot the points.

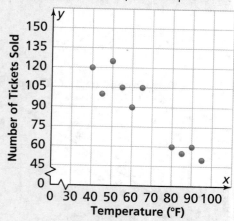

There are clusters between 40°F and 65°F, and between 80°F and 95°F. The scatter plot shows that when temperatures are 80°F or above, there are fewer tickets sold.

Practice

The table shows the distance in miles and price of airfare in dollars.

Distance (mi)	Airfare ($)
200	250
250	300
300	275
350	150
400	400
450	425
500	350
550	250
600	475
700	325
750	200

1. Construct a scatter plot.

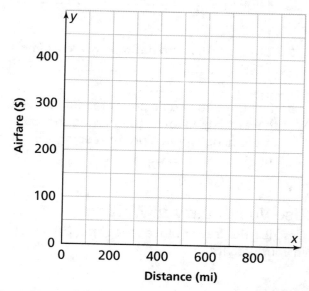

2. Is there a relationship between distance and airfare? Explain.

LESSON 4-2 Analyze Linear Associations

Quick Review

The association between the data in a scatter plot can be linear or nonlinear. A **trend line** is a line on a scatter plot, drawn near the points, which approximates the association between paired data. If the data are linear, the association can be positive or negative, and strong or weak.

Example

Identify the association between the data.

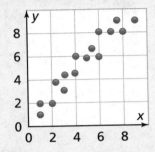

Points are close to a trend line, so the association is linear and strong. The y-values increase as x-values increase, so the association is positive.

Practice

Identify the association between the data on each scatter plot.

1.

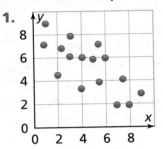

2.

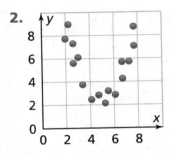

LESSON 4-3 Use Linear Models to Make Predictions

Quick Review

To make predictions, substitute known values into the equation of a linear model to solve for an unknown.

Example

Predict the volume of a tank after 24 minutes.

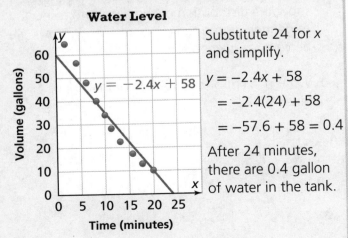

Substitute 24 for x and simplify.

$y = -2.4x + 58$

$= -2.4(24) + 58$

$= -57.6 + 58 = 0.4$

After 24 minutes, there are 0.4 gallon of water in the tank.

Practice

The scatter plot shows the wages of employees.

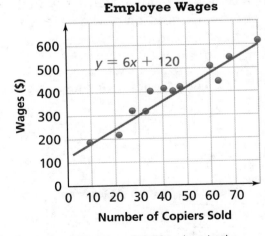

1. If an employee earns $570, what is the expected number of copiers sold?

2. If an employee sells 100 copiers, what is the expected wage?

Interpret Two-Way Frequency Tables

Quick Review

A two-way frequency table displays the relationship between paired **categorical data.**

Example

The two-way frequency table shows the results of a random survey about the favorite drink of boys and girls. Mr. Marcum said that boys are more likely than girls to prefer milk. Is the statement true or false? Explain.

	Milk	Water	Juice	Total
Boys	10	8	12	30
Girls	7	3	10	20
Total	17	11	22	50

The statement is not true because 10 out of 30 boys prefer milk, which is less than 7 out of 20.

Practice

1. The two-way frequency table shows the results of a random survey of movies watched by 100 students. Mrs. Leary said that according to the data, girls are more likely than boys to watch movie A. Is the statement true or false? Explain.

	A	B	C	Total
Boys	14	12	19	45
Girls	16	22	17	55
Total	30	34	36	100

LESSON **4-5**   Interpret Two-Way Relative Frequency Tables

Quick Review

Relative frequency is the ratio of a data value to the total of a row, a column, or the entire data set. It is expressed as a percent.

Example

Make a two-way relative frequency table to show the distribution of the data with respect to all 150 students polled. What percent of students take Spanish?

	Spanish	French	German	Total
Boys	21	36	15	72
Girls	33	15	30	78
Total	54	51	45	150

	Spanish	French	German	Total
Boys	14%	24%	10%	48%
Girls	22%	10%	20%	52%
Total	36%	34%	30%	100%

$$\frac{54}{150} \cdot 100 = 36\%$$

Thirty-six percent of students take Spanish.

Practice

The two-way table shows the eye color of 200 cats participating in a cat show.

	Green	Blue	Yellow	Total
Male	40	24	16	80
Female	30	60	30	120
Total	70	84	46	200

1. Make a two-way relative frequency table to show the distribution of the data with respect to gender. Round to the nearest tenth of a percent, as needed.

2. What percent of cats that are female have blue eyes?

Hidden Clue

For each ordered pair, solve the equation to find the unknown coordinate. Then locate and label the corresponding point on the graph. Draw line segments to connect the points in alphabetical order. Use the completed picture to help you answer the riddle below.

I can...
solve multistep equations that involve collecting like terms.

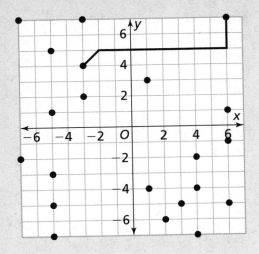

How do you make
a seven even?

A $(6, -0.5y + 20 - 0.5y = 13)$ 6,

B $(4 - 3x - 7x = -8, 7)$, 7

C $(2x + 4 - 6x = 24, 5)$, 5

D $(5x + 6 - 10x = 31, 1)$, 1

E $(7x - 3 - 3x = 13, -2)$, -2

F $(4, -12y + 8y - 21 = -5)$ 4,

G $(44 = 6x - 1 + 9x, -5)$, -5

H $(-5, 4y + 14 - 2y = 4)$ -5,

I $(-5, 15 + y + 6 + 2y = 0)$ -5,

J $(4, 3y + 32 - y = 18)$ 4,

K $(6, 5y + 20 + 3y = -20)$ 6,

L $(9x - 14 - 8x = -8, -1)$, -1

M $(-3, -5y + 10 - y = -2)$ -3,

N $(-13 + x - 5 - 4x = -9, 4)$, 4

GLOSSARY

ENGLISH

SPANISH

alternate interior angles Alternate interior angles lie within a pair of lines and on opposite sides of a transversal.

ángulos alternos internos Los ángulos alternos internos están ubicados dentro de un par de rectas y a lados opuestos de una secante.

Example ∠1 and ∠4 are alternate interior angles. ∠2 and ∠3 are also alternate interior angles.

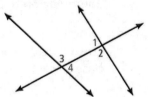

angle of rotation The angle of rotation is the number of degrees a figure is rotated.

ángulo de rotación El ángulo de rotación es el número de grados que se rota una figura.

Example The angle of rotation is 180°.

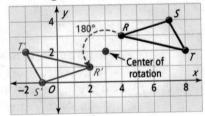

categorical data Categorical data consist of data that fall into categories.

datos por categorías Los datos por categorías son datos que se pueden clasificar en categorías.

Example Data collected about gender is an example of categorical data because the data have values that fall into the categories "male" and "female."

center of rotation The center of rotation is a fixed point about which a figure is rotated.

centro de rotación El centro de rotación es el punto fijo alrededor del cual se rota una figura.

Example O is the center of rotation.

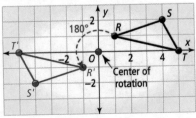

ENGLISH

cluster A cluster is a group of points that lie close together on a scatter plot.

Example This graph shows two clusters.

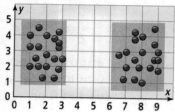

SPANISH

grupo Un grupo es un conjunto de puntos que están agrupados en un diagrama de dispersión.

---

composite figure A composite figure is the combination of two or more figures into one object.

figura compuesta Una figura compuesta es la combinación de dos o más figuras en un objeto.

---

cone A cone is a three-dimensional figure with one circular base and one vertex.

cono Un cono es una figura tridimensional con una base circular y un vértice.

Example

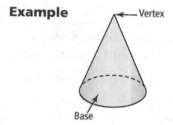

Vertex

Base

---

congruent figures Two two-dimensional figures are congruent (≅) if the second can be obtained from the first by a sequence of rotations, reflections, and translations.

figuras congruentes Dos figuras bidimensionales son congruentes ≅ si la segunda puede obtenerse a partir de la primera mediante una secuencia de rotaciones, reflexiones y traslaciones.

Example $\triangle SRQ \cong \triangle ABC$

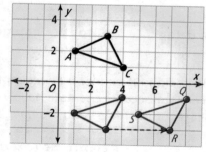

ENGLISH

SPANISH

converse of the Pythagorean Theorem If the sum of the squares of the lengths of two sides of a triangle equals the square of the length of the third side, then the triangle is a right triangle. If $a^2 + b^2 = c^2$, then the triangle is a right triangle.

expresión recíproca del Teorema de Pitágoras Si la suma del cuadrado de la longitud de dos lados de un triángulo es igual al cuadrado de la longitud del tercer lado, entonces el triángulo es un triángulo rectángulo. Si $a^2 + b^2 = c^2$, entonces el triángulo es un triángulo rectángulo.

Example Since $3^2 + 4^2 = 25$, or 5^2, the triangle is a right triangle.

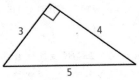

corresponding angles Corresponding angles lie on the same side of a transversal and in corresponding positions.

ángulos correspondientes Los ángulos correspondientes se ubican al mismo lado de una secante y en posiciones correspondientes.

Example $\angle 1$ and $\angle 3$ are corresponding angles. $\angle 2$ and $\angle 4$ are also corresponding angles.

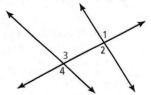

cube root The cube root of a number, n, is a number whose cube equals n.

raíz cúbica La raíz cúbica de un número, n, es un número que elevado al cubo es igual a n.

Example The cube root of 27 is 3 because $3 \cdot 3 \cdot 3 = 27$. The cube root of -27 is -3 because $(-3) \cdot (-3) \cdot (-3) = -27$.

cylinder A cylinder is a three-dimensional figure with two parallel circular bases that are the same size.

cilindro Un cilindro es una figura tridimensional con dos bases circulares paralelas que tienen el mismo tamaño.

Example

ENGLISH

SPANISH

D

dilation A dilation is a transformation that moves each point along the ray through the point, starting from a fixed center, and multiplies distances from the center by a common scale factor. If a vertex of a figure is the center of dilation, then the vertex and its image after the dilation are the same point.

dilatación Una dilatación es una transformación que mueve cada punto a lo largo de la semirrecta a través del punto, a partir de un centro fijo, y multiplica las distancias desde el centro por un factor de escala común. Si un vértice de una figura es el centro de dilatación, entonces el vértice y su imagen después de la dilatación son el mismo punto.

Example $\triangle A'B'C'$ is the image of $\triangle ABC$ after a dilation with center A and scale factor 2.

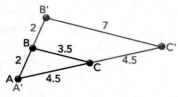

E

enlargement An enlargement is a dilation with a scale factor greater than 1. After an enlargement, the image is bigger than the original figure.

aumento Un aumento es una dilatación con un factor de escala mayor que 1. Después de un aumento, la imagen es más grande que la figura original.

Example The dilation is an enlargement with scale factor 2.

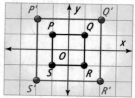

exterior angle of a triangle An exterior angle of a triangle is an angle formed by a side and an extension of an adjacent side.

ángulo externo de un triángulo Un ángulo externo de un triángulo es un ángulo formado por un lado y una extensión de un lado adyacente.

Example $\angle 1$ is an exterior angle of $\triangle ABC$.

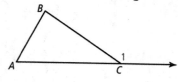

ENGLISH

SPANISH

function A function is a rule for taking each input value and producing exactly one output value.

función Una función es una regla por la cual se toma cada valor de entrada y se produce exactamente un valor de salida.

G

gap A gap is an area of a graph that contains no data points.

espacio vacío o brecha Un espacio vacío o brecha es un área de una gráfica que no contiene ningún valor.

Example This graph shows one gap.

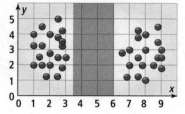

H

hypotenuse In a right triangle, the longest side, which is opposite the right angle, is the hypotenuse.

hipotenusa En un triángulo rectángulo, el lado más largo, que es opuesto al ángulo recto, es la hipotenusa.

Example

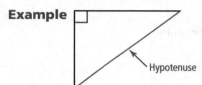

Hypotenuse

I

image An image is the result of a transformation of a point, line, or figure.

imagen Una imagen es el resultado de una transformación de un punto, una recta o una figura.

Example

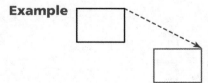

The blue figure is the image of the black figure.

initial value The initial value of a linear function is the value of the output when the input is 0.

valor inicial El valor inicial de una función lineal es el valor de salida cuando el valor de entrada es 0.

Example The initial value of the function $y = 2x + 4$ is 4 because when $x = 0$, $y = 2(0) + 4 = 4$.

ENGLISH	SPANISH
interval An interval is a period of time between two points of time or events.	**intervalo** Un intervalo es un período de tiempo entre dos puntos en el tiempo o entre dos sucesos.

Example A 3-hour interval is between 2:00 PM and 5:00 PM.

ENGLISH	SPANISH
irrational numbers An irrational number is a number that cannot be written in the form $\frac{a}{b}$, where a and b are integers and $b \neq 0$. In decimal form, an irrational number cannot be written as a terminating or repeating decimal.	**números irracionales** Un número irracional es un número que no se puede escribir en la forma $\frac{a}{b}$ donde a y b, son enteros y $b \neq 0$. Los números racionales en forma decimal no son finitos y no son periódicos.

Example The numbers π and $\sqrt{2}$ are irrational numbers.

ENGLISH	SPANISH
leg of a right triangle In a right triangle, the two shortest sides are legs.	**cateto de un triángulo rectángulo** En un triángulo rectángulo, los dos lados más cortos son los catetos.

Example

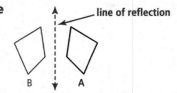

ENGLISH	SPANISH
line of reflection A line of reflection is a line across which a figure is reflected.	**eje de reflexión** Un eje de reflexión es una línea a través de la cual se refleja una figura.

Example

Figure B is a reflection of Figure A.

ENGLISH	SPANISH
linear function A linear function is a function whose graph is a straight line. The rate of change for a linear function is constant.	**función lineal** Una función lineal es una función cuya gráfica es una línea recta. La tasa de cambio en una función lineal es constante.

Example

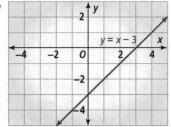

ENGLISH

SPANISH

measurement data Measurement data consist of data that are measures.

datos de mediciones Los datos de mediciones son datos que son medidas.

Example Data collected about heights are an example of measurement data because the data are measures, such as 62 inches or 5 ft 2 inches.

negative association There is a negative association between two data sets if the y-values tend to decrease as the x-values increase.

asociación negativa Existe una asociación negativa entre dos conjuntos de datos si los valores de y tienden a disminuir mientras de los valores de x a aumentar.

Example

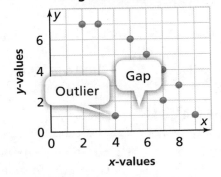

Negative Association

negative exponent property For every nonzero number a and integer n, $a^{-n} = \frac{1}{a^n}$.

propiedad del exponente negativo Para todo número distinto de cero a y entero n, $a^{-n} = \frac{1}{a^n}$.

Example $8^{-5} = \frac{1}{8^5}$

nonlinear function A nonlinear function is a function that does not have a constant rate of change.

función no lineal Una función no lineal es una función que no tiene una tasa de cambio constante.

Example

Input Time (sec)	Output Height (ft)
0	3
1	5
2	6
3	5
4	3

1 → 2
1 → 1
1 → −1
1 → −2

ENGLISH

outlier An outlier is a piece of data that doesn't seem to fit with the rest of a data set.

SPANISH

valor extremo Un valor extremo es un valor que parece no ajustarse al resto de los datos de un conjunto.

Example This data set has two outliers.

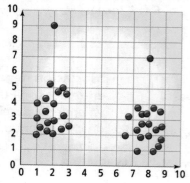

P

perfect cube A perfect cube is the cube of an integer.

cubo perfecto Un cubo perfecto es el cubo de un entero.

Example Since $64 = 4^3$, 64 is a perfect cube.

perfect square A perfect square is the square of an integer.

cuadrado perfecto Un cuadrado perfecto es el cuadrado de un entero.

Example Since $25 = 5^2$, 25 is a perfect square.

positive association There is a positive association between two data sets if the y-values tend to increase as the x-values increase.

asociación positiva Existe una asociación positiva entre dos conjuntos de datos si los valores de y tienden a aumentar mientras de los valores de x a aumentar.

Example

Positive Association

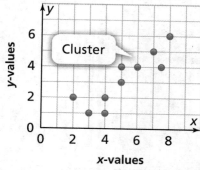

power of powers property To find the power of a power, keep the base and multiply the exponents.

propiedad de la potencia de una potencia Para hallar la potencia de una potencia, se deja la misma base y se multiplican los exponentes.

ENGLISH

power of products property To multiply two powers with the same exponent and different bases, multiply the bases and keep the exponent.

product of powers property To multiply two powers with the same base, keep the common base and add the exponents.

proof A proof is a logical, deductive argument in which every statement of fact is supported by a reason.

Pythagorean Theorem In any right triangle, the sum of the squares of the lengths of the legs equals the square of the length of the hypotenuse. If a triangle is a right triangle, then $a^2 + b^2 = c^2$, where a and b represent the lengths of the legs, and c represents the length of the hypotenuse.

SPANISH

propiedad de la potencia de productos Para multiplicar dos potencias que tienen el mismo exponente y bases diferentes, se multiplican las bases y se deja el mismo exponente.

propiedad del producto de potencias Para multiplicar dos potencias con la misma base, se deja la misma base y se suman los exponentes.

comprobación Una comprobación es un argumento lógico y deductivo en el que cada enunciado de un hecho está apoyado por una razón.

Teorema de Pitágoras En cualquier triángulo rectángulo, la suma del cuadrado de la longitud de los catetos es igual al cuadrado de la longitud de la hipotenusa. Si un triángulo es un triángulo rectángulo, entonces $a^2 + b^2 = c^2$, donde a y b representan la longitud de los catetos, y c representa la longitud de la hipotenusa.

Example $6^2 + 8^2 = 10^2$

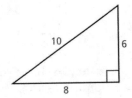

Q

qualitative graph A qualitative graph is a graph that represents important qualities or features of situations without using quantities, or numbers.

quotient of powers property To divide two powers with the same base, keep the common base and subtract the exponents.

R

rate of change The rate of change of a linear function is the ratio $\frac{\text{vertical change}}{\text{horizontal change}}$ between any two points on the graph of the function.

gráfica cualitativa Gráfica que representa cualidades o atributos importantes de una situación sin usar cantidades o números.

propiedad del cociente de potencias Para dividir dos potencias con la misma base, se deja la misma base y se restan los exponentes.

tasa de cambio La tasa de cambio de una función lineal es la razón del $\frac{\text{cambio vertical}}{\text{cambio horizontal}}$ que existe entre dos puntos cualesquiera de la gráfica de la función.

Example The rate of change of the function $y = \frac{2}{3}x + 5$ is $\frac{2}{3}$.

ENGLISH

SPANISH

---

reduction A reduction is a dilation with a scale factor less than 1. After a reduction, the image is smaller than the original figure.

reducción Una reducción es una dilatación con un factor de escala menor que 1. Después de una reducción, la imagen es más pequeña que la figura original.

Example The dilation is a reduction with scale factor $\frac{1}{2}$.

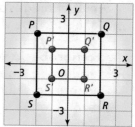

---

reflection A reflection, or flip, is a transformation that flips a figure across a line of reflection.

reflexión Una reflexión, o inversión, es una transformación que invierte una figura a través de un eje de reflexión.

Example

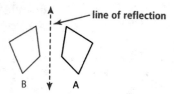

Figure B is a reflection of Figure A.

---

relation Any set of ordered pairs is called a relation.

relación Todo conjunto de pares ordenados se llama relación.

Example {(0, 0), (1, 8), (2, 16), (3, 24), (4, 32)}

---

relative frequency table A relative frequency table shows the ratio of the number of data in each category to the total number of data items. The ratio can be expressed as a fraction, decimal, or percent.

mesa relativa de frecuencia Una mesa relativa de la frecuencia muestra la proporción del número de datos en cada categoría al número total de artículos de datos. La proporción puede ser expresada como una fracción, el decimal, o el por ciento.

Example

Cars in Parking Lot

Color	Relative Frequency
Red	45%
Blue	25%
Silver	30%
Total	100%

ENGLISH

SPANISH

remote interior angles Remote interior angles are the two nonadjacent interior angles corresponding to each exterior angle of a triangle.

ángulos internos no adyacentes Los ángulos internos no adyacentes son los dos ángulos internos de un triángulo que se corresponden con el ángulo externo que está más alejado de ellos.

Example ∠1 and ∠2 are remote interior angles of ∠3.

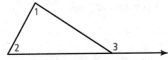

rotation A rotation is a rigid motion that turns a figure around a fixed point, called the center of rotation.

rotación Una rotación es un movimiento rígido que hace girar una figura alrededor de un punto fijo, llamado centro de rotación.

Example A rotation about the origin maps triangle *RST* to triangle *R'S'T'*.

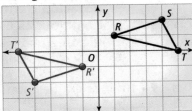

S

same-side interior angles Same-side interior angles are in the interior of two lines on the same side of a transversal.

ángulos internos del mismo lado Los ángulos internos del mismo lado se ubican dentro de dos rectas que están del mismo lado de una secante.

scale factor The scale factor is the ratio of a length in the image to the corresponding length in the original figure.

factor de escala El factor de escala es la razón de una longitud de la imagen a la longitud correspondiente en la figura original.

Example △A'B'C' is a dilation of △ABC with center A. The scale factor is 4.

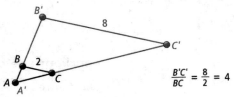

$$\frac{B'C'}{BC} = \frac{8}{2} = 4$$

ENGLISH	SPANISH
scatter plot A scatter plot is a graph that uses points to display the relationship between two different sets of data. Each point can be represented by an ordered pair.	**diagrama de dispersión** Un diagrama de dispersión es una gráfica que usa puntos para mostrar la relación entre dos conjuntos de datos diferentes. Cada punto se puede representar con un par ordenado.

Example

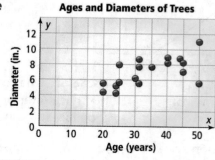

Ages and Diameters of Trees

ENGLISH	SPANISH
scientific notation A number in scientific notation is written as the product of two factors, one greater than or equal to 1 and less than 10, and the other a power of 10.	**notación científica** Un número en notación científica está escrito como el producto de dos factores, uno mayor que o igual a 1 y menor que 10, y el otro una potencia de 10.

Example 37,000,000 is $3.7 \cdot 10^7$ in scientific notation.

ENGLISH	SPANISH
similar figures A two-dimensional figure is similar ($\sim$) to another two-dimensional figure if you can map one figure to the other by a sequence of rotations, reflections, translations, and dilations.	**figuras semejantes** Una figura bidimensional es semejante ($\sim$) a otra figura bidimensional si puedes hacer corresponder una figura con otra mediante una secuencia de rotaciones, reflexiones, traslaciones y dilataciones.

Example Rectangle *ABCD* $\sim$ Rectangle *EFGH*

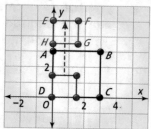

slope of a line

$$\text{slope} = \frac{\text{change in } y\text{-coordinates}}{\text{change in } x\text{-coordinates}} = \frac{\text{rise}}{\text{run}}$$

pendiente de una recta

$$\text{pendiente} = \frac{\text{cambio en las coordenadas } y}{\text{cambio en las coordenadas } x}$$

$$= \frac{\text{distancia vertical}}{\text{distancia horizontal}}$$

Example The slope of the line is $\frac{2}{4} = \frac{1}{2}$.

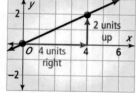

ENGLISH	SPANISH

slope-intercept form An equation written in the form $y = mx + b$ is in slope-intercept form. The graph is a line with slope m and y-intercept b.

forma pendiente-intercepto Una ecuación escrita en la forma $y = mx + b$ está en forma de pendiente-intercepto. La gráfica es una línea recta con pendiente m e intercepto en y b.

Example The equation $y = 2x + 1$ is written in slope-intercept form with slope 2 and y-intercept 1.

solution of a system of linear equations A solution of a system of linear equations is any ordered pair that makes all the equations of that system true.

solución de un sistema de ecuaciones lineales Una solución de un sistema de ecuaciones lineales es cualquier par ordenado que hace que todas las ecuaciones de ese sistema sean verdaderas.

Example $(-4, -11)$ is the solution of $y = 3x + 1$ and $y = 2x - 3$ because it makes both equations true.

sphere A sphere is the set of all points in space that are the same distance from a center point.

esfera Una esfera es el conjunto de todos los puntos en el espacio que están a la misma distancia de un punto central.

Example

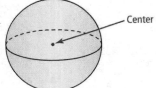

Center

square root A square root of a number is a number that, when multiplied by itself, equals the original number.

raíz cuadrada La raíz cuadrada de un número es un número que, cuando se multiplica por sí mismo, es igual al número original.

Example $\sqrt{9} = 3$, because $3^2 = 9$.

system of linear equations A system of linear equations is formed by two or more linear equations that use the same variables.

sistema de ecuaciones lineales Un sistema de ecuaciones lineales está formado por dos o más ecuaciones lineales que usan las mismas variables.

Example $y = 3x + 1$ and $y = 2x - 3$ form a system of linear equations.

theorem A theorem is a conjecture that is proven.

teorema Un teorema es una conjetura que se ha comprobado.

Example The Pythagorean Theorem states that in any right triangle, the sum of the squares of the lengths of the legs equals the square of the length of the hypotenuse.

ENGLISH

transformation A transformation is a change in position, shape, or size of a figure. Three types of transformations that change position only are translations, reflections, and rotations.

SPANISH

transformación Una transformación es un cambio en la posición, la forma o el tamaño de una figura. Tres tipos de transformaciones que cambian sólo la posición son las traslaciones, las reflexiones y las rotaciones.

Example

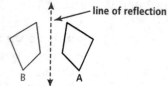

Figure B is a reflection, or flip, of Figure A.

---

translation A translation, or slide, is a rigid motion that moves every point of a figure the same distance and in the same direction.

traslación Una traslación, o deslizamiento, es un movimiento rígido que mueve cada punto de una figura a la misma distancia y en la misma dirección.

Example A translation 5 units down and 3 units to the right maps square *ABCD* to square *A'B'C'D*.

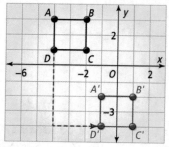

---

transversal A transversal is a line that intersects two or more lines at different points.

transversal o secante Una transversal o secante es una línea que interseca dos o más líneas en distintos puntos.

Example

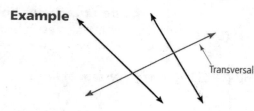

Transversal

ENGLISH

SPANISH

trend line A trend line is a line on a scatter plot, drawn near the points, that approximates the association between the data sets.

línea de tendencia Una línea de tendencia es una línea en un diagrama de dispersión, trazada cerca de los puntos, que se aproxima a la relación entre los conjuntos de datos.

Example

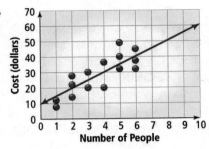

Y

y-intercept The *y*-intercept of a line is the *y*-coordinate of the point where the line crosses the *y*-axis.

intercepto en y El intercepto en *y* de una recta es la coordenada y del punto por donde la recta cruza el eje de las *y*.

Example The *y*-intercept of the line is 4.

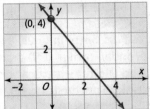

Z

zero exponent property For any nonzero number a, $a^0 = 1$.

propiedad del exponente cero Para cualquier número distinto de cero a, $a^0 = 1$.

Example $4^0 = 1$
$(-3)^0 = 1$
$x^0 = 1$

ACKNOWLEDGEMENTS

Photographs

CVR: Phonlamai Photo/Shutterstock, ESOlex/Shutterstock, Picsfive/Shutterstock, Laborant/Shutterstock, Onchira Wongsiri/Shutterstock, Christianto/Shutterstock, Peangdao/Shutterstock, Tortoon/Shutterstock, D and D Photo Sudbury/Shutterstock, Grasycho/Shutterstock, Christian Bertrand/Shutterstock/Shutterstock; **3** Hywards/Fotolia; **4** (bulb) Robertovich/Fotolia, (faucet) LYA AKINSHIN/Fotolia, (girl) Maridav/Fotolia, (globe) Somchai Som/Shutterstock, (mineral) marcel/Fotolia, (oil) ptasha/Fotolia, (pump) phive215/Fotolia, (solar panel) lily/Fotolia, (tablet) yossarian6/Fotolia, (tree rings) oscar0/Fotolia, (tree) Givaga/Fotolia, (water) 31moonlight31/Fotolia, (wood) Kletr/Fotolia; **7** (T) Syda Productions/Shutterstock, (B) Ppa/Shutterstock; **8** (T) Denis Belitsky/Shutterstock, (B) Realstock/Shutterstock; **9** (C) Yuri Bizgaimer/Fotolia, (CL) yurakp/Fotolia, (L) Photka/Fotolia, (TC) Jane Kelly/Fotolia; **12:** Castleski/Shutterstock; **13:** Injenerker/Fotolia; **15** (C) Pongmoji/Fotolia, (CR) Sunnysky69/Fotolia, (TC) Alex Stokes/Fotolia, (TL) Xalanx/Fotolia; **20:** Doko/Shutterstock; **21** (TC) Aelita2/123RF, (TL) Richard Laschon/123RF, (TR) Pavel Losevsky/Fotolia; **24:** Sakdam/Fotolia; **25** (BCR): Trentemoller/Shutterstock; **27** (C) hrerickson/Fotolia, (CL) Leah Anne Thompson/Fotolia, (TC) andreusK/Fotolia; **31:** Perytskyy/Fotolia; **34** (CL) Monkey Business Images/Shutterstock, (TL) Warut Prathaksithorn/123RF; **35** (TCR) Wildarun/Fotolia, (TR) Dirk Ercken/Shutterstock; **41** (C) michaeljung/Fotolia, (CL) Jeka84/Fotolia, (L) Edyta Pawlowska/Fotolia, (TCL) larygin Andrii/Fotolia; **42:** evelyng23/Shutterstock; **47** (TL) Voyagerix/Fotolia, (TR) mimagephotos/Fotolia; **57:** Lev/Fotolia; **60:** Tarik GOK/Fotolia; **62:** Frender/Fotolia; **63** (C) Jeanne McRight/Fotolia, (TC) Stillfx/Fotolia; **65:** Royaltystockphoto/Fotolia; **68:** PRinMD68/Fotolia; **69** (C) neirfy/Fotolia, (CL) Brocreative/Fotolia, (CR) Kletr/Fotolia; **72:** GRIN/NASA; **81:** RapidEye/iStock/Getty Images Plus/Getty Images; **84** (BCR) Photobank/Fotolia, (BR) yossarian6/Fotolia, (C) Sergiy Serdyuk/Fotolia, (CL) eranda/Fotolia, (CR) eranda/Fotolia, (TC) Gelpi/Fotolia, (TCR) iagodina/Fotolia, (TR) Yongtick/Fotolia; **87** (T) Wicked Digital/Shutterstock, (B) Veera/Shutterstock; **88** (T) Monkey Business Images/Shutterstock, (B) Galyna Andrushko/Shutterstock; **89** (C) Pack/Fotolia, (CL) annexs2/Fotolia, (TC) opka/Fotolia; **91:** vladimirs/Fotolia, Taylon/Shutterstock; **95** (C) Chones/Fotolia, (CL) Claireliz/Fotolia, (T) Kurhan/Fotolia; **106:** Freeskyline/Fotolia; **107:** TAlex/Fotolia; **117:** Mihai Simonia/Shutterstock; **121** (CR): S_Photo/Shutterstock, (CL) S_Photo/Shutterstock, (T) S_Photo/Shutterstock; **127:** WavebreakMediaMicro/Fotolia; **133:** Minicel73/Fotolia; **136:** Ljupco Smokovski/Fotolia; **139** (CL) Razoomanetu/Fotolia, (CR) Zuzule/Fotolia, (TC) vladvm50/Fotolia; **143:** kraska/Fotolia; **145:** RobertoC/Fotolia; **159:** Gemenacom/Shutterstock; **163** (T) Monkey Business Images/Shutterstock, (B) SpeedKingz/Shutterstock; **164** (T) Andrey_Popov/Shutterstock, (B) Chaosamran_Studio/Shutterstock; **165** (C) Maxximmm/Fotolia, (CL) WavebreakmediaMicro/Fotolia; **169** (BCR) Anatolii/Fotolia, (BR) Photology1971/Fotolia, (C) Begiz/Fotolia, (CR) SkyLine/Fotolia; **171:** Alce/Fotolia; **174:** Hugo Félix/Fotolia; **176:** Alekss/Fotolia; **178** (C) Markobe/Fotolia, (CL) Dmitry Vereshchagin/Fotolia; **194** (TCR) Paleka/Fotolia, (TR) Giuseppe Porzani/Fotolia; **195** (BCR) lilu13/Fotolia, (C) Aleksei Kurguzov/123RF, (CR) Francesco Italia/Fotolia; **196:** Cherezoff/Shutterstock; **197** (TC) Ryanking999/Fotolia, (TCR) Alekss/Fotolia, (TR) Efks/Fotolia; **200:** Stefano Cavoretto/Shutterstock; **201** (C) Airdone/Fotolia, (TC) Cherezoff/Shutterstock; **202** (Bkgrd) Lonely/Fotolia, (L) Photosvac/Fotolia, (R) Photosvac/Fotolia; **204** (CR): Mohammad Ikhtiar Sobhan/Shutterstock, (CL) irabel8/Shutterstock, DK Arts/Shutetrstock; **213:** StepanPopov/Shutterstock; **214** (B) pkproject/Fotolia, (BCL) Jürgen Fälchle/Fotolia, (BCR) leonardogonzalez/Fotolia, (Bkgrd) adimas/Fotolia, (BL) StepStock/Fotolia, (BR) yossarian6/Fotolia, (C) Daniel Thornberg/Fotolia, (C) Deepspacedave/Fotolia, (CL) Daniel Thornberg/Fotolia, (CR) jfunk/Fotolia, (CR) Lucky Dragon/Fotolia, (T) sergiy1975/Fotolia, (TC) GVS/Fotolia, (TC) vlorzor/Fotolia, (TCR) brm1949/Fotolia, (TR) Luis Louro/Fotolia; **217** (T) Stephen Coburn/Shutterstock, (B) Mikhail Grachikov/Shutterstock; **218** (T) MaxShutter/Shutterstock, (B) YP_Studio/Shutterstock; **223:** Uwimages/Fotolia; **229** (C): Dan Kosmayer/Shutterstock, (R) Valua Vitaly/Shutterstock, (CR) iko/Shutterstock; **230:** Maxim Safronov/Shutterstock; **231:** Lucadp/Fotolia; **232:** Shock/Fotolia; **233** (C) Comstock Images/Stockbyte/Getty Images, (TC) Denyshutter/Fotolia; **241** (BL) Samott/Fotolia, (BR) Frinz/Fotolia, (C) Fantasticrabbit/Fotolia, (T) Jayzynism/Fotolia, (TC) Jovannig/Fotolia, (TL) Kadmy/Fotolia, (TR) Echo/Cultura/Getty Images; **243:** DigiClack/Fotolia; **245:** WavebreakMediaMicro/Fotolia; **246** (TC) dallasprice_120/Fotolia, (TCR) vadymvdrobot/Fotolia, (TR) vadymvdrobot/Fotolia; **249:** Ermolaev Alexandr/Fotolia; **259:** Ryan Burke/DigitalVision Vectors/Getty Images.